"I believe this will become the [?] clear, concise, and eminently r[?] this, and now we have it. Thank you Dr. Jones!

Daniel L. Akin
President, Southeastern Baptist Theological Seminary

"David W. Jones has written a well-informed, readable, and practical introduction to the study of Christian ethics. For every important ethical topic, he carefully documents and summarizes a number of different Christian views and then argues graciously and effectively for the position he favors. He constantly returns to Scripture as his ultimate standard and makes many practical applications to ordinary life. Readers will find this to be an excellent introduction to biblical ethics for many years to come."

Wayne Grudem
Research professor of Theology and Biblical Studies, Phoenix Seminary

"It is always a joy to see books that tackle the issue of ethics in our day, but that also deliberately approach the topic from a biblical standpoint. Therefore, it is my privilege to commend to you this volume. May it enjoy the success it deserves, for there are too few who have had the courage to use the Scriptures in confronting such hard ethical questions in our times."

Walter C. Kaiser Jr.
President emeritus, Gordon-Conwell Theological Seminary

"David W. Jones is a distinctive evangelical scholar, anointed with biblical wisdom and gospel passion. This book will teach, rebuke, and encourage, and it will provoke conversations that will linger long after the last page is turned."

Russell D. Moore, Ph.D.
President, SBC Ethics & Religious Liberty Commission

B&H Studies in Christian Ethics

Volumes Available

Taking Christian Moral Thought Seriously edited by Jeremy A. Evans
Moral Apologetics for Contemporary Christians by Mark Coppenger
An Introduction to Biblical Ethics by David W. Jones
Christian Bioethics by C. Ben Mitchell and D. Joy Riley

Forthcoming Volumes

Basic Christian Ethics by Daniel R. Heimbach

כִּי יְיָ לֹא תִרְצָח

עֲנָה

An Introduction to
Biblical Ethics

David W. Jones

אֶת לֹא תַחְמֹד

B&H
ACADEMIC
Nashville, Tennessee

For Johnathan, Laura, Alison, Madeline,
and Kimberly, with hope (Prov 22:6)

Contents

Series Preface

The greatest challenge to the life and witness of the church in our age is widespread moral confusion and denial of moral authority. This condition has been greatly influenced by a number of factors, including postmodern denial of objective truth, secularization of common life, pluralization of worldviews, and privatization of religion—all accompanied by growing hostility toward anything Christian. In fact, claims of objective moral authority and understanding are openly contested by our culture more than any other aspects of Christian faith and witness. Those who are redefining justice, character, and truth are working hard to deconstruct essential social institutions to justify a variety of ends: pursuing sensuality, elevating lifestyle over protecting innocent human life, stealing what others have fairly acquired, ridiculing the rule of law, abandoning the needy for self-fulfillment, and forsaking lifelong commitments. They reject the Judeo-Christian values on which the institutions of Western civilization were erected (i.e., marriage, property ownership, free-market enterprise, justice, law, education, and national security) and without which they cannot endure. Never in the history of the church has there been a more critical need for scholarship, instruction, and application of Christian ethics in ways that equip Christian men and women to engage the surrounding culture in prophetic moral witness.

This series aims to promote understanding and respect for the reality and relevance of God's moral truth—what Francis Schaeffer called "true truth"—in contrast to truth claims that are false or distorted. We hope these books will serve as a resource for Christians to resist compromise and to contend with the moral war raging through our culture and tormenting the church. Some authors in this series will address the interpretation of biblical teachings; others will focus on the history, theological integration, philosophical analysis, and application of Christian moral understanding. But all will use and apply God's moral truth in ways that convince the mind, convict the heart, and consume the soul.

In *An Introduction to Biblical Ethics*, David W. Jones introduces readers to the field of biblical ethics. Readers may wonder how biblical ethics relates to Christian ethics. Are these different terms for one thing or terms for two different things? The answer is, they are different things that are closely connected. All worthy teaching of Christian ethics should be biblical in the sense of being faithful to biblical moral revelation, centered on biblical content, and compatible with biblical framing of reality and truth. But biblical ethics is distinct in that it focuses on exactly what the Bible says in matters of right or wrong moral action, good and bad moral character, and worthy or unworthy moral goals. So while Christian ethics includes biblical ethics, centers on biblical ethics, and builds on biblical ethics, the fields have different boundaries. As a field of study, biblical ethics is part of the larger field of Christian ethics; and Christian ethics is larger because it addresses philosophical thinking, theological doctrines, historical movements, and applying God's moral standards to moral issues of the day—as well as what the Bible specifically says on moral matters.

This introduction to biblical ethics is bibliocentric, theocentric, and Christocentric. This means the author: (1) not only describes what the Bible says but treats what it says as authoritative, inerrant, relevant, and necessary; (2) not only accepts biblical teaching as a good way of doing things but as applying eternal, divine, moral laws to everyday life; and (3) not only embraces a theistic worldview but affirms the uniqueness of Christ as the way, the truth, and the life—not only for Christians but for everyone everywhere.

While other books sometimes reduce biblical ethics to a version of human philosophy or just one of various humanly generated religious traditions, this text assumes and defends the view that biblical ethics is a matter of truth that cannot be reduced to humanly defined terms whether philosophical or religious. It is a matter of theology, not philosophy, and not just a matter of human speculation about theology but of true and reliable communication from the only God who exists. It comes from a source of truth and authority in a category to itself, one transcending all others including those defined by philosophical reason or arising from religious imagination. In other words this book treats biblical ethics as truth authoritatively and reliably revealed by the one true God for all humanity regarding the only standards that will matter at the end of time when each individual stands before the judgment seat of God.

An Introduction to Biblical Ethics by David W. Jones will prepare students, teachers, and scholars for moral battle; resource churches to inspire holiness and expose corruption; equip parents to raise children who pursue righteousness and virtue; and challenge all of us to grow in the fear of God, motivated by love for God as directed by the Word of God.

Daniel R. Heimbach
Series Editor

Preface

I took my first class in biblical ethics in college more than twenty years ago. My memories about that class are not good. I recall that the professor clearly did not want to teach the course (it was a Monday night class that interfered with his desire to watch football). I remember that the lectures were monotone, philosophical presentations that I had a tough time finding relevant to my life. I also recall that the textbook was bad—exceptionally bad. The writing was dry, the content was way over my head, and the author seemed to have a way of muddling even the simplest of issues. Honestly, I quit reading the textbook about a third of the way through the course and just held on for a passing grade. In fact, I sold the book back to the campus bookstore at the end of the semester for laundry money. So much for the great beginnings of my career as a professional ethicist.

It was not until I enrolled in an ethics course in seminary that I came to understand that ethics is not to be equated with tedious legalism, works-based salvation, or some type of self-sanctification project. Rather, ethics is Christian living; it is the blueprint for a Christian worldview; it is applied theology. With this new and correct perspective I began to embrace the field of ethics, with a special interest in biblical ethics. For more than a decade now I have been teaching undergraduate and graduate students in the field of Christian ethics at Southeastern Seminary (Wake Forest, NC), as well as at other institutions as a visiting professor. It has been my goal to provide those who take my classes with a more interesting and thorough introduction to the field of ethics than I had in college. You would have to ask some of my former students to learn whether I have succeeded in teaching ethics winsomely; yet, I have been blessed to see a handful of former students go on to earn doctorates in the field. Perhaps this has been in spite of my classes, but I like to think that, in part, it has been because of them.

This book is essentially the content of my biblical ethics class in book form. In writing this text I have purposely tried to keep the discussion at an introductory level. I am not assuming that the reader has any knowledge in the field of ethics prior to reading this book. I envision this volume being well within reach of college and seminary students, as well as, perhaps, motivated laypeople. For the most part, in this book I have chosen the authors of other introductory-level textbooks as my discussion partners. Classic works and figures in the field of ethics are also incorporated into the dialogue that follows. I have intentionally suppressed tangential and more advanced discussions into the footnotes. Additionally, you will find summary points at the end of each chapter, as well as a glossary in the back of this book. I hope that this approach and writing style will hold the attention of readers unfamiliar with the field, while at the same time providing a comprehensive introduction to this discipline.

As with any book, many individuals contributed their time and talents in order to make this project possible. I would like to thank all of those who read parts or all of this manuscript and offered many helpful corrections and insights. Special thanks are due to Billie Goodenough, Daniel Heimbach, Dawn Jones, Matthew Shores, Andrew Spencer, John Tarwater, and Chris Thompson, among others who are too numerous to name. Additionally, I would like to thank the hundreds of students who have taken my classes over the years and, through their questions and comments, unknowingly helped shape this book. Of course, any errors in content or form in the following pages are solely the responsibility of the author.

Chapter 1

Introduction

I n his discourse on morality recorded in Plato's *Republic*, the storied philosopher Socrates declared, "We are discussing no small matter, but how we ought to live."[1] Indeed, the discussion of ethics is important, for on a daily basis humans are confronted with questions of right and wrong. In practice, when ethical encounters arise, individuals with the capacity for moral evaluation do not usually make decisions arbitrarily; rather, people tend to make ethical choices that conform to certain patterns or models.[2] This is so because, whether consciously or not, everyone with the ability to make moral judgments has a system of ethics out of which he or she operates. On account of this truth, as well as the inevitability of moral encounters, it is important to be aware of and to understand one's own system of ethics.

This is a book about biblical ethics. Biblical ethics is a subcategory of the discipline of Christian ethics, which is sometimes called

---

[1] Plato, *Republic*, 1.352d.

[2] Traditionally, Protestants have held that those without the capacity to make moral choices, such as infants and those with severely diminished mental capacity, are not accountable for otherwise immoral acts. The *Westminster Confession of Faith* teaches, "Elect infants, dying in infancy, are regenerated, and saved by Christ, through the Spirit, who works when, and where, and how He pleases: so also are all other elect persons who are incapable of being outwardly called by the ministry of the Word" (10.3). For more on the eternal fate of deceased infants, see Daniel L. Akin and R. Albert Mohler, "The Salvation of 'Little Ones': Do Infants Who Die Go to Heaven?" *SBC Life* (May 1998): 12–13; John MacArthur, *Safe in the Arms of God* (Nashville: Thomas Nelson, 2003); and Ronald Nash, *When a Baby Dies* (Grand Rapids: Zondervan, 1999).

moral theology.[3] Biblical ethics differs from secular ethics, which is sometimes referred to as moral philosophy, in that it is distinctively Christian in its approach to ethical evaluation as it uses the Bible as its source of moral authority.[4] Moreover, biblical ethics is more specific than Christian ethics proper in that it specifically focuses on the study, structure, and application of the moral law as it is revealed in Scripture. In order to appreciate the uniqueness of the discipline of biblical ethics, especially as it differs from non-Christian systems of ethics, it will be helpful to sketch out several distinctives of biblical ethics at the outset of this discussion.

Distinctives of Biblical Ethics

ONE MAJOR DISTINCTIVE OF BIBLICAL ETHICS is that it is built on an objective, theistic worldview. In other words, biblical ethics assumes the presence of a fixed moral order in the world that proceeds from God. Therefore, advocates of biblical ethics affirm the existence of universal, moral absolutes. In contrast, secular ethics rests on a subjective, anthropocentric worldview that stems from the heart and mind of man. Since it is a man-centered enterprise, advocates of secular ethics usually deny the existence of universal moral absolutes.[5] Stated another way, biblical ethics seek to identify and to follow a universal, divine *ought*, whereas secular ethics tend to focus on a local, human *should*. As Frame and others have noted,[6] if one

---

[3] In saying biblical ethics is a subcategory of the discipline of Christian ethics, it should not be inferred that Christian ethics proper is not biblical. Rather, the umbrella of Christian ethics, which is biblical, contains many more specific fields of study such as biblical ethics and historical ethics, as well as many topic-focused disciplines such as the ethics of wealth and poverty, environmental ethics, and the ethics of church-state relations, to name a few.

[4] The fact that secular ethics is derived from philosophy ought not to lead one to the conclusion that philosophy is either juxtaposed to or of no use in Christian ethics. Indeed, philosophical ethics that stem from a biblical worldview and rely upon Scripture as a source of moral authority are a subcategory of the discipline of Christian ethics.

[5] Often this denial is evident more by omission than by overt statement. For example, many secular ethics texts lack a discussion of meta-ethics in favor of case-based situational ethics. There is no real discussion of why anything might be a worthy principle. The same is true of many corporate ethics codes.

[6] After defining ethics as "a means of determining which persons, acts, and attitudes receive God's blessing and which do not," Frame observes, "Many will find this objectionable. Given this definition, for example, Aristotle's *Nicomachean Ethics* is not about ethics! . . . The same could be said of any non-Christian thinker." John M. Frame, *The Doctrine of the Christian Life* (Phillipsburg, NJ: P&R, 2008), 10. Others who have made a similar claim include: Karl Barth, *Ethics*, ed. Dietrich Braun, trans. Geoffrey W. Bromiley (New York: Seabury Press, 1981), 16, 18; Dietrich Bonhoeffer, *Ethics*, ed. Eberhard Bethge, trans. Neville Horton Smith (New York: Macmillan,1962), 244–46; Jacques Ellul, *The Ethics of*

accepts the idea that ethics are by definition objective and universal in nature, then in a sense nontheistic ethics are really not ethics at all. Indeed, while secular ethics serve to promote order, oftentimes they are merely a means by which people further their own self-interests and ideas under the guise of morality, "call[ing] evil good and good evil" (Isa 5:20).

A second distinctive of biblical ethics is that it is not a means of earning favor with God but rather is the natural result of righteousness already imputed by God. To elaborate, secular systems of ethics are often tied to an attempt to earn favor with others or to create a more advantageous environment for oneself. In contrast, biblical ethics understands Jesus Christ to have perfectly modeled righteousness (cf. Heb 2:17–18; 4:15); yet, through his substitutionary atonement, God imputes Jesus' righteousness to man. As believers gradually adopt biblical ethics, then, they do not accumulate righteousness or merit; rather, they practically become like that which they are already considered to be.[7] Moreover, this pursuit of sanctification brings glory to God. The apostle Paul described this process as follows, "He made the One who did not know sin to be sin for us, so that we might become the righteousness of God in Him. . . . [I desire to be] found in Him, not having a righteousness of my own from the law, but one that is through faith in Christ— the righteousness from God based on faith" (2 Cor 5:21; Phil 3:9; cf. 1 Pet 3:18).

A third distinctive of biblical ethics is that it seeks to recognize and to participate in God's moral order already present within the created order and in special revelation. In other words, biblical ethics is revelatory and participatory in nature, not constructive and formative. Secular systems of ethics tend to view the task of man as constructing and obeying a moral framework. This is especially true in regard to novel or as-yet-addressed ethical issues. By way of contrast, biblical ethics seeks to discover and to be a part of God's

Freedom, trans. and ed. Geoffrey W. Bromiley (Grand Rapids: Eerdmans, 1976), 7–8; Carl F. H. Henry, _Christian Personal Ethics_ (Grand Rapids: Eerdmans, 1957), 146–47; Oliver O'Donovan, _Resurrection and Moral Order: An Outline for Evangelical Ethics_ (Grand Rapids: Eerdmans, 1986), viii; Paul Ramsey, _Basic Christian Ethics_ (Louisville, KY: Westminster/ John Knox, 1950), 1; and Francis A. Schaeffer, _Whatever Happened to the Human Race?_ in _The Complete Works of Francis A. Schaeffer_, vol. 5 (Wheaton, IL: Crossway, 1982), 290.

[7] Interestingly, following Charles Sheldon's classic work _In His Steps_, concerning moral choices, many modern evangelicals ask the question, "What would Jesus do?" Yet perhaps a better question to ask would be, "What _did_ Jesus do?" See Charles Sheldon, _In His Steps_ (Nashville, TN: Broadman, 1896).

moral order that is ever present, especially as it is revealed in the Word of God. Said differently, within biblical ethics the task of the moral agent is to think God's thoughts after him and to act accordingly. Additionally, biblical ethics holds that God's moral order is comprehensive and sufficient for all ethical encounters—past, present, and future. As will be explored in chapters 7 and 8 of this volume, there is no topic that cannot be addressed by moral law within biblical ethics. While topics for ethical discussion change with time, technology, and culture, moral norms remain the same.

A fourth distinctive of biblical ethics is that it affirms immorality stems from human depravity, not primarily from man's ignorance of ethics or from socioeconomic conditions. Since secular systems of ethics generally endorse the goodness of the human heart, remedies for immorality frequently include external fixes such as education and financial provision. Given the presupposition of man's favorable estate, these seem to be logical, if not self-evident, solutions for moral evil. A practical problem with these cures, however, is that experience testifies they rarely do more than produce a temporary veneer of morality at best. By way of contrast, a scriptural evaluation of man's moral condition includes the following: "Every scheme [of man's] mind . . . [is] nothing but evil all the time" (Gen 6:5). "Man's inclination is evil from his youth" (Gen 8:21). And, "No one is good but One—God" (Luke 18:19).[8] Therefore, biblical ethics proposes the solution for immorality, both personal and societal (or structural), is a change of man's heart, not merely a modification of man's environment.[9]

---

[8] Additional verses that speak to man's moral condition include: "All of us have become like something unclean, and all our righteous acts are like a polluted garment; all of us wither like a leaf, and our iniquities carry us away like the wind" (Isa 64:6). "I am the vine; you are the branches. The one who remains in Me and I in him produces much fruit, because you can do nothing without Me" (John 15:5). And, "Those [whose lives] are in the flesh cannot please God" (Rom 8:8). By way of contrast, note the scriptural charges and description of the moral capacity of the regenerate: "Be perfect, therefore, as your heavenly Father is perfect" (Matt 5:48). "Be holy, because I am holy" (1 Pet 1:16). And, "For His divine power has given us everything required for life and godliness through the knowledge of Him who called us by His own glory and goodness" (2 Pet 1:3). Of course, this is not to say redeemed man will be perfect. Experience testifies Christians, like the unregenerate, will continue to sin. Yet, in light of believers' regenerate condition and divine resources (cf. 1 Cor 10:13), it must be concluded that sin is always by choice, never of necessity. As Martin Luther famously noted, Christians are *simul justus et peccator*—that is, at the same time both righteous and sinful. Cf. WA 39.523; 56.270.9–11; 343.16–23; 351.23–352.7.

[9] Although a bit hyperbolic, the words of missionary David Brainerd are instructive here: "I never got away from Jesus and him crucified. When my people were gripped by the great evangelical doctrine of Christ and him crucified, I had no need to give them instructions

A fifth and final distinctive of biblical ethics is that in the process of assigning moral praise or blame, biblical ethics incorporates conduct (i.e., the what), character (i.e., the who), and goals (i.e., the why) of individuals involved in moral events. While this distinctive will be examined in greater detail later in this chapter and again in chapter 5, for the present it will suffice to note that non-Christian systems of ethics tend to reduce morality to the level of conduct. Although conduct certainly is an important factor in moral evaluation, especially since character and goals are intangible, to ignore the who and/or the why of a moral event will often result in ethical distortions, including legalism and license, among many others. Moreover, such an approach to ethics can marginalize important moral concepts including volition and motive. The system of biblical ethics, then, seeks to incorporate conduct, character, and goals into the process of moral evaluation.

Defining Biblical Ethics

IN EVERYDAY CONVERSATION THE TERMS *ETHICS* and *morality* are frequently used interchangeably. Indeed, even in many introductory-level textbooks—the present one included—the terms *ethics* and *morality*, along with their cognates, are used in a parallel manner. While this is true, it should be noted that in advanced, specialized, or technical discussions of ethics, a distinction is oftentimes made between the two terms.[10] To elaborate, the word *ethics*, which comes from the Greek term *ethos*, is a broad term that refers to a manner of living. The word *morals*, which is derived from the Latin word *mos*, is a more focused term that is used in reference to specific customs, habits, or conduct.[11] In other words, ethics emphasizes an entire

---

about morality." Philip E. Howard, ed., *The Life and Diary of David Brainerd* (Grand Rapids: Baker, 1989), 179.

[10] See the discussions of the differences between ethics and morality in J. Douma, *Responsible Conduct*, trans. Nelson D. Kloosterman (Phillipsburg, NJ: P&R, 2003), 2–5; John S. Feinberg and Paul D. Feinberg, *Ethics for a Brave New World* (Wheaton, IL: Crossway, 1993), 17–18; Frame, *The Doctrine of the Christian Life*, 10–12; John Murray, *Principles of Conduct: Aspects of Biblical Ethics* (Grand Rapids: Eerdmans, 1957), 11; and Scott B. Rae, *Moral Choices*, 2nd ed. (Grand Rapids: Zondervan, 2000), 15.

[11] The difference between "ethics" and "morality" can also be seen in the *Oxford English Dictionary* explanation of the two terms. The *Oxford English Dictionary* defines ethics as "the science of morals; the department of study concerned with the principles of human conduct," while noting that morality pertains to "the distinction between right and wrong, or good and evil, in relation to actions, volitions, or character of responsible being." *Oxford English Dictionary*, 2nd ed. (1989), s.v. "ethic," "moral."

belief system and gives a general perspective; morality emphasizes individual acts and gives specific principles. The distinction between these two terms can be seen further in Moreland and Craig's explanation that "ethics can be understood as the . . . study of morality."[12] So, then, while the terms *ethics* and *morals* will be used interchangeably in this text out of convention, the reader should be aware that the words are not strictly synonymous.

Having covered several of the foundational distinctives of biblical ethics, as well as some of the nuances in ethical terminology, it is now possible to turn to defining *biblical ethics*. Simply put, *biblical ethics* can be understood as the attempt to understand what it means both to live and to think biblically. A more formal definition of *biblical ethics*, however, can be found in Murray's classic work *Principles of Conduct*, the standard twentieth-century text on biblical ethics in the Protestant tradition. Here Murray wrote, "Biblical ethics is concerned with the manner of life and behavior which the Bible requires and which the faith of the Bible produces."[13] Following Murray's lead, an even more specific working definition of *biblical ethics* is as follows: *Biblical ethics is the study and application of the morals prescribed in God's Word that pertain to the kind of conduct, character, and goals required of one who professes to be in a redemptive relationship with the Lord Jesus Christ.* This is referred to

---

[12] J. P. Moreland and W. L. Craig, *Philosophical Foundations for a Christian Worldview* (Downers Grove, IL: IVP, 2003), 393.

[13] Murray, *Principles of Conduct*, 12. In his book *Biblical Christian Ethics*, Jones has a similar definition of biblical ethics as he writes: "Given the assumption that the holy Scriptures of the Old and New Testaments are the only infallible rule of faith and practice, the Bible is the source and norm of Christian ethics as well as Christian doctrine. On this view ethics and dogmatics are not properly separate disciplines but integral parts of the whole study of God's revelation of himself and his will for humankind. Christian ethics is properly a subdivision of systematic theology; it could be called the doctrine of the Christian life." David Clyde Jones, *Biblical Christian Ethics* (Grand Rapids: Baker, 1994), 7. In his *Introduction to Biblical Ethics*, another popular, late-twentieth-century, biblical ethics text, McQuilkin defines *biblical ethics* as follows, "The approach of this book is turning to Scripture and examining all texts that deal with each ethical question. . . . We shall treat the Bible as our final authority. And we will seek to apply biblical principles as well as direct mandates, but we will attempt to go only as far as Scripture itself goes and maintain the emphases of the Bible itself. So we call our study *biblical ethics*." Robertson McQuilkin, *Introduction to Biblical Ethics*, 2nd ed. (Wheaton, IL: Tyndale, 1995), ix. Yet another definition of biblical ethics comes from Walter C. Kaiser's recent work in the field. Kaiser writes: "A biblical ethic begins with the light of Scripture. . . . Thus for Christians, biblical ethics is the reflection on human acts and conduct from the perspective given to us in Holy Scripture from our Lord." Walter C. Kaiser Jr., *What Does the Lord Require? A Guide for Preaching and Teaching Biblical Ethics* (Grand Rapids: Baker, 2009), 9.

as a "working definition," for its component parts will be unpacked and analyzed in the pages that follow in this chapter.

Consequential and Deontological Systems of Ethics

IN THE WORKING DEFINITION OF BIBLICAL ETHICS just given it was noted, "Biblical ethics is the study and application of the morals *prescribed . . . .*" In the process of assigning moral praise or blame, then, biblical ethics focuses upon the acts that are committed (or omitted) and their conformity (or lack thereof) to prescribed morals. Yet, this is only one of two possible, normative ways of engaging in moral assessment. To elaborate, in evaluating a moral event, there are two logical possibilities: one can either focus upon the acts that are committed or upon the consequences that result.[14] Stated differently, the age-old question asks, "Do the ends justify the means, or are the means sufficient apart from the ends?"[15] In the formal study of ethics means-based systems are referred to as deontological theories, while ends-based systems are classified as consequentialist or utilitarian theories.

Consequentialist Theories

CONSEQUENTIALIST OR UTILITARIAN SYSTEMS OF ETHICS assign moral praise or blame based on the end results of moral events. That which is moral within a consequentialist system of ethics, then, is the course of action that produces the greatest amount of overall good. Jones summarizes this approach to ethics well, noting that according to "a consequentialist theory of ethics . . . an act is right if it is intended to produce a greater balance of good over evil than any available alternative."[16] Advocates of this approach to ethics, including classic

---

[14] Some may want to identify the school of thought known as "virtue ethics" as a third type of ethical system. This, however, is a misunderstanding of virtue ethics, for virtue ethics does not describe a moral event but the character of a moral agent. Indeed, a given virtue cannot be evaluated apart from its manifestation in a moral event. Such evaluation of virtues will be tied to a moral agent's act and conformity to norms (deontology) or the results of a moral agent's act (consequentialism). See the discussion of character later in this chapter and in chapter 5.

[15] The first recorded instance of the idea of the ends justifying the means in western literature is in the Greek poet Sophocles' work *Electra* (c. 409 BC) in which he had his character Orestes remark, "The end excuses any evil."

[16] Jones, *Biblical Christian Ethics*, 127. Rae offers a similarly concise definition, "Utilitarianism commonly argues that the moral choice is the one that produces the greatest good for the greatest number of people, or the moral choice is the course of action that produces more good consequences than harmful ones." Rae, *Moral Choices*, 85.

proponents such as Jeremy Bentham (1748–1832) and John Stuart Mill (1806–73),[17] usually define "greatest good" in terms of individual or corporate human flourishing. Options for such anthropocentric flourishing include an increase in pleasure, the maximization of happiness, a decrease in pain, the attainment of power, the lowering of financial cost, the feeling of self-actualization, or some similar idea. Therefore, since morality is determined by evaluating results, there is no inherently good or bad act within a pure consequentialist system of ethics.

One should not confuse, however, a consequentialist approach to ethics with a teleological emphasis within a system of ethics. Simply put, teleology refers to "the doctrine of design and purpose."[18] At first glance, then, to act in a teleological manner appears similar to consequentialism, for both concepts are forward looking. Yet to proceed with design, purpose, and goals in mind is not necessarily synonymous with assigning moral praise or blame based on the results of moral events. As Jones has noted, the similarities of the ideas of teleology and utility have led to "modern confusion of [identifying] teleological ethics with consequentialism."[19] Yet, while some scholars have made the error of conflating teleology with utility,[20] this is a false association, for the concepts are not identical. Moreover, as will be discussed later in this chapter and again in chapter 5, it is possible to have a teleological emphasis within a deontological system of ethics. Indeed, this is true of biblical ethics. Said differently, then, the opposite of a deontological approach to ethics is a consequentialist approach to ethics, not a teleological emphasis within a system of ethics.

---

[17] Jeremy Bentham, *An Introduction to the Principles of Morals and Legislation* (London: T. Payne, 1789); John Stuart Mill, *Utilitarianism and Other Essays* (London: Penguin, 1987).

[18] *Oxford English Dictionary*, 2nd ed. (1989), s.v. "teleology."

[19] Jones, *Biblical Christian Ethics*, 20–21. Jones also notes: "The ambiguity of the term teleological is the source of some confusion in ethics. Its classic use for the perfection of human nature in conformity with right precepts should be distinguished from the modern use for the view that the rightness or wrongness of an action is determined solely by its consequences." Ibid., 18 n. 5.

[20] For example, Rae writes: "Teleological systems are systems that are based upon the end result produced by an action. . . . The primary form of teleological ethics is called utilitarianism. . . . Utilitarianism and teleological ethics are used interchangeably." Rae, *Moral Choices*, 17, 84–85. Similarly, Geisler notes: "Ethical systems can be broadly divided into two categories, deontological (duty-centered) and teleological (end-centered). Christian ethics is deontological. Utilitarianism is an example of a teleological ethic." Norman L. Geisler, *Christian Ethics: Options and Issues* (Grand Rapids: Baker, 1998), 24. See also Feinberg and Feinberg, *Ethics for a Brave New World*, 27–28.

There are many practical benefits of consequentialist systems of ethics, such as avoiding the supposed strictness of deontological systems, a perceived ease and simplicity of application (e.g., just determine the greatest good), and the popularity of consequentialism in the public square,[21] as well as the ability ostensibly to make moral judgments apart from divine revelation or even the need for a belief in God. Indeed, consequentialist theories abound, including ethical egoism (egoistic utilitarianism), which teaches the right choice is the one that advances one's own self-interest; ethical universalism (altruistic universalism), which holds the correct path is the one that produces the greatest amount of good for the greatest number of people; epicureanism (hedonistic utilitarianism), which posits the correct choice is the one that produces the most pleasure; situationalism (idealistic utilitarianism), which teaches the right thing to do is to take the path that upholds a given ideal; and there are many other manifestations of consequentialism.

Yet, despite the popularity and apparent benefits of this approach to morality, there are a number of significant limitations to consequentialist systems of ethics. For example, consequentialism relies heavily on man's ability to perform what Geisler calls the "utilitarian calculus."[22] To elaborate, within this approach to ethics man must be able to predict accurately the results of a given action in order to provide moral guidance. Yet, since humans are not omniscient, it seems the only sure way for a consequentialist system of ethics to operate is retrospectively.[23] Such an approach, of course, is impractical and raises questions about the real usefulness and viability of consequentialist moral systems. Indeed, while consequentialism could possibly describe how man *did* live, it appears it cannot answer the fundamental moral question Schaeffer posed, "How shall we *then* live?"[24]

A second related challenge for consequentialist systems of ethics is that for any given action there are a myriad of results, some

---

[21] Frame observes, "Utilitarianism seems to be almost routinely assumed in contemporary discussion of ethical issues." Frame, *Doctrine of the Christian Life*, 97.

[22] Geisler, *Christian Ethics*, 31. Cf. John Jefferson Davis, *Evangelical Ethics: Issues Facing the Church Today*, 3rd ed. (Phillipsburg, NJ: P&R, 2004), 282. In referring to a "utilitarian calculus," Geisler seems to be playing off of John Stuart Mill's advocation of a so-called "hedonistic calculus." Cf. Mill, *Utilitarianism and Other Essays*.

[23] Frame observes, "It turns out, then, that utilitarianism though advertised as a simple and practical method for evaluating courses of action, in fact requires divine omniscience." Frame, *Doctrine of the Christian Life*, 99.

[24] Francis A. Schaeffer, *How Shall We Then Live?* (Grand Rapids: Revell, 1979).

immediate and others in the distant future. Regarding this challenge Davis observes: "Human beings have an imperfect ability to fully anticipate the consequences of a given action. . . . The long term consequences of a given action may be especially difficult to foresee."[25] Moreover, even if advocates of a consequentialist approach to ethics were able to identify correctly all of the results of a given action (which is doubtful), a related concern is mankind's ability to evaluate properly such consequences. The issue here, which Douma refers to as the "principle of measurability,"[26] is the prospect of identifying good and bad results relying solely on the criteria within the moral event itself. Indeed, it seems that in order to make moral judgments, consequentialist systems must use deontological moral principles—that is, prior concepts about right and wrong. As Rae has observed: "The utilitarian must appeal to [deontological] principles to determine what constitutes a good or harmful consequence. What makes an outcome harmful or beneficial depends on a prior commitment to [deontological] principles."[27] Taken at face value, then, consequentialism does not appear to be internally coherent.

Historically, the way consequentialism has operated is that the presiding authority is privileged with the position of defining good and bad for a given moral event. Concerning personal ethics this authority can be oneself; in regard to societal ethics, the authority is usually those in power—or, at least, those with power. Such arrangements, however, can lead to serious problems. For instance, on a personal level consequentialist systems can become myopic and result in incongruent concepts of good and bad between different individuals. On a societal level utilitarian moral arrangements have proven disastrous, resulting in the endorsement of all varieties of injustice, ranging from environmental destruction to ethnic cleansing. Frame refers to this as the "swine trough" objection to utilitarianism—that is, the observation that a consequentialist approach to ethics allows for the justification of all types of

---

[25] Davis, *Evangelical Ethics*, 282. Frame writes, "To measure the consequences of an action, we would have to trace its effects into the indefinite future and throughout the universe. One action, after all, can have enormous effects, years later and miles away." Frame, *Doctrine of the Christian Life*, 98.

[26] Douma, *Responsible Conduct*, 10.

[27] Rae, *Moral Choices*, 87. Likewise, Geisler writes, "Even utilitarians take the end as a universal good, showing that they cannot avoid a universal good. Otherwise from whence do they derive the concept of a good that should be desired for its own sake?" Geisler, *Christian Ethics*, 37–38.

deplorable acts as long as such acts are in the interest of the majority or at least the authority.[28] Moreover, this objection highlights
the inability of consequentialist systems to protect minorities, as
well as its failure to account for individual merit.[29]

One final limitation of consequentialism is that on a personal
level such an approach to ethics is not inherently satisfying. To
elaborate, experience testifies that acting in one's own self-interest
is not always fulfilling, especially given the perspective that comes
with the passage of time. In fact, oftentimes embarking on a course
of action that requires great personal sacrifice—including the giving of one's finances, one's time, and even one's own blood, sweat,
and tears—can be satisfying. This is so because mankind is made
in the image of God. While the *imago Dei* is surely a complex
theological topic, for the purposes of the present discussion, it can
be simply noted that, in part, image-bearing involves acting like
God.[30] This functional aspect of the *imago Dei* is clearly emphasized in the creation narrative, as well as elsewhere in Scripture, for
mankind was commanded to act like God (cf. Gen 1:26–28; Ps
8:3–8). Just as God is sovereign over all, so in the first chapters of
the Bible God's image-bearers are commanded to have dominion
over the creation; just as God is a creator, so God's image-bearers
are told to procreate. True morality, then, involves functionally
bearing God's image, not acting consequentially so as always to fulfill one's own interests or to satisfy an anthropocentric concept of
good. Moreover, since the Lord made man to do what he told him
to do (i.e., keep his commands), one would expect utilitarian-type
ethics to be unfulfilling.

Deontological Theories

IN CONTRAST TO UTILITARIANISM, DEONTOLOGICAL THEORIES make
ethical judgments based on the morality of actions themselves.
When evaluating a moral event within a deontological system of

---

[28] Frame, *Doctrine of the Christian Life*, 98.

[29] Rae claims that in secular society, "The most common charge against utilitarianism is
that it cannot protect the rights of minorities." Rae, *Moral Choices*, 86, 88.

[30] While a thorough discussion of the *imago Dei* falls beyond the scope of this work, helpful resources include G. C. Berkouwer, *Man: The Image of God* (Grand Rapids: Eerdmans,
1962); Anthony A. Hoekema, *Created in God's Image* (Grand Rapids: Eerdmans, 1986);
Philip Edgcumbe Hughes, *The True Image: The Origin and Destiny of Man in Christ* (Grand
Rapids: Eerdmans, 1989); and Meredith Kline, *Images of the Spirit* (Grand Rapids: Baker,
1980).

ethics, moral praise or blame is assigned based on the conformity (or lack thereof) of specific actions to prescribed morals. As such, deontological theories are usually described as action-based ethical systems. The term *deontological* is derived from the Greek word *deon*, which is usually translated *duty* or *obligation*. Therefore, deontological theories are often called duty-based ethics.

While deontological ethics focus on actions and moral norms, it is important to note, as the Feinbergs do: "Deontologists do not ignore consequences altogether. They only claim that consequences are not the basis for deciding the moral rightness or wrongness of an action."[31] To elaborate, given that the Lord is benevolent toward mankind and biblical norms are a reflection of God's character, it is logical to conclude that moral acts will produce good consequences (cf. Gen 4:7). While this is true, a potential problem with this equation is that the good produced by moral actions is not always immediate, nor is man always capable of evaluating divinely defined good.[32] Indeed, many moral choices require self-sacrifice and/or a degree of suffering.[33] While Christians can affirm that in God's economy "all things work together for the good" (Rom 8:28; cf. Heb 12:11), it is difficult to construct a utilitarian ethic based on human perception of this process. In sum, then, while consequences are relevant within deontological moral systems, as Davis has observed, it is best to view the results of moral events as "secondary considerations."[34]

---

[31] Feinberg and Feinberg, *Ethics for a Brave New World*, 28. Similarly, Geisler observes: "Christian ethics does not neglect results. Simply because results do not determine what is right does not mean that it is not right to consider results. Indeed, results of actions are important in Christian ethics." Geisler, *Christian Ethics*, 25.

[32] Man's inability to define good eternally and theistically—in fact, man's tendency to define good temporally and selfishly—can lead to a skewed view of morality and evil. As Frame observes in his defense of a so-called greater good theodicy: "It is important for us to define *greater good* theistically. The greater good should be seen, first of all, not as greater pleasure or comfort for us, but as greater glory for God. . . . Unless God's standards govern our concept of goodness, there can be no talk of good or evil at all." John M. Frame, *The Doctrine of God* (Phillipsburg, NJ: P&R, 2002), 171.

[33] For a fuller treatment on the doctrine of suffering, see my chapter on the topic entitled "The Biblical Teaching on Suffering" in David W. Jones and Russell S. Woodbridge, *Health, Wealth and Happiness: Has the Prosperity Gospel Overshadowed the Gospel of Christ?* (Grand Rapids: Kregel, 2011), 107–22.

[34] Davis, *Evangelical Ethics*, 281. Note the Feinbergs' description of their own deontological ethical system: "It is not that we think God is disinterested in consequences. In fact, we think his nature inclines him to act in his creatures' best interests. Moreover, we hold that if his commands are followed, the creatures' best interests will be served." Feinberg and Feinberg, *Ethics for a Brave New World*, 30. Rae writes: "It is important to take the consequences of actions and decisions seriously. . . . Consequences may force us to realize that

In the formal study of ethics deontological moral systems are not as numerous as those that are consequentialist in orientation; nevertheless, several noteworthy ethical theories fall into this category. The two most significant deontological systems are divine command theory and natural law theory, which is sometimes called ethical rationalism. Divine command theory holds that God has commanded what is moral and what is immoral.[35] Biblical ethics is an example of a divine command moral system. Natural law theory, which has recently enjoyed a renaissance of sorts among Protestants,[36] teaches that humans either innately know what is moral and what is immoral, or they can glean such knowledge from means embedded within the created order. Natural law theory, which will be briefly discussed in the following chapter, looks to general revelation as a source for moral principles, whereas divine command theory appeals to special revelation. Both divine command theory and natural law theory, then, make ethical judgments based on the conformity of actions to revealed moral norms.

Source of Moral Authority

In the aforementioned working definition of biblical ethics, it was noted, "Biblical ethics is the study and application of the morals prescribed *in God's Word*." Within the system of biblical ethics, then, the Word of God is the source of moral authority—that is, in

---

sometimes there are exceptions to our deontological principles." Rae, *Moral Choices*, 88. In describing how consequentialist and deontological systems are related, Douma appears to go too far as he asserts: "We should choose neither utilitarianism nor deontology as the basis for our ethics. Our conduct must be deontological, but never one-sidedly so. We always look at and weigh the benefit, as utilitarians do." Douma, *Responsible Conduct*, 28.

[35] *The Westminster Dictionary of Christian Ethics* defines *divine command theory* as follows, "The name applied to any moral system or theory in which central moral elements are related directly to the commands of the deity." *The Westminster Dictionary of Christian Ethics* (1986), s.v. "divine command morality."

[36] While natural law theory has been a staple of Roman Catholic moral thought, Protestants have traditionally neglected this approach to ethics. This tendency, however, appears to be changing. Examples of recent Protestant studies of natural law theory include: J. Daryl Charles, *Retrieving the Natural Law: A Return to Moral First Things* (Grand Rapids: Eerdmans, 2008); Stephen J. Grabill, *Rediscovering the Natural Law in Reformed Theological Ethics* (Grand Rapids: Eerdmans, 2006); and David VanDrunen, *Natural Law and the Two Kingdoms: A Study in the Development of Reformed Social Thought* (Grand Rapids: Eerdmans, 2009). Also of note is the work of Protestant turned Roman Catholic, J. Budziszewski. Budziszewski's readable texts on natural law, both of which were written prior to his conversion to the Roman Catholic faith, include, *Written on the Heart: The Case for Natural Law* (Downers Grove, IL: IVP, 1997), and *What We Can't Not Know: A Guide* (Dallas, TX: Spence, 2003).

biblical ethics Scripture is the origin and wellspring of moral norms. All ethical systems, whether deontological or consequentialist in orientation, have a source of moral authority. Indeed, a source of moral authority is a critical component in ethical evaluation, as it will both inform the standards of conduct in a given moral system and, as will be explored in the ensuing discussion, speak to the life-orientation of system participants.

Actual forms or expressions of sources of moral authority vary among ethical systems. For example, one can look to a written law code as a source of moral authority, one can make an unspoken ideal a source of moral authority, or authority can be vested in the directives of an individual—including oneself, one's leaders, or even God.[37] Yet, while sources of moral authority abound, Rae notes that all sources of moral authority can be classified under two broad headings: human constructions or transcendent sources.[38] Moreover, taking a historical perspective, Rae observes, "The major figures in the history of ethics can be grouped into [these] two primary categories."[39] As examples of those whose source of moral authority is a human construction, Rae cites Aristotle, Hobbes, Hume, Bentham, and Mill. Rae's examples of transcendent source ethicists include Plato, Augustine, Aquinas, and Kant.[40] While sources of moral authority can be packaged up differently, every ethical system gets its moral standards either from a supernatural source or from man.[41] The difference between ethical systems that rely solely upon a human construction for moral authority and those with a transcendent orientation is great, for with an anthropocentric source of moral authority, ethics are subjective, created, and changeable, while with a divine source of moral authority, ethical standards are objective, discovered, and unchanging.

---

[37] See the Feinbergs for a thorough discussion of differing sources of moral authority, which they group into reason-based systems, prescription-based systems, and relation-based systems. Feinberg and Feinberg, *Ethics for a Brave New World*, 24–27.

[38] Rae, *Moral Choices*, 12–13.

[39] Ibid., 47.

[40] Ibid.

[41] One ought not to confuse the *source* of moral authority with the *agent* of moral authority. For example, God invests his moral authority in man. This may be expressed in the example of a father exercising authority over his children or a pastor exercising authority over his church (cf. Eph 5:22–6:9; 1 Pet 2:13–3:7). In fact, even in regard to secular authority, there is a sense in which this is true as Paul notes such rulers are "God's servant[s] for your good" (Rom 13:4). Additionally, note that Jones has a brief discussion of authority that is derived from divinely ordained structure and the need of right exercise of such authority. Cf. Jones, *Biblical Christian Ethics*, 154–55.

Summum Bonum

AMONG OTHER REASONS, THE SOURCE OF moral authority within an ethical system is important, for it will ultimately determine the *summum bonum*, or highest good, of system participants. In other words, the source of moral authority within a moral system will indicate whom the system is designed to please. For example, biblical ethics has God's Word as a source of moral authority. Since the Bible reveals God's glory, the *summum bonum* of biblical ethics is the glorification of God. This transpires as system participants are conformed to God's image as they keep his moral standards. In a secular system of ethics such as ethical egoism, which teaches the right choice is the path that advances one's own self-interest, the *summum bonum* is self-glorification. The concept of *summum bonum*, then, which has long been a topic of discussion among both secular and religious ethicists,[42] is important, for it introduces the idea that ethical evaluation involves more than just the acts that are committed. As will be explored shortly, events that qualify for moral evaluation always involve conduct, character, and goals. The process of ethical evaluation, then, must incorporate the *summum bonum* of participants in moral events. The *summum bonum* is inherently tied to the source of moral authority in an ethical system.

The earlier observation that sources of moral authority can be logically reduced to two—namely, God and man—has profound implications for moral evaluation. Indeed, assuming freedom of choice and ability,[43] this observation means moral defenses such as

---

[42] See Jones, *Biblical Christian Ethics*, 17–18; Frame, *Doctrine of the Christian Life*, 28. Also, in an often overlooked ethics text, Cornelius Van Til has a lengthy discussion of the importance of the *summum bonum* of ethical systems. Van Til writes, "In a most general way we may say that God is man's *summum bonum*." Cornelius Van Til, *Christian Theistic Ethics* (Phillipsburg, NJ: P&R, 1980), 41. See pp. 41–121 for Van Til's entire discussion.

[43] The idea and parameters of free will are topics theologians have debated for centuries. As the concept is commonly understood, at a minimum having a free will entails the ability to choose freely from among available options given one's ability. As theologians have debated free will, two general positions have emerged. Some have espoused the idea of a so-called "volitional free will," which is the understanding that people are free to choose from the available options. Others have adopted a wider view, holding a so-called "libertarian free will" or a "contra-causal free will." This is the idea that humanity's will is completely free—that is, free to choose any option. Of course, there are a myriad of hybrid views and other options. Regardless of one's position on this complicated topic, though, ethicists have long affirmed that intention or volition is a nonnegotiable component of moral evaluation. In other words, in order for moral praise or blame to be assigned, one must act with free will (however, it is defined within one's theological system). Indeed, even secular civil laws recognize accidental or forced acts should not be evaluated in the same way as are intentional acts. For more information on this topic, especially as it relates to salvation, see: R. C.

"The Devil made me do it" are not valid excuses for immorality; for whether consciously or not, participants in moral events always act with a *summum bonum* in mind. So, while the Devil may introduce temptation into a moral equation (cf. Gen 3:1–5; 1 Thess 3:5), ultimately free moral agents make the choice to act morally or immorally. In so doing, the *summum bonum* of the moral agent is revealed. Given the two ultimate sources of moral authority in view, the *summum bonum* will be either pleasing God or pleasing man—usually oneself. Within the system of biblical ethics, to act morally is to have God as the source of moral authority and his glorification as the *summum bonum*. To act immorally is to have man as the source of moral authority and the glorification of man as the *summum bonum*.

While it is perhaps a bit peripheral to the present discussion of biblical ethics, the concept of *summum bonum* raises the interesting question of whether a system of ethics that has man as its source of moral authority can ever produce purely benevolent, altruistic acts. In other words can a nontheistic, secular system of ethics ever not have the glorification of man as its *summum bonum*? For the sake of the present discussion, Christians can at least affirm the following. First, as was previously reviewed, the testimony of Scripture regarding natural man's moral abilities reveals a bleak picture, at best (cf. Gen 6:5; 8:21; Isa 64:6; Luke 18:19; John 15:5; Rom 8:8). Second, experience testifies that unregenerate men have the ability to perform seemingly meritorious acts. As Jesus even observed, "You then, who are evil, know how to give good gifts to your children" (Matt 7:11). Yet, note good works, such as the giving of gifts to children, are not morally praiseworthy if they are done for immoral reasons (e.g., as a precursor to child abduction). Indeed, Augustine taught such good works are nothing more than "splendid sins."[44]

As the question of unregenerate man's ability to act in a benevolent manner is set aside, consider the following narrative from Josiah Gilbert Holland's *The Life of Abraham Lincoln*. In this text,

---

Sproul, *Willing to Believe: The Controversy over Free Will* (Grand Rapids: Baker, 2002); David Basinger, ed., *Predestination and Free Will: Four Views of Divine Sovereignty and Human Freedom* (Downers Grove, IL: InterVarsity Press, 1985); and Robert Kane, *A Contemporary Introduction to Free Will* (New York: Oxford University Press, 2005).

[44] Robert Jamieson, A. R. Fausset, and David Brown, *A Commentary: Critical, Practical and Explanatory on the Old and New Testaments* (Toledo, OH: Jerome B. Names, 1884), 347. See Jerry Bridges, *Respectable Sins: Confronting the Sins We Tolerate* (Colorado Springs: NavPress, 2007).

which was the first biography of President Lincoln published after his death, Holland recounts an occasion on which Lincoln was ruminating about his own moral ability to act in a completely altruistic, selfless manner, apart from Christ. Holland writes:

> Lincoln was riding by a deep slough, in which, to his exceeding pain, he saw a pig struggling, and with such faint efforts that it was evident that he could not extricate himself from the mud. Mr. Lincoln looked at the pig and the mud which enveloped him, and then looked at some new clothes with which he had but a short time before enveloped himself. Deciding against the claims of the pig, he rode on, but he could not get rid of the vision of the poor brute, and, at last, after riding two miles, he turned back, determined to rescue the animal at the expense of his new clothes. Arrived at the spot, he tied his horse, and coolly went to work to build of old rails a passage to the bottom of the hole. Descending on these rails, he seized the pig and dragged him out, but not without serious damage to the clothes he wore. Washing his hands in the nearest brook, and wiping them on the grass, he mounted his gig and rode along. He then fell to examining the motive that sent him back to the release of the pig. At the first thought, it seemed to be pure benevolence, but, at length, he came to the conclusion that it was selfishness, for he certainly went to the pig's relief in order, as he said to the friend to whom he related the incident, to "take a pain out of his own mind."[45]

Moral Pitfalls

REGARDLESS OF ONE'S VIEW OF MAN'S natural ability to act altruistically, most Christians would agree an ethical system that has God as its source of moral authority puts one in a better position to act in a God-glorifying manner than do competing ethical systems. Following a moral system such as biblical ethics, however, does not guarantee that one's *summum bonum* will continually remain theocentric. Indeed, while believers may affirm "man's chief end is to glorify God,

---

[45] Josiah Gilbert Holland, *The Life of Abraham Lincoln* (Springfield, MA: Gurdon Bill, 1866), 78–79.

and to enjoy him forever,"[46] all too often advocates of Christian moral systems such as biblical ethics fall prey to distractions that put self in the place of moral authority. These distractions or moral pitfalls of biblical ethics abound, yet three are prominent: personal emotions, past experiences, and perceived practicality.[47]

As an example of the moral pitfalls of biblical ethics, one could consider the issue of divorce and remarriage. While the ethics of divorce and remarriage vary among evangelical Christians,[48] for the sake of the present discussion, assume one believes that Scripture forbids divorce and remarriage in all circumstances.[49] It is one thing to hold this position intellectually, yet if an advocate of this position found his son or daughter in a difficult marriage, there may be an emotional temptation to adjust one's ethics in order to satisfy the pragmatics of the moment. This would be especially true in a context where divorce in the case of a difficult marriage is accepted both by the culture and by the community of faith. Or consider the moral issue of ordaining women into the pastorate. If someone was converted under the ministry of a female pastor or evangelist, such an experience would likely influence one's interpretation of passages such as 1 Cor 14:34–35 and 1 Tim 2:9–15. Of

---

[46] *Westminster Shorter Catechism*, answer 1.

[47] While the biblical ethicist views emotions, experiences, and pragmatic intentions as moral pitfalls, secular ethicists have built entire moral systems around these ideas. For example, "Emotivism is the view that the primary element in the meaning of moral judgments consists in their function of expressing the emotions or attitudes of the speaker." *The Westminster Dictionary of Christian Ethics* (1986), s.v. "emotivism." See also, the explanation and critiques of emotivism in Frame, *Doctrine of the Christian Life*, 82–84; Geisler, *Christian Ethics*, 32–35; and Rae, *Moral Choices*, 88–89. An example of a moral system built around perceived practicality is pragmatism, which is "considered by many to be America's most important contribution to philosophy." *The Westminster Dictionary of Christian Ethics* (1986), s.v. "pragmatism."

[48] Several surveys of the various positions are available. For example, see H. Wayne House, ed., *Divorce and Remarriage: Four Christian Views* (Grand Rapids: InterVarsity Press, 1990); Mark L. Strauss, ed., *Remarriage After Divorce in Today's Church: Three Views* (Grand Rapids: Zondervan, 2006); and Bruce Vawter has a shorter yet well-written summary of the major views of divorce and remarriage in "The Divorce Clauses in Mt 5.32 and 19.9," *Catholic Biblical Quarterly* 16 (1954): 155–67. For the author's personal view on the ethics of divorce and remarriage, see David W. Jones, "The Betrothal View of Divorce and Remarriage," *Bibliotheca Sacra* 165, no. 1 (Jan. 2008): 68–85. See also Andreas J. Köstenberger and David W. Jones, *God, Marriage, and Family: Rebuilding the Biblical Foundation*, 2nd ed. (Wheaton, IL: Crossway, 2010), 223–38.

[49] The idea that Scripture prohibits divorce (in the sense of the dissolution of a marriage) and remarriage is the historic view of the church from the cross until at least the sixteenth century. See Gordon J. Wenham and William E. Heth, *Jesus and Divorce*, 2nd ed. (Carlisle, UK: Paternoster, 2002); and Henri Crouzel, *L'eglise primitive face au divorce du premier au cinquième siècle* (Paris: Beauchesne, 1971).

course, it is not possible to separate emotions and experiences from ethical evaluation. Indeed, even if it were possible, it would not be advisable, for emotions and experience are parts of being human. Therefore, within biblical ethics the goal is not to divest oneself of emotions, experiences, and/or pragmatic intentions.[50] Rather, the challenge is not to let anything trump the Word of God and become the conduit though which self usurps the place of moral authority.[51]

Given the fallen state of the human heart, however, even with a theocentric system of ethics in place, it is difficult to avoid the moral pitfalls that usher self into the place of moral authority. Indeed, it seems believers often find themselves in situations where there is a temptation to make an ethical decision based on an anthropocentric motive or rationale rather than on the Word of God. Moreover, given the degree of man's depravity, believers usually become aware they have made such self-centered choices only in retrospect. How can this be avoided? In answer to this question it may be noted the ability to remain faithful to Scripture increases with sanctification. Yet, beyond this general observation, two more specific suggestions can be offered. First, a practical way to discern one's source of moral authority in a given situation is that moral choices tend to be defended in the same manner in which they are held. For example,

---

[50] Frame has an excellent and lengthy section in which he calls for more emphasis being placed on emotion in Christian systems of ethics. While he recognizes the fallacy of letting emotion usurp the place of moral authority, nevertheless Frame chides Protestant ethicists for marginalizing emotion. See Frame, *Doctrine of the Christian Life*, 370–82. Likewise, Douma calls for Protestants to place a higher emphasis on emotion, writing, "The good moral act is unimaginable apart from the emotional involvement of the person who acts." Douma, *Responsible Conduct*, 19–20. See, also, *The Westminster Dictionary of Christian Ethics* (1986), s.v. "emotion;" and *New Dictionary of Christian Ethics and Pastoral Theology* (1995), s.v. "emotion."

[51] The writings of eighteenth-century revivalist John Wesley are particularly instructive in this regard. While he did not write a systematic theology or ethics text, a reading of Wesley's sermons reveals that he identified four sources of moral authority: Scripture, tradition, reason, and experience. This is the so-called "Wesleyan Quadrilateral," a term coined by the twentieth-century American Methodist Albert C. Outler in his introduction to the 1964 collection of John Wesley's writings entitled *John Wesley* (New York: Oxford University Press, 1964). It is interesting to note Outler's remarks as he later reflected on his creation of the term *Wesleyan Quadrilateral*. Outler lamented: "There is one phrase I wish I had never used: the Wesleyan Quadrilateral. It has created the wrong image in the minds of so many people and, I am sure, will lead to all kinds of controversy." Paul Wesley Chilcote, "Rethinking the Wesleyan Quadrilateral," *Good News Magazine* (January/February 2005), n.p. The problem to which Outler is alluding is the tendency of some readers to view the four pillars of the Wesleyan Quadrilateral as equal sources of moral authority. For Wesley, Scripture was the only true source of moral authority and the lens through which tradition, reason, and experience should be viewed.

if one's immediate reaction to a contrary moral stance is unrighteous anger,[52] then it is possible that the original ethical position was based more on one's emotions than on Scripture. Conversely, if one's stance on a moral issue arises from a careful study of the Word of God, then it should be possible to articulate winsomely such a view even in the face of opposition and calmly (albeit sometimes passionately) to dialogue with those who hold dissenting opinions.

A second suggestion that may help identify or reveal one's source of moral authority in a particular scenario is the ethical formula: stated belief, plus actual practice, equals actual belief. To elaborate by way of example, a believer may confess a belief that embezzlement is wrong because the Word of God prohibits stealing. Yet, if this same person cheats on his taxes, then (at that moment, at least) he does not actually believe stealing is wrong, nor is the Bible his source of moral authority, for indeed the Word of God prohibits stealing. Concerning the dynamics behind this scenario, the testimony of Scripture is clear, "For as [a man] thinks within himself, so he is" (Prov 23:7 NASB; cf. 27:19), and in regard to one's actions Jesus taught, "For the mouth speaks from the overflow of the heart. . . . But what comes out of the mouth comes from the heart" (Matt 12:34; 15:18). In other words, the actions of a man betray his heart; the externals expose the internals; profession shows confession; and ethics reveal theology. In sum, then, by observing the way moral positions are defended, as well as the congruity (or lack thereof) between stated beliefs and actual practice, believers can monitor their own source of moral authority and return to the Word of God when necessary.

Conduct, Character, and Goals

IN THE WORKING DEFINITION OF *BIBLICAL ethics* given earlier in this chapter, it was noted, "Biblical ethics is the study and application of the morals prescribed in God's Word that pertain to the kind of *conduct, character, and goals* required of one who professes to be in a redemptive relationship with the Lord Jesus Christ." As has been

---

[52] Anger in and of itself is not immoral. While Scripture does classify anger as a work of the flesh (cf. Gal 5:20) and warns believers about the dangers of unrighteous anger (cf. Eccl 7:9; Matt 5:22; Rom 12:19; Eph 4:26; Col 3:8), nevertheless, there are many examples of righteous anger in the Bible. Examples include Jesus (cf. Mark 3:5), Moses (cf. Exod 32:19), and Nehemiah (cf. Neh 13:25), among many others.

touched upon in this chapter, biblical ethics is not just concerned with practice but also with the person and the purpose of moral events. In the assigning of moral praise or blame within the system of biblical ethics, this focus on conduct, character, and goals is what C. S. Lewis referred to as considering the three parts of morality,[53] Frame calls having a tri-perspectival approach to ethics,[54] Beach and Niebuhr refer to as the "triadic relation" of ethics,[55] and Bahnsen labels the three basic perspectives in decision making.[56] Indeed, within the Protestant tradition most ethicists have engaged in moral evaluation by considering conduct, character, and goals.[57] In fact, a focus on the three parts of morality can even be seen in the ethics chapter of the most famous of all Protestant confessions of belief, the *Westminster Confession of Faith.* The *Confession* speaks of good works being done with a "heart purified by faith [i.e., right character] . . . done in a right manner [i.e., right conduct] . . . to a right end, the glory of God [i.e., right goal]."[58]

It may be helpful to think of the three parts of morality as three points on a triangle that represent a single moral event. The first corner of the triangle corresponds to conduct (i.e., the "practice" of moral events), which is deontological in orientation and focuses

---

[53] Cf. C. S. Lewis, *Mere Christianity* (New York: Macmillan, 1943), 69–73. In his trademark conversational tone, Lewis avoids the terms *conduct, character,* and *goals* and refers to the three parts of morality as: (1) relations between man and man, (2) the things inside each man, and (3) relations between man and the power that made him.

[54] Frame, *Doctrine of the Christian Life,* 33–36. Frame's terminology for the three parts of morality is somewhat confusing as he uses differing nomenclature for non-Christian and Christian moral systems. In reference to non-Christian systems, Frame refers to the deontological tradition, the existential tradition, and the teleological tradition. In regard to Christian ethics, Frame refers to a normative perspective, an existential perspective, and a situational perspective.

[55] Waldo Beach and H. Richard Niebuhr, *Christian Ethics: Sources of the Living Tradition* (New York: Ronald Press, 1955), 5.

[56] Cf. Greg L. Bahnsen, *By This Standard: The Authority of God's Law Today* (Tyler, TX: Institute for Christian Economics, 1985), 78–84. Bahnsen's labels for the three parts of morality are the normative approach, motivational approach, and consequential approach.

[57] Another example is theologian Samuel E. Waldron. In his exposition of the ethics chapter of the 1689 *London Baptist Confession,* Waldron writes that a good work must have "the right *root* (it must proceed from a heart purified by faith); the right *manner* (God's work must be done in God's way) and the right *end* (the glory of God must be its ultimate end)." Samuel E. Waldron, *A Modern Exposition of the 1689 Baptist Confession of Faith* (Durham, UK: Evangelical Press, 1989), 212. Jones refers to the direction, the motive, and the goal. Cf. Jones, *Biblical Christian Ethics,* 5. Van Til's terminology for the three parts of morality is the standard, the virtue, and the ideal. Cf. Van Til, *Christian Theistic Ethics,* 125. O'Donovan refers to the objective order, the subjective order, and the end of the moral life. Cf. Oliver O'Donovan, *Resurrection and Moral Order,* 2nd ed. (Grand Rapids: Eerdmans, 1994), 5.

[58] *Westminster Confession of Faith* 16.7.

on external acts and behavior. Conduct usually deals with relations between man and man. The second corner of the triangle stands for character (i.e., the "person" of moral events), which is ontological in orientation and focuses on motives and internal disposition. Character deals with the things inside each man—that is, man's self-relations. The third corner of the triangle represents goals (the "purpose" of moral events), which is teleological in orientation and focuses on design or intended end. In biblical ethics goals deal with relations between man and God. Consideration of any one corner of the triangle—that is, any one part of morality—apart from the others will provide insufficient information in order to engage in informed, responsible, ethical evaluation. Perhaps this idea can be communicated by conceiving of the three parts of morality as being three circles in a Venn diagram (see chart 1.1). Within this rubric, moral events transpire in the area of the diagram where the three circles of conduct, character, and goals overlap.

In his classic work *Mere Christianity* C. S. Lewis emphasized the importance of considering conduct, character, and goals in ethical evaluation. In his chapter entitled "The Three Parts of Morality" Lewis gave the following illustration:

> There are two ways in which the human machine goes wrong. One is when human individuals drift apart from

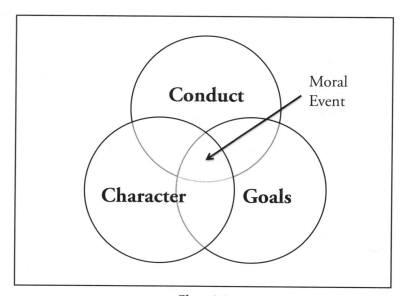

Chart 1.1

one another, or else collide with one another and do one another damage, by cheating or bullying. The other is when things go wrong inside the individual—when the different parts of him (his different faculties and desires and so on) either drift apart or interfere with one another. You can get the idea plainly if you think of us as a fleet of ships sailing in formation. The voyage will be a success only, in the first place, if the ships do not collide and get in one another's way; and secondly, if each ship is seaworthy and has her engines in good order. As a matter of fact, you cannot have either of these two things without the other. If the ships keep on having collisions they will not remain seaworthy very long. On the other hand, if their steering gears are out of order they will not be able to avoid collisions. . . . But there is one thing we have not yet taken into account. We have not asked where the fleet is trying to get to. . . . And however well the fleet sailed, its voyage would be a failure if it were meant to reach New York and actually arrived at Calcutta. Morality, then, seems to be concerned with three things. Firstly, with fair play and harmony between individuals. Secondly, with what might be called tidying up or harmonizing the thing inside each individual. Thirdly, with the general purpose of human life as a whole: what man was made for: What course the whole fleet ought to be on.[59]

As was previously noted, both in the formal study and in the casual practice of ethics many people tend to focus on conduct.[60] Indeed, this is natural, for conduct is quantifiable and may be legislated, while character and goals are intangible and difficult to evaluate—even within oneself (cf. 1 Cor 4:1–4). This is why conduct is

---

[59] Lewis, *Mere Christianity*, 70–71.

[60] Recently, there has been an increase in Christian scholars who have sought to emphasize character in moral evaluation. While such thinkers are in the minority, their works are instructive. For example, see Daniel J. Harrington and James F. Keenan, *Jesus and Virtue Ethics: Building Bridges Between New Testament Studies and Moral Theology* (Lanham, MD: Sheed and Ward, 2002); Stanley Hauerwas, *Christians Among the Virtues: Theological Conversations with Ancient and Modern Ethics* (Notre Dame, IN: University of Notre Dame Press, 1997); Stanley Hauerwas, *A Commentary of Character* (Notre Dame, IN: University of Notre Dame Press, 1991); Joseph J. Kotva, *The Christian Case for Virtue Ethics* (Washington, DC: Georgetown University Press, 1996); Alasdair MacIntyre, *After Virtue: A Study in Moral Theory* (Notre Dame, IN: University of Notre Dame Press, 1984); and N. T. Wright, *After You Believe: Why Christian Character Matters* (New York: HarperOne, 2010).

the level upon which moral and legal judgments are usually made in the public square. Yet, as has been observed, to limit moral evaluation solely to conduct will inevitably result in ethical distortions such as legalism and license, among others. Moreover, truncating morality to the assessment of conduct, apart from a consideration of character and goals, not only is unorthodox but also will leave one unable to explain certain portions of Scripture. For instance, to cite just a few examples, ethical systems that are solely based on conduct cannot explain why:

- Murder is prohibited (cf. Exod 20:13), yet capital punishment is prescribed (cf. Gen 9:5–6; Rom 13:4).
- Premarital sex is immoral if done consensually (cf. Deut 22:25–27) but not immoral for the violated party if it occurs against one's will (cf. Deut 22:23–25).
- Eating meat sacrificed to idols is both allowed (cf. 1 Cor 10:25–26) and prohibited (cf. Rom 14:6, 15, 21; 1 Cor 8:13; Rev 2:14, 20).
- Under Old Testament civil law, usury was forbidden in dealings with Jews but permitted in transactions with foreigners (cf. Deut 23:19–20).[61]
- The prophet Balaam was commanded by God to accompany the Midianite princes (cf. Num 22:20) but then was nearly killed by the Lord for doing so (cf. Num 22:22–35).
- Paul circumcised Timothy (cf. Acts 16:3) but refused to circumcise Titus (cf. Gal 2:3)—both in view of his Jewish onlookers.
- Truth-telling is normative for the Christian life (cf. Col 3:9), yet truth that is not spoken out of love can be sinful (cf. Eph 4:15, 25).

Given most people's default, conduct-based moral systems, the idea that the same act could be either moral or immoral seems tenuous at best. Yet, in regard to conduct, Paul taught, "I know and am persuaded by the Lord Jesus that nothing is unclean in itself. Still, to someone who considers a thing to be unclean, to that one it is unclean" (Rom 14:14; cf. Rom 14:20; 1 Tim 4:4;

---

[61] Readers interested in moral information on the topic of usury are directed toward my text on the topic. Cf. David W. Jones, *Reforming the Morality of Usury: A Study of Differences that Separated the Protestant Reformers* (Lanham, MD: University of America, 2004).

Titus 1:15).[62] In understanding this concept it is important not to confuse conduct with moral events. For example, murder and capital punishment both entail the same conduct—that is, the willful taking of human life. Yet certain assumptions about character and goals are loaded or incorporated into the terms *murder* and *capital punishment*. To elaborate, *murder* is defined as the malicious taking of human life—that is, murder consists of the willful killing of another human being out of anger (or wrath, jealousy, selfishness, etc.) in order to satisfy one's own sense of justice. *Capital punishment*, however, is understood to be the plaintive taking of human life by the state in obedience to God's law, out of respect for the image of God, as an expression of divine justice. Therefore, both murder and capital punishment involve the same conduct—that is, the purposeful taking of human life—however, considered in isolation, this conduct is neither moral nor immoral in and of itself. The character and goals of the moral agent, along with the conduct, provide one with the information necessary in order to assign moral praise or blame for moral events.

Several words of warning, however, are in order. First, in saying conduct, isolated from other factors, is neither moral nor immoral, the reader ought not to understand that behavior such as adultery could ever be considered ethical. This is so because adultery is not just conduct, but rather adultery is a moral event that involves the conduct of sexual intercourse, willfully engaged in by individuals of corrupt character, done with the goal of self-glorification. Consequently, adultery is always immoral. While the corrupt human heart may be convinced adultery is engaged in for meritorious reasons, this could never be so. The moral event of adultery is prohibited in Scripture; thus, it can never be committed for the glory of God. Second, in moving the locus of assigning moral

---

[62] Another example of this concept comes from Jesus' interchange with the Pharisees and scribes about their tradition of hand-washing. Mark records on one occasion the religious leaders asked Jesus, "Why don't Your disciples live according to the tradition of the elders, instead of eating bread with ritually unclean hands?" (Mark 7:5). In his response Jesus instructed his disciples by asking, "Are you also as lacking in understanding? Don't you realize that nothing going into a man from the outside can defile him? . . . What comes out of a person—that defiles him. For from within, out of people's hearts, come evil thoughts, sexual immoralities, thefts, murders, adulteries, greed, evil actions, deceit, promiscuity, stinginess, blasphemy, pride, and foolishness. All these evil things come from within and defile a person" (Mark 7:18, 20–23). In other words, Jesus taught the conduct of hand-washing (or the lack thereof) was neither moral nor immoral. Rather, as Christ shifted the illustration from hand-washing to speaking, the conduct, character, and goals of an individual defile or not.

praise or blame away from a legalistic focus on conduct, there exists the risk of opening up a Pandora's box of moral license. This error is committed when conduct is completely eliminated from the moral equation. Biblical ethics, however, seeks to incorporate conduct, character, and goals in understanding moral norms without neglecting any one of the three parts of morality.

Conclusion

BIBLICAL ETHICS IS THE STUDY AND application of the morals prescribed in God's Word that pertain to the kind of conduct, character, and goals required of one who professes to be in a redemptive relationship with the Lord Jesus Christ. This means biblical ethics is deontological in orientation, as it focuses on the conformity of moral events to divine moral norms. Furthermore, biblical ethics looks to the Word of God as its source of moral authority. Within the pages of Scripture, biblical ethics draws its substance. Finally, biblical ethics seeks to incorporate conduct, character, and goals in the assignment of moral praise or blame. Biblical ethics holds that moral norms are more than just legalistic, wooden rules that govern action. Indeed, moral norms are comprehensive life directives that speak to the whole person and have the glorification of God as their goal.

Summary Points

- Biblical ethics is the study and application of the morals prescribed in God's Word that pertain to the kind of conduct, character, and goals required of one who professes to be in a redemptive relationship with the Lord Jesus Christ.
- The distinctives of biblical ethics include:
  o Being built on an objective, theistic worldview.
  o Being the natural result of merit imputed by God rather than a means of earning merit with God.
  o Seeking to recognize and to participate in God's moral order already present within the created order and in special revelation.
  o Affirming that immorality stems from human depravity, not primarily from man's ignorance of ethics or from socioeconomic conditions.

- ○ Incorporating three elements of a moral event: conduct, character, and goals.
- Two main types of ethical systems exist:
  - ○ Consequentialist or utilitarian ethics, which assigns moral praise or blame based upon the end results of a moral event.
  - ○ Deontological ethics, which makes ethical judgments based on the morality of actions themselves when evaluated for conformity of the actions to prescribed morals.
- Scripture is the source of moral authority for biblical ethics.
  - ○ The source of moral authority will determine the *summum bonum*.
  - ○ Moral pitfalls related to the source of moral authority include personal emotions, past experiences, and perceived practicality.
- Conduct, character, and goals are the three parts of morality.

Chapter 2

The Nature of the Law

T he previous chapter proposed a working definition of
biblical ethics and examined several of the foundational
components of the discipline. In exploring the definition
given, chapter 1 covered some of the major differences between
deontological and consequential (or utilitarian) theories of ethics, explained the importance of a source of moral authority in
the formulation of ethical systems, and examined the significance
and distinctives of the three parts of morality: conduct, character,
and goals. With this foundational material in place, the next four
chapters will focus on the core element in a system of biblical
ethics—that is, the law of God. The present chapter will cover
the nature of the law as it looks at how the law relates to God.
Chapter 3 will examine the relevancy of the law as it focuses on
how the law relates to the gospel. The subject of chapter 4 is the
coherency of the law as it examines how the various laws are interrelated. Finally, chapter 5 will review the structure of the law as it
focuses on how the law relates to man.

Before embarking upon a study of the nature of the law, it
will be helpful to have a working definition of the term *law*. The
Bible uses the word *law* in a number of different ways. Indeed,
McQuilkin suggests there are as many as twelve distinct uses of the
term in Scripture.[1] While the concept of law will be refined over

---

[1] Robertson McQuilkin, *An Introduction to Biblical Ethics*, 2nd ed. (Wheaton, IL:
Tyndale, 1995), 31. McQuilkin notes that one of his father's books identifies twelve uses

the next several chapters, for the sake of the present discussion, *law* can simply be defined as the moral standards God has revealed to man.[2] In other words, the law specifies the moral standards of God. It reveals the behavior the Lord desires of all mankind. The law is the measure by which God will judge the deeds of men. This, of course, raises the important question of how mankind can know the law of God.

Historically, most Christians have held that God reveals himself to humanity via two methods of self-disclosure: general revelation and special revelation. Both of these forms of revelation are useful in the broad discipline of Christian ethics. General revelation, which is sometimes called natural or universal revelation, includes the created order, the conscience of man, and the events of history.[3] Special revelation includes the Bible and other supernatural, scriptural means of divine communication. Since biblical ethics looks to the law of God as revealed in Scripture for moral authority, special revelation is naturally prominent within this book. Nevertheless, since some have held that aspects of God's moral law are reflected in general revelation, it will be helpful to this study to examine the topic briefly. Indeed, such a review of general revelation will be useful in understanding the nature of the law.

General Revelation and the Law

GENERAL REVELATION CAN BE DEFINED AS God's revelation of himself to all peoples, at all times, in all places. In the field of secular ethics, there is a long tradition of engaging in moral theory by appealing

---

of the law. The text in view is Robertson C. McQuilkin, *God's Law and God's Grace* (Grand Rapids: Eerdmans, 1958), 13–17. In his own book, however, the younger McQuilkin only lists six uses of the term "law" in Scripture. These are law as the expressed will of God that people be like him morally, law as the Mosaic legal system, law as obedience to the law, law as the Old Testament, law as specific laws, and law as an operating principle. McQuilkin, *Biblical Ethics*, 31–37.

[2] The *New Dictionary of Christian Ethics and Pastoral Theology* notes, for Christians the law can be conceptually thought of as "the ethical imperatives of the gospel." *New Dictionary of Christian Ethics and Pastoral Theology* (1995), s.v. "Law."

[3] While the three sources listed here are standard, some theologians would expand, divide, or perhaps even compress this list to include or omit other sources of revelation. For example, J. Budziszewski, one of the leading contemporary natural law ethicists, identifies five forms of general revelation. They are the creation, the image of God, man's physical and emotional design, conscience, and the order of causality. J. Budziszewski, *Written on the Heart: The Case for Natural Law* (Downers Grove, IL: InterVarsity, 1997), 180–81.

to general revelation,[4] although the term *general revelation* is seldom used. In the West this school of thought, known as natural law theory or ethical rationalism,[5] dates back to Greco-Roman times. Key historical proponents include the philosophers Socrates, Plato, and Aristotle, the tragedians Aeschylus and Sophocles, the statesman Cicero, as well as followers of the Stoic tradition.[6] More recent secular thinkers who have relied on or made use of general revelation in the formation of their ethics (whether they use the term *natural law* or not) include Hobbes, Butler, Hume, Locke, Kant, and Sartre.[7] Likewise, many Christians have mentioned and, in varying degrees, made use of general revelation in the construction of their ethical systems. Among others, key historical thinkers include Augustine, Aquinas, and even Calvin.[8] Examples of more recent Christian ethicists who have engaged in moral theory using general revelation include J. Budziszewski, Alasdair MacIntyre, and many within the Roman Catholic tradition.[9]

Subjectively speaking, the use of general revelation in moral theory can be defined as knowing *that* something is right or wrong

---

[4] Perhaps overstating the case, the *Baker Dictionary of Christian Ethics* claims, "Throughout the entire history of Western philosophy, appeals to laws of nature have been used to establish an authoritative basis for ethical judgments." *Baker Dictionary of Christian Ethics* (1973), s.v. "natural law."

[5] While natural law theory and ethical rationalism are often used synonymously in introductory level ethics texts, as they are here, the reader should note the methodology of ethical rationalism extends beyond natural law theory.

[6] Cf. Socrates, *Apology*; Sophocles, *Antigone*. A passage in Cicero's *De republica* is often cited by both secular and Christian ethicists in discussions of general revelation and natural law. In this passage Cicero writes, "There is in fact a true law—namely, right reason—which is in accordance with nature, applies to all men, and is unchangeable and eternal. By its commands this law summons men to the performance of their duties; by its prohibitions it restrains them from doing wrong. . . . It will not lay down one rule at Rome and another at Athens, nor will it be one rule today and another tomorrow. But there will be one law, eternal and unchangeable, binding at all times upon the peoples; and there will be, as it were, one common master and ruler of men, namely God, who is the author of this law, its interpreter, and its sponsor." Cicero, *De republica* 3.22.

[7] Cf. John Locke, *Essays on the Law of Nature*, ed. W. von Leyden (New York: Oxford University Press, 2002); Immanuel Kant, *Foundations of the Metaphysics of Morals* (Indianapolis: Bobbs-Merrill, 1959).

[8] Augustine, *Confessions* 2.4.9; Aquinas, *Summa* 1ae2ae. 98–105; Calvin, *Institutes* 2.2.13, 22; 2.8.1–2; 4.20.16. For more on Calvin's citation of natural law see Stephen J. Grabill, *Rediscovering the Natural Law in Reformed Theological Ethics* (Grand Rapids: Eerdmans, 2006), 70–97.

[9] Cf. J. Budziszewski, *What We Can't Not Know: A Guide* (Dallas, TX: Spence, 2003); Budziszewski, *Written on the Heart*; Alasdair MacIntyre, *After Virtue* (Notre Dame, IN: University of Notre Dame Press, 1981); and Alasdair MacIntyre, *First Principles, Final Ends, and Contemporary Philosophical Issues* (Milwaukee, WI: Marquette University Press, 1990).

without knowing exactly *why* it is right or wrong. Murray writes that the "moral consciousness . . . has an intuitive sense of what is right and good."[10] More specifically, though, in appealing to general revelation, ethicists have attempted to discern and define what has become known as "natural law." Rae writes that "natural law is simply general revelation in the area of moral values."[11] While this definition is correct, a survey of ethicists who have appealed to natural law reveals a lack of consensus as to the specifics of the concept.[12] Indeed, given the wide use of the term in moral literature, readers must be careful to discern what a given author means when referring to natural law. For the sake of the present discussion, natural law can simply be understood as the basic framework of moral order discernible through general revelation.

Modes of General Revelation

AS WAS PREVIOUSLY NOTED, WITHIN ORTHODOX theology there are three classic modes of general revelation, the first being the created order. Christian ethicists have found support for this concept in passages such as Ps 19:1–4, which reads, "The heavens declare the glory of God, and the sky proclaims the work of His hands. Day after day they pour out speech; night after night they communicate knowledge. There is no speech; there are no words; [where] their voice is not heard. Their message has gone out to all the earth, and their words to the ends of the world." Another oft-cited passage in support of creation being a source of general revelation is Rom 1:18–20. Here, as he examines the spiritual state of those who lack access to the written law, Paul writes,

> For God's wrath is revealed from heaven against all god-
> lessness and unrighteousness of people who by their
> unrighteousness suppress the truth, since what can be
> known about God is evident among them, because God
> has shown it to them. For His invisible attributes, that is,

---

[10] John Murray, *Principles of Conduct: Aspects of Biblical Ethics* (Grand Rapids: Eerdmans, 1955), 19.

[11] Scott B. Rae, *Moral Choices: An Introduction to Ethics*, 2nd ed. (Grand Rapids: Zondervan, 2000), 33.

[12] Most standard Christian ethics encyclopedias contain an overview of the various streams within natural law theory. Cf. *Baker Dictionary of Christian Ethics* (1973), s.v. "natural law;" *New Dictionary of Christian Ethics and Pastoral Theology* (1995), s.v. "natural law;" *The Westminster Dictionary of Christian Ethics* (1986), s.v. "natural law."

His eternal power and divine nature, have been clearly seen
since the creation of the world, being understood through
what He has made. As a result, people are without excuse.

The message of these passages, as well as others,[13] is clear: the
created order itself reveals both the existence and the character of
God. Given the biblical teaching that one's actions reveal one's
being (cf. Prov 23:7; 27:19; Matt 12:34; 15:18), since God created
the world, one would expect the creation to reflect its Maker.[14]
Stated differently, God's laws are an expression of his character,
which is "clearly seen" (Rom 1:20) in the world; therefore, aspects
of God's moral order are discernable through that which the Lord
has made. While thinkers differ on the exact details, in ethical theory this moral knowledge available through the created order is
what is meant by the term *natural law*. Furthermore, since God
created the world good, some ethicists, especially those within the
Roman Catholic tradition, have suggested morality can be viewed
in terms of interacting with the world in accord with its teleological
design. While most would agree there is indeed a type of natural
order within the creation (in addition to revelation of God's moral
character), the subjective nature of discerning such design leads
most Protestant thinkers to resist the idea of defining morality in
terms of following a perceived creational blueprint.

A second mode of general revelation by which God's moral
standards may be known is the conscience of man. Wolters writes:

> Even without God's explicit verbal positivization of the
> creational norms . . . people have an intuitive sense of nor-
> mative standards for conduct. One word for that intui-
> tive attunement to creational normativity is *conscience*. . . .
> This does not refer to some innate virtue of "natural man,"
> unaffected by sin, but to the finger of the sovereign Creator

---

[13] Citing Prov 6:6–11 as an example, Rae writes, "The book of Proverbs defines right
and wrong (wisdom and folly) by observations drawn from nature." Rae, *Moral Choices*, 33.
Another passage to which some theologians have appealed as an example of creation being
a source of general revelation is Acts 14:15–17. Here Paul refers to "God, who made the
heaven, the earth, the sea, and everything in them. . . . He did not leave Himself without a
witness, since He did what is good by giving you rain from heaven and fruitful seasons." Cf.
Millard J. Erickson, *Christian Theology* (Grand Rapids: Baker, 1985), 169; Wayne Grudem,
Systematic Theology: An Introduction to Biblical Doctrine (Grand Rapids: Zondervan, 1994),
122–23.

[14] Cf. C. S. Lewis' discussion of natural law as a proof for the existence of God. Lewis,
Mere Christianity, 27–39.

engraving reminders of his norms upon human sensibilities even in the midst of apostasy.[15]

Christian ethicists have found support for this idea in Rom 2:14–15 where Paul writes, "So, when Gentiles, who do not have the law, instinctively do what the law demands, they are a law to themselves even though they do not have the law. They show that the work of the law is written on their hearts. Their consciences confirm this. Their competing thoughts will either accuse or excuse them."

The idea that the conscience resonates with God's moral law is common in the New Testament.[16] Indeed, Scripture speaks of having a "good conscience" (Acts 23:1; 1 Tim 1:5, 19; 1 Pet 3:21), a "clear conscience" (Acts 24:16; 1 Tim 3:9; 2 Tim 1:3; Heb 13:18; cf. 1 Pet 3:16), and a cleansed conscience (cf. Heb 9:14). The New Testament also mentions the possibility of an "evil conscience" (Heb 10:22), a defiled conscience (cf. Titus 1:15; Heb 9:9), and a weak conscience (cf. 1 Cor 8:7, 10), as well as a seared conscience (cf. 1 Tim 4:2). Moreover, Paul writes about the testimony of his own conscience, which he observed was Spirit led and without guilt (cf. Rom 9:1; 2 Cor 1:12). The apostle Paul also encourages believers to submit to their authorities "because of your conscience" (Rom 13:5; cf. 1 Cor 10:25) and exhorts his readers to order their conduct aright in view of the consciences of others (cf. 1 Cor 8:12; 10:29; 2 Cor 4:2). While many of these verses are written to believers with access to the written law, it is clear that the conscience is a tool God uses to regulate (if not to reveal) his moral standards to all of mankind.[17]

A third mode of general revelation is history or, in theological terminology, the record of divine providence. The idea here is that a review of history, on both a personal and a worldwide level, will

---

[15] Albert M. Wolters, *Creation Regained: Biblical Basics for a Reformational Worldview* (Grand Rapids: Eerdmans, 1985), 25.

[16] The word *conscience* does not appear in many English translations of the Old Testament as most versions prefer the term *heart*. Yet in the HCSB see Gen 20:5, 6; 1 Sam 24:5; 25:31; 2 Sam 24:10; Job 27:6; Ps 16:7; Jer 2:2.

[17] Interestingly, most modern, evangelical ethics textbooks do not address conscience. But for a brief treatment of conscience, see the chapter on the topic in J. Douma, *Responsible Conduct*, trans. Nelson D. Kloosterman (Phillipsburg, NJ: P&R, 2003), 145–55; the section in John Frame, *The Doctrine of the Christian Life* (Phillipsburg, NJ: P&R, 2008), 362–64; and the short but rich treatment in David Clyde Jones, *Biblical Christian Ethics* (Grand Rapids: Baker, 1994), 72–76.

testify to the existence of God and his law. This includes the Lord's providential supervision of individuals, as well as the revelation and confirmation of God's moral standards through the events of history. Among other passages,[18] scriptural support for this concept can be found in Acts 14:17. Here, when speaking in the city of Lystra, Paul explained to a pagan crowd that God "did not leave Himself without a witness, since He did what is good by giving you rain from heaven and fruitful seasons." Another passage that speaks of general revelation in the events of history is Acts 17:24–27. These verses record that as Paul spoke to the Athenians at the Areopagus he taught:

> The God who made the world and everything in it—He is Lord of heaven and earth. . . . He Himself gives everyone life and breath and all things. From one man He has made every nationality to live over the whole earth and has determined their appointed times and the boundaries of where they live. He did this so they might seek God, and perhaps they might reach out and find Him, though He is not far from each one of us.

In summary, creation, conscience, and history are three classic modes of general revelation. Yet, while Scripture testifies to these as valid means of revelation, it does not spell out clearly their exact use in moral theory. Given the subjective nature of this process, perhaps the use of general revelation in ethical formulation can best be understood by way of illustration. Consider, for example, the topic of homosexuality.[19] The discipline of biblical ethics would conclude that homosexuality is immoral based on passages such as Gen 18:17–19:29; Lev 18:22; 20:13; Rom 1:18–32; 1 Cor 6:9–11;

---

[18] Other passages used to support this concept include: Dan 2:21–22, "He changes the times and seasons; He removes kings and establishes kings. He gives wisdom to the wise and knowledge to those who have understanding. He reveals the deep and hidden things; He knows what is in the darkness, and light dwells with Him." And Matt 5:45, "Your Father in heaven . . . causes His sun to rise on the evil and the good, and sends rain on the righteous and the unrighteous."

[19] Another example is procreation. Whereas biblical ethics would conclude that procreation is good based on passages such as Deut 7:13–14; Pss 113:9; 127:3–5; and Prov 17:6, among others, natural law theory could reach the same conclusion apart from the Bible. Indeed, a consideration of general revelation may lead one to view procreation as moral, for it is the natural result of sexual intercourse (i.e., an appeal to creation); human beings innately know it is good and are inclined toward it (i.e., an appeal to conscience); and historically it has resulted in happiness and the furtherance of the human race when practiced (i.e., an appeal to history).

and 1 Tim 1:10, among others. Natural law theory, however, could potentially reach a similar conclusion without appealing to Scripture. For instance, reflection on general revelation may lead one to the opinion that homosexuality is immoral because the act is contrary to the design of the human body (i.e., an appeal to creation); human beings seem innately to know it is wrong (i.e., an appeal to conscience);[20] and historically it has almost always been considered immoral and resulted in death and disease when practiced (i.e., an appeal to history).[21]

Limitations of Natural Law

IT SEEMS, THEN, THAT AN APPEAL to creation, conscience, and history may be helpful in the formation of one's ethics. Yet, while the example just cited appears to confirm this notion, the use of general revelation in moral theory has not been accepted uncritically by all Christian thinkers. Indeed, as will be explored over the following pages, natural law theory is not without its limitations and its detractors. In fact, some have suggested the challenges incumbent to ethical rationalism so handicap the discipline that perhaps it is best to abandon it altogether. While some may view this sentiment to be an overreaction, historically this has been the stance of many Protestant ethicists.

One of the most oft-cited limitations of ethical rationalism is the ability of fallen man to receive and to make use of natural law via general revelation. This is not a challenge to the ontological existence of natural law. Rather, this critique raises the question of natural man's ability to discern and to keep spiritual and moral truths apart from divine enablement. The underlying issue in view here is the extent of the fall of mankind as recorded in Genesis 3.

---

[20] Concerning this topic, the words of J. Budziszewski are arresting, "Conjugal sex means self-giving, making one flesh out of two. By contrast, when a man puts the part of himself which represents life into the cavity of another man which represents decay and expulsion, at the most basic of all possible levels he is saying, 'Life be swallowed in death.' We cannot overwrite such meanings with different ones just because we want to." Budziszewski, *What We Can't Not Know*, 86–87.

[21] According to the controversial study by Cameron et al., the median age of death of married American males is 75; however, for sexually active homosexual American males it is 42. While 80 percent of married American men lived to age 65 or older, less than 2 percent of homosexual men lived as long. Cf. Paul Cameron, W. L. Playfair, and S. Wellum, "The Longevity of Homosexuals: Before and After the AIDS Epidemic," *Omega* 29 (1994): 249–72. For a more recent, confirmatory study, see: Paul Cameron and Kirk Cameron, "Gay Obituaries Closely Track Officially Reported Deaths from Aids," *Psychological Reports* 96, no. 3 (June 2005): 693–97.

How marred by sin is man's nature? How depraved is humanity? To what degree did the fall affect man's spirit, his mind, and his soul? Speaking generally about moral systems yet particularly addressing ethical rationalism, Jones writes, "The problem is that every system of laws presupposes some view of human nature."[22] Since Protestants have traditionally held to the total depravity of mankind, the use of natural law theory apart from Scripture has not been widespread. Roman Catholic theologians, however, who generally hold a more optimistic view of the epistemological abilities of natural man, have embraced and developed ethical rationalism.

Of course, many of those who eschew natural law theory admit some awareness of the moral law by fallen man. Indeed, this seems to be an inescapable conclusion in view of passages such as Psalm 19 and Romans 1–2. Yet, as Frame correctly observes, "It is difficult to understand how best to coordinate depravity with common grace."[23] Since an in-depth study of human depravity lies beyond the scope of this book, perhaps it is best to conclude with this general observation: in ethical formation, the degree to which one makes use of natural law apart from Scripture will be inversely proportional to one's view of the fallen estate of man. This being said, in his discussion of natural law, it is worth noting that Paul does call general revelation "truth" (Rom 1:18, 25). While this truth is "known" (Rom 1:19, 21), "seen" (Rom 1:20), and "understood" (Rom 1:20), it is nevertheless "suppressed" (Rom 1:18); thus, it cannot be employed by unregenerate man in any significant way for moral guidance.[24] Indeed, there is a difference between the *existence* of natural law, mankind's potential to *know* natural law, and his desire and ability to *keep* natural law.

---

[22] Jones, *Biblical Christian Ethics*, 82. *The Westminster Dictionary of Christian Ethics* echoes Jones's observation as it notes the problem with any moral system is that "its view of human nature is likely to be at least as controversial as the moral conclusions at which it arrives." *The Westminster Dictionary of Christian Ethics* (1986), s.v. "Natural Law."

[23] Frame, *Doctrine of the Christian Life*, 244.

[24] Natural law advocates often seem to overlook the thrust of Paul's discussion in Romans 1–2 where he cites general revelation. Contextually it is clear that the apostle's main goal is to demonstrate man's lost condition. Natural law reveals God's character. In light of this revelation and mankind's rejection of the law, man's lost condition and need for a Savior are communicated. Note, however, Paul never holds natural law up as a means of attaining righteousness, as only the gospel accomplishes this (cf. Rom 1:16–17). Some have held that if natural law does not have the potential to save, then God is unjust. Yet God's judgment is not based on the viability of general revelation for salvation or on man's ability to keep the law. Rather, it is based on man's knowledge of the law and subsequent willful breaking of it. Man is not judged for what he cannot do but for what he does do.

A second limitation of using natural law in ethical formation is the ability to reach moral conclusions without committing the so-called *naturalistic fallacy*. This objection, clearly articulated in G. E. Moore's *Principia Ethica*,[25] states that one cannot reach a moral conclusion (an *ought*) from a factual observation (an *is*).[26] In other words, Moore argued that to base ethical theory solely on observations about the world or man is flawed. This is because ethics necessarily entails an *ought*, while natural law is by definition an *is*. For example, one can say, "Adultery causes a guilty conscience." This is an observation about how someone might feel after being unfaithful to a spouse. Yet the naturalistic fallacy says there is then no way to make the moral claim, "Adultery is wrong." For just because unfaithfulness causes guilt does not make it wrong. This same rubric could be applied to moral conclusions drawn from any part of natural law, for all natural law comes from observations that stem from general revelation.

A third limitation of ethical rationalism concerns the vague nature of natural law. Said differently, since natural law must be discerned through general revelation, it tends to be imprecise in both its content and its form. This raises the question of whether natural law (or at least man's perception of it) is specific enough to be useful in ethical formation, especially in regard to addressing complex moral issues. Indeed, the apostle Paul hinted at this challenge as he wrote, "I would not have known sin if it were not for the law. For example, I would not have known what it is to covet if the law had not said, 'Do not covet'" (Rom 7:7). So, while general revelation may communicate aspects of moral law, it is questionable as to whether such revelation (i.e., natural law), considered in isolation, is comprehensive enough to be useful in moral theory.

In response to this problem, one may be tempted to appeal to mankind's ostensible, universal awareness and acceptance of natural law. Yet, as Van Til writes, "The common consciousness of man is not nearly so common as its name would seem to indicate. Aside from the differences that obtain between nation and nation at the present time or at any other time, it is notorious that at different

---

[25] G. E. Moore, *Principia Ethica* (Cambridge: Cambridge University Press, 1903). Note that Moore was developing the line of thought suggested by David Hume in his *Treatise of Human Nature*.

[26] Frame argues that an exception, of sorts, to the naturalistic fallacy is Christian ethics. This is so, he argues, because there is an implicit "ought" present in the "is" of God's commands. Cf. Frame, *Doctrine of the Christian Life*, 60–61.

ages the 'common consciousnesses' has changed its verdict about the actions of men."[27] Van Til's comments summarize this objection well. While it seems natural law theory can produce a general framework for morality that is agreeable to most men in a given time and place, it has difficulty in regard to the timeless, universal specifics of ethics. Comprehensive ethical theories, however, must operate in the realm of complex particulars and not just provide general trajectories.

It appears, then, that in order to be useful in ethical formation, natural law theory may need to be supplemented by a more objective form of revelation—namely, the Word of God.[28] Even Budziszewski, one of the leading contemporary advocates of natural law theory, seems to arrive at this conclusion as he writes:

> There is a natural law, and it can be known and philosophically analyzed. But that which is beside the Scripture can be vindicated only with the help of Scripture; that which is revealed before the gospel can be secured against evasion only in light of the gospel. The doctrine of natural law is best grounded not in the study of nature independent of God's Word but in the Word of God itself.[29]

[27] Cornelius Van Til, *Christian Theistic Ethics* (Phillipsburg, NJ: P&R, 1980), 126. Along these same lines, the *New Dictionary of Christian Ethics and Pastoral Theology* notes, "[While] it may be said that human nature as God's creation affords indications of his good purposes for us . . . it is too optimistic to suppose we can logically derive specific moral rules unambiguously from generalizations about human nature. . . . In a pluralistic society with no universal recognition of natural law, how can we expect it to be the basis for human laws?" *New Dictionary of Christian Ethics and Pastoral Theology*, ed. David J. Atkinson and David H. Field (Downers Grove, IL: IVP, 1995), s.v. "natural law."

[28] Supplementing general revelation with special revelation is not as complex as it might seem, for both reveal the same *quantity* (i.e., God). The difference in modes of revelation is one of *quality*, with special revelation being superior. In regard to viewing general revelation through the lens of special revelation, Frame notes, "Natural-law arguments often cry out for scriptural supplementation." Frame, *Doctrine of the Christian Life*, 248. Yet many who appeal to natural laws in moral theory do so in order to avoid Scripture and the implications of divine command theory. This approach to ethical formation seems illogical, for the moral "ought-ness" of natural law must come from somewhere. For a thought-provoking critique of the attempts of some to use natural law, apart from Scripture, as a basis for public policy, see Daniel R. Heimbach, "Natural Law in the Public Square," *Liberty University Law Review* 2, no. 3 (Spring 2008): 685–702.

[29] Budziszewski, *Written on the Heart*, 183–84. Note Frame's comments on Budziszewski's statement, "If 'that which is beside the Scripture can be vindicated only with the help of Scripture,' then appeals to natural law depend on Scripture. If one presents a natural-law argument to someone who doesn't believe in natural law, who keeps challenging the authority on which the law is based, ultimately the argument must have recourse to Scripture. So natural-law arguments ultimately depend on arguments from Scripture." Frame, *Doctrine of the Christian Life*, 245.

It is, then, to special revelation that this study on the nature of law now turns.

Special Revelation and the Law

IN THE PRECEDING DISCUSSION IT WAS suggested that general revelation alone is insufficient to communicate moral law to mankind in such a way so as to produce a viable system of ethics. Nevertheless, this brief review was helpful in that it hinted at the true nature of law—namely, that it is a reflection of God's moral character. But, to hold fast to that conclusion without a review of special revelation would be premature, especially in a book about biblical ethics.

In this book special revelation is equated with the Bible. Therefore, references to the law in special revelation ought to be understood as references to the moral standards of God as revealed in Scripture. While in his sovereignty God is surely able to communicate through special, supernatural means apart from Scripture,[30] the Bible is the only normative, objective, and timeless mode of special revelation. Moreover, since that which is recorded in Scripture is sufficient for Christian living (cf. Ps 119:1; 2 Tim 3:16–17; 2 Pet 1:3), there is no need to depart from the Bible in seeking divine moral imperatives. So the question of the nature of the law as revealed in special revelation is the question of how the moral standards revealed in Scripture relate to God.

It is somewhat surprising that the nature of the law is overlooked in many modern, introductory-level ethics textbooks. Indeed, this is an important issue, for one's answer to this question will lay the groundwork for addressing a number of other foundational issues in biblical ethics. Such issues, which will be explored over the following chapters, include the relevancy of the law, the coherency of the law, and the structure of the law. In regard to the importance of this subject, John Bunyan, the famed author of *Pilgrim's Progress*, explained: "The man who does not know the nature of the law cannot know the nature of sin. And he who does not know the

---

[30] Supernatural means of revelation are numerous in the narrative of Scripture, although not normative. Examples include prophets (cf. Heb 1:1–2), Urim and Thummim (cf. Exod 28:30), casting of lots (cf. Lev 16:8), dreams and visions (cf. Joel 2:28), angels (cf. Luke 1:26–38), audible communication (cf. Rev 1:8), and other supernatural means such as the burning bush (cf. Exod 3:1–22).

nature of sin cannot know the nature of the Savior."[31] Given that the cross is the remedy for sin and that sin entails transgressing the law, Bunyan's argument is that to misunderstand the nature of the law will lead to a wrong idea about Christ and the atonement. High stakes, indeed.

In discussions of ethics prolegomena—both secular and Christian—the question of how the law and God (or, in the case of secular ethics, the civil authorities) are related is often explored in conjunction with the so-called "Euthyphro Dilemma." This is the name given to a conversation on the nature of law recorded by Plato in his text entitled *Euthyphro*. This discussion, which is part of a much larger dialogue between Socrates and a young Athenian named Euthyphro, is as follows:

> *Socrates*: And what do you say of law-keeping, Euthyphro? Is not law-keeping, according to your definition, loved by all the gods?
>
> *Euthyphro*: Certainly.
>
> *Socrates*: Because it is pious or holy, or for some other reason?
>
> *Euthyphro*: No, that is the reason.
>
> *Socrates*: So then, law-keeping is loved because it is holy, not holy because it is loved?[32]

The issue being raised by Socrates, albeit in a somewhat obtuse manner, is the question of the nature of law—that is, assuming a deontological, divine command system of ethics, Socrates is inquiring into the essence of the relationship between the law and God. Socrates is posing the question, "What makes the law right and good?" While some may view this as an esoteric question, Rae notes that this issue "must be addressed by every adherent of divine command theory."[33] The two seemingly logical options Socrates offers Euthyphro are that law can be right and good because God (or in Socrates's case, more than one god) commands them, or that

---

[31] Quoted in Philip Graham Ryken, *Written in Stone: The Ten Commandments and Today's Moral Crisis* (Wheaton, IL: Crossway, 2003), 9.

[32] Plato, *Euthyphr* 10d.

[33] Rae, *Moral Choices*, 32.

the law can be right and good because God only commands that which is right and good. In Socrates's words, the law is either "holy because it is loved" or "loved because it is holy." This is referred to as a dilemma because, as will be explored in the following discussion, serious challenges have been raised in regard to both of these options. In fact, the two horns of this dilemma are so sharp that some thinkers, such as famed atheists Bertrand Russell and Anthony Flew among others,[34] have even used them as rationale for rejecting Christianity altogether.

The Authority over Law Paradigm

ALTHOUGH IT APPEARS AS THE SECOND option in Plato's dialogue, the most widely held view of the nature of the law is the idea that the law is right and good simply because God commanded it. Almost by default, this position seems to be held by most people, especially those in the evangelical community. In Socrates's words, the law is "holy because it is loved," or in contemporary T-shirt and bumper-sticker jargon: "God said it. I believe it. That settles it." This view of the nature of law is referred to as the authority *over* law paradigm for it places the authority (i.e., God) over the law.[35] According to this paradigm, the true power of the law—that is, what makes the law right and good—rests on God's ability to espouse moral legislation. This position teaches that the law is right and true simply because God commanded it. In technical terms this view is known as ethical voluntarism.[36] While this paradigm is widely held and has many benefits, such as safeguarding the sovereignty of God and stressing

---

[34] In his book *Why I Am Not a Christian* Bertrand Russell wrote, "If you are quite sure there is a difference between right and wrong, you are then in this situation: Is that difference due to God's fiat or is it not? If it is due to God's fiat, then for God Himself there is no difference between right and wrong, and it is no longer a significant statement to say that God is good. If you are going to say, as theologians do, that God is good, you must then say that right and wrong have some meaning which is independent of God's fiat, because God's fiats are good and not good independently of the mere fact that he made them. If you are going to say that, you will then have to say that it is not only through God that right and wrong came into being, but that they are in their essence logically anterior to God." Bertrand Russell, *Why I Am Not a Christian* (New York: Simon and Schuster, 1957), 12. According to Baggett and Walls, famed atheist Anthony Flew also makes use of the Euthyphro Dilemma as a barometer for one's aptitude for philosophy. Cf. David Baggett and Jerry L. Walls, *Good God: The Theistic Foundations of Morality* (New York: Oxford University Press, 2011), 32.

[35] Levin calls this the "pure will theory." Michael Levin, "Understanding the Euthyphro Problem," *International Journal for Philosophy of Religion* 25, no. 2 (1989): 83.

[36] Rae notes, with some explanation, that Islamic ethics is the best example of this approach to morality. Cf. Rae, *Moral Choices*, 32–33.

the limits of human freedom,[37] some significant challenges to this view have been raised.[38]

To elaborate, the most often cited critique of this position is that under this paradigm the law seems to be arbitrary, for God could have given the opposite laws, and then those laws would be correct. Rae writes, "If things are good because God commands them, then he could command that we torture babies, and that would be good simply because he commanded it."[39] Thankfully, however, torturing babies seems intuitively wrong to most people. Indeed, the larger rubric supporting this idea seems to reduce God's rule to a legalistic or perhaps even tyrannical "might makes right" kind of authority.[40] Moreover, within this paradigm God would apparently be free to alter his moral laws at any time. Geisler emphasizes this point as he observes that this view "provides no security that God will remain constant in his ethical concerns, since he could change his mind at any time and will that hate is right rather than love."[41] This, of course, raises questions about the infallibility and the authority of Scripture in which moral law is found.

A second related problem for the authority over law position involves the goodness of God. This limitation, which Piers Benn

---

[37] *New Dictionary of Christian Ethics and Pastoral Theology* (1995), s.v. "voluntarism;" *The Westminster Dictionary of Christian Ethics* (1986), s.v. "voluntarism." Note that the *Westminster Dictionary of Christian Ethics* incorrectly identifies the early Protestant Reformers, such as John Calvin, as proponents of this view.

[38] For more in-depth analysis of this view see Baggett and Walls, *Good God*, 33–38; Louise Anthony, "Atheism as Perfect Piety," in *Is Goodness Without God Good Enough? A Debate on Faith, Secularism and Ethics*, ed. Robert K. Garcia and Nathan L. King (Lanham, MD: Roman & Littlefield), 67–84; Geisler, *Christian Ethics*, 21–22, 30–31, 37; Richard Joyce, "Theistic Ethics and the Euthyphro Dilemma," *Journal of Religious Ethics* 30, no. 1 (March 1, 2002): 49–75; and John Millikin, "Euthyphro, the Good, and the Right," *Philosophia Christi* 11, no. 1 (2009): 145–55.

[39] Rae, *Moral Choices*, 32.

[40] A practical problem with the authority over law paradigm is the legalistic ecclesiology it tends to foster. When the truth of the law is divorced from the character of the lawgiver and instead is invested in the authority of the lawgiver, distortions often result. Such distortions include the proliferation of extrabiblical rules, the fostering of pride and self-righteousness, and a tendency to separate from perceived lawbreakers. Examples of those who have fallen into this error include the Pharisees in biblical times and legalistic churches in modern times.

[41] Geisler, *Christian Ethics*, 37. Similarly, Baggett and Walls write, "If God has no reasons for his commands, then we can't anticipate what his commands will be, since they are liable to be whatever divine whim dictates, irrespective of prior reasons or the intrinsic features of the actions involved." Baggett and Walls, *Good God*, 34. Those who respond to this critique by appealing to passages such as Isa 40:8 and Mark 13:31 to argue that God's Word will never pass away misunderstand this view, for under this paradigm what God says triumphs what God has said.

notes is "potentially devastating,"[42] is that in connecting the nature of the law to God's authority (and not to his character) there does not appear to be a necessary and meaningful difference for God between good and evil—at least not in the expression of law. Adherents of this view certainly may affirm the scriptural teaching that "everything created by God is good" (1 Tim 4:4) and "no one is good but One—God" (Luke 18:19). Yet, since this position holds that the law is right and true simply because it originates from God, in the giving of the law there is not a requisite connection between God's goodness and the law. Indeed, under this paradigm God's goodness is somewhat peripheral to his lawgiving or perhaps is synonymous with or reduced to his power. While this critique does not rule out God's essential goodness, it does raise the issue of how divine goodness may be known as well as the question of the rationale for which to praise God for his goodness. In regard to this notion, Leibniz rhetorically asked, "Why praise him [i.e., God] for what he has done, if he would be equally praiseworthy in doing just the contrary?"[43]

A third, significant critique of the authority over law paradigm relates to the atonement of Christ. Questions often asked by unbelievers and immature believers alike are: "Why did Jesus have to die a cruel, bloody death on the cross? Why couldn't God, in his infinite power, just declare man's sins forgiven?" Upon reflection, though, it becomes clear that these questions regarding the means of the atonement rest on the assumed validity of the authority over law paradigm. Perhaps unconsciously, the thought process behind this question seems to be that since man's sin problem involves a violation of laws God has declared to be right and true, then God should simply be able to remedy this problem by declaring man's sins to be forgiven. However, Jesus did die a cruel, bloody death on the cross—a death that was ordained of God (cf. Acts 2:23; 4:27–28). Therefore, this ought to lead one to the conclusion that God could not remedy man's sin problem by divine fiat.[44] Indeed, if it were

---

[42] Piers Benn, *Ethics* (Montreal: McGill-Queen's University Press, 1998), 48.

[43] Gottfried Wilhelm Leibniz, *Discourse on Metaphysics*, trans. Peter G. Lucas and Leslie Grint (Manchester, U.K.: Manchester University Press, 1968), 5.

[44] There are, of course, many things that God cannot do, including lie (cf. Titus 1:2; Heb 6:18), break his covenants (cf. Ps 89:34), change (cf. Mal 3:6), change his mind (cf. Num 23:19), be unjust (cf. Exod 34:7), tire (cf. Isa 40:28), deny himself (cf. 2 Tim 2:13), reject the elect (cf. John 6:37), be tempted (Jas 1:13), do wickedness (Job 34:10), and share his glory (cf. Isa 42:8), among others.

possible to remedy sin and to make man righteous apart from Jesus'
cruel, bloody death on the cross, there would have been no substitutionary atonement (cf. Matt 26:39; Mark 14:36; Gal 3:21).

The Authority Under Law Paradigm

IN LIGHT OF THE AFOREMENTIONED PROBLEMS with the authority over
law paradigm, some have opted for the second horn of the Euthyphro Dilemma. This position, which was the first option offered by
Socrates to Euthyphro, holds that the law is "loved because it is holy."
In other words, this paradigm teaches God's laws are right and true
because God commanded that which is right and true. According to
this view, then, the true power of the law rests within the law's own
fundamental, intrinsic rightness and goodness. This position is called
the authority *under* law paradigm for it places the authority (i.e.,
God) under the law. According to this paradigm the law is external
and antecedent to God; God is obedient to the law;[45] and God wisely
restates the law to man. Others have called this the "guided will theory" of the nature of law,[46] or the "divine independence theory" of
the relationship between God and the law.[47] In technical terms, since
this position is usually discussed in conjunction with and in contrast
to ethical voluntarism, this view is known as ethical nonvoluntarism.

While the authority under law paradigm has both benefits and
proponents[48] akin to the authority over law view, this position is
not without limitations.[49] The most obvious and often mentioned
critique of this view is that it appears to infringe on God's sovereignty as the law is external to and even transcends God. Indeed,
under this paradigm God himself conforms to the law before passing it on to man. Moreover, if one defines God as that which is

---

[45] Mouw writes that advocates of this position "hold that there is only one perfectly
rational and enlightened (i.e., omniscient) being, and that this being is benevolent, that is,
he has 'adopted' the moral point of view . . . the situation has never been otherwise and that
it will never change." Richard J. Mouw, "The Status of God's Moral Judgments," *Canadian
Journal of Theology* 16 (1970): 65.

[46] Levin, "Understanding the Euthyphro Problem," 83.

[47] Anthony, "Atheism as Perfect Piety," 71.

[48] Cf. Levin, "Understanding the Euthyphro Problem," 83–97; and Mouw, "The Status
of God's Moral Judgments," 61–66. In his article Mouw interacts with another advocate of
this position, Wallace I. Matson, *The Existence of God* (Ithaca, NY: Cornell University Press,
1965), 233–34. Note that Rae, either misunderstanding or conflating this view, incorrectly
claims, "This is the view of historic, rabbinic Judaism and of Roman Catholic ethics." Rae,
Moral Choices, 33.

[49] For a more in-depth analysis of this position and its adherents, see Baggett and Walls,
Good God, 38–45.

ultimate, in a sense, this position makes the law itself a god, for the law is antecedent to God. Baggett and Walls articulate this problem well as they write:

> If God merely registers the conditions of the moral climate, so to speak, and then factually reports such conditions to us (perhaps via imperatives), he may be the divine moral meteorologist, but he is hardly the one responsible for the content of ethics. To think otherwise is to confuse categories; we might as well blame the weather radar for the thunderstorm that ruined our tennis match. . . . The guided will view denies that God, even if he exists, is relevant to ethics in anything more than an ancillary role of filling us in on its details.[50]

A second problem with the authority under law paradigm is similar to the aforementioned critique of the authority over law position—that is, this view calls into question the goodness of God. This is not a challenge to the essential goodness of God, for Scripture is clear regarding this fact (cf. Ps 25:8; Nah 1:7). Rather, this critique raises the question of how man may know and learn the goodness of God through the law, if at all. To elaborate, according to this paradigm, the law—which the Bible univocally teaches is right and good (cf. Rom 7:12, 16; 1 Tim 1:8)—exists apart from God. God, then, in his infinite wisdom confers the law to man. However, under this paradigm there is no requisite connection between God's goodness and his revelation of the law. Proponents of this view may claim that God's act of giving the law to man was benevolent, but this is merely an evaluation of divine action, not a statement about divine being. In sum, then, from this position one may conclude the law is good, and perhaps even that God is wise, but not that God is essentially good. Indeed, this view seems to violate the connection that Scripture makes between God's goodness and the law (cf. Ps 119:68; Matt 19:17). Historically, this tie has

---

[50] Baggett and Walls, *Good God*, 38–39. In a similar manner Levin writes: "If God wills what he does because it is antecedently right, moral standards become independent of God and in this instance God's will becomes a function of something beyond itself. If moral standards are as ultimate as God, God loses his unique independence." Levin, "Understanding the Euthyphro Problem," 84. Additionally, note that the supremacy of God (not the law) could be argued from passages such as Eccl 3:14 and John 1:1–3.

been a fundamental component of ethical theory in the Christian tradition.[51]

A third problem with the authority under law paradigm is the implication this view has for Jesus' atonement. Perhaps the most concise explanation of the atonement in Scripture is found in 2 Cor 5:21 where Paul writes, "He made the One who did not know sin to be sin for us, so that we might become the righteousness of God in Him." Furthermore, other passages in the Bible describe the atonement as being foreordained (cf. 1 Pet 1:20), foretold (cf. Isa 53:4–6), reconciliatory (cf. Col 1:22), redemptive (cf. Heb 9:12), voluntary (cf. John 10:18), loving (cf. Gal 2:20), necessary (cf. Heb 9:22), sanctifying (cf. Heb 10:10), glorifying (cf. 1 Cor 6:20), and acceptable (cf. Eph 5:2). Yet, given the dynamics of the authority under law paradigm, the atonement does not even seem possible, let alone as glorious as it is described in Scripture. This is so because if the law is antecedent to God, and God himself must obey it, it does not seem that God could make atonement for violations of a law to which he himself is bound. In fact, even if this were possible under this paradigm, there would apparently be no need for God to become incarnate in order to accomplish this feat.

In summary it seems that the two horns of the Euthyphro Dilemma—namely, the authority over law paradigm and the authority under law paradigm—each have serious flaws, challenges, and liabilities. Both explanations of the nature of law appear to impugn God's character, cannot explain God's goodness, and either challenge the necessity or the possibility of Jesus' atonement. Indeed, it is not surprising that the Euthyphro Dilemma has historically been used as a foil against divine command theories of morality, including biblical ethics. Yet there is another option—a third paradigm that may help to explain the nature of law and avoid the horns of the Euthyphro Dilemma.

The Authority Is Law Paradigm

A THIRD, SOMETIMES OVERLOOKED, OPTION FOR how the law and God relate can be termed the authority *is* law paradigm. This view of the nature of law teaches that the law is right and true simply because it reflects and reveals God's moral character, which is right and true.

---

[51] Cf. Paul Chamberlain, *Can We Be Good Without God?* (Downers Grove, IL: InterVarsity Press, 1996); and Dennis P. Hollinger, *Choosing the Good: Christian Ethics in a Complex World* (Grand Rapids: Baker, 2002).

According to this position, then, the true power of the law rests in the fact that it is a revelation of God's moral character. To be clear, under this paradigm the law itself is not God; the law is ontologically separate from God, as it appears in Scripture. Yet, according to this view the content of the law is a faithful representation and expression of God's moral character. As Geisler explains: "The ethical imperatives that God gives are in accord with his unchangeable moral character. That is, God wills what is right in accordance with his own moral attributes. . . . God is absolutely perfect and his law is a reflection of his character."[52] This position, then, understands the law not only to be revelation *from* God but also to be a revelation *of* God. Just as a man's actions reflect his being, so God's actions—including his giving of the law—reveal his being (cf. Prov 23:7; Matt 12:34; 15:18).[53] Technically speaking, this position is known as Christian essentialism.

One of the clearest arguments in support of this paradigm is the process of sanctification. Scripture is replete with exhortations to practical holiness.[54] For example, Jesus taught his disciples, "Be perfect, therefore, as your heavenly Father is perfect" (Matt 5:48); Paul commanded his readers, "Therefore, be imitators of God, as dearly loved children" (Eph 5:1); and Peter wrote, "As the One who called you is holy, you also are to be holy in all your conduct; for it is written, Be holy, because I am holy" (1 Pet 1:15–16; cf. Lev 11:44). Scripture teaches the way in which believers can attain practical holiness, and thus become like God, is to keep the law (cf. Deut 10:12–13; Pss 19:8–9; 119:105; John 14:21). However, assuming a Protestant understanding of grace, the process of sanctification would not be possible through law-keeping if the law did

---

[52] Geisler, *Christian Ethics*, 22, 101. In a similar vein Frame writes: "If God says something, it is never a mere fact; it is also a norm. God's word bears his lordship attributes of control, authority, and presence, and his authority makes whatever he says normative for us. . . . God is not only a fact, but also a norm. . . . God's very nature is normative. . . . Our ultimate ethical authority is God himself. He is law in the highest sense." Frame, *Doctrine of the Christian Life*, 61, 133, 224. Puritan Thomas Watson notes, "The moral law is the copy of God's will, our spiritual directory; it shows us what sins to avoid, what duties to pursue." Thomas Watson, *The Ten Commandments* (Carlisle, PA: Banner of Truth, 1965), 14.

[53] Note that Paul describes God's law as holy, just, good, and glorious (cf. Rom 7:12; 2 Cor 3:7–9; 1 Tim 1:8), all of which are fundamental attributes of God. Indeed, God alone is holy and good (cf. Mark 10:18; Rev 15:4).

[54] The classic work on this topic is J. C. Ryle, *Holiness: Its Nature, Hindrances, Difficulties, and Roots* (Moscow, ID: Charles Nolan, 2002).

not reflect God's moral character.[55] In other words, if the law is merely a collection of rules God favors, or if the law is antecedent to God, then it could not impart holiness when kept. However, if the law reflects God's holiness and moral character, as believers keep the law, they naturally will become like him. Under this paradigm, then, the process of sanctification is as follows: God gives his self-reflecting law to mankind and calls believers to be sanctified; in obedience believers keep the law of God and consequently become holy like God. As will be explored in the following chapter, Protestants have traditionally referred to this as the third or proper use of the law.[56]

A second piece of evidence for the authority is law paradigm is that this view supports and explains the biblical teaching that Christians sin against God when they break his law. Question 14 in the Shorter Catechism of the *Westminster Confession of Faith* teaches, "Sin is any want of conformity unto, or transgression of, the law of God."[57] While few Christians would argue with this definition, in practice believers often seem to conceive of sin in terms of breaking sterile rules. The example of many in Scripture, however, offers a different perspective. For instance, when Potiphar's wife invited Joseph into her bed, Joseph rhetorically asked, "How could I do such a great evil and sin against God?" (Gen 39:9). In a similar fashion, in his prayer of repentance concerning his adultery with Bathsheba and murder of her husband Uriah, David confessed to God, "Against You—You alone—I have sinned and done this evil in Your sight" (Ps 51:4). What these citations, as well as the example of others in Scripture,[58] reveal is that to sin is not merely to break sterile rules; rather, to sin is to transgress and offend the very character and being of God. Indeed, to sin is to attempt to usurp the place of God by practically legislating laws reflective of oneself (cf. Rom 8:7; Jas 4:4). Sin is not ancillary to God or to man; rather, it involves the hearts of both.

---

[55] Readers ought not to confuse justification, which entails the *imputation* of holiness, with sanctification, which involves the *impartation* of holiness.

[56] John Calvin, *Institutes* 2.7.12.

[57] Robert Steel, *The Shorter Catechism with Proofs, Analyses, and Illustrative Anecdotes for Teachers and Parents* (London: T. Nelson and Sons, 1885), 52.

[58] Another example is Abimelech who, after protesting his innocence in regard to taking Sarah as his wife, was told by the Lord: "Yes, I know that you did this with a clear conscience. I have also kept you from sinning against Me" (Gen 20:6). Note, too, that when David was first confronted by Nathan the prophet in regard to his adultery with Bathsheba, he confessed, "I have sinned against the LORD" (2 Sam 12:13).

A third argument for the authority is law paradigm relates to Paul's discussion of the fate of the unevangelized. To elaborate, as he examined the spiritual state of all men in his letter to the Romans, Paul wrote:

> For God's wrath is revealed from heaven against all god-lessness and unrighteousness of people who by their unrighteousness suppress the truth, since what can be known about God is evident among them, because God has shown it to them. For His invisible attributes, that is, His eternal power and divine nature, have been clearly seen since the creation of the world, being understood through what He has made. As a result, people are without excuse. (Rom 1:18–20)

Clearly, then, Paul concludes that all men—even the unevangelized—are objects of God's wrath and without excuse. Yet note the apostle's reasoning. Paul writes that since unregenerate men reject God's attributes as manifest in the created order, they are condemned. This conclusion, however, would not be possible if the law were not an expression of God's moral character. Yet, since the law is a revelation of God's character, to suppress knowledge of God's attributes is tantamount to breaking the law.[59] As Paul writes, even though the unevangelized do not have the written law, in suppressing knowledge of God, "They are a law to themselves even though they do not have the law" (Rom 2:14).[60] Stated succinctly, then, since the law is a reflection of God's character, to reject God's character is to break the law.

Finally, unlike the views of the nature of law that stem from the two horns of the Euthyphro Dilemma, the authority is law paradigm can help explain the necessity and sufficiency of the

---

[59] This also explains Paul's teaching that "sin was in the world before the law" (Rom 5:13).

[60] Paul highlights an interesting corollary to this idea that also supports the authority is law paradigm—that is, the phenomena that people who reject God's law always reinvent God. Paul writes: "For though they knew God, they did not glorify Him as God or show gratitude. Instead, their thinking became nonsense, and their senseless minds were darkened. Claiming to be wise, they became fools and exchanged the glory of the immortal God for images resembling mortal man, birds, four-footed animals, and reptiles" (Rom 1:21–23). On a base level, then, man realizes God's law reflects and reveals God. Consequently, when man replaces God's law with his own law, he then creates a God who would give the law that he has already predetermined to hold. This is why the God of any niche theology (e.g., liberation theology, feminist theology) always resembles its proponents.

atonement of Christ. If "sin is the breaking of the law" (1 John 3:4), and the law is a reflection of God's moral character, then God himself can make propitiation for man's sin. When men sin, the law is broken, and God is offended. While God's justice will not allow sin to be overlooked, in his mercy and grace God can atone for man's sin by paying the penalty for sin himself. That the law is an expression of God's own character is one of the factors that make the substitutionary atonement possible. As the writer of the book of Hebrews explains, Jesus voluntarily chose to become "like His brothers in every way, so that He could become a merciful and faithful high priest in service to God, to make propitiation for the sins of the people" (Heb 2:17). Indeed, given man's lost condition, not only can God provide substitutionary atonement, but this is the only way man can be saved (cf. Acts 4:12). Just as sin is man substituting himself for God, so salvation is God substituting himself for man.

Conclusion

IN SUMMARY, THIS CHAPTER HAS FOCUSED on the nature of law as it has looked at how the law relates to God. The opening pages of this chapter looked at general revelation and the manifestation of natural law within the created order. In this section it was noted that the use of general revelation in ethical formation, a discipline known as natural law theory, is a viable moral system. Indeed, as was reviewed, there is a long tradition—within both secular and Christian ethics—of employing natural law in the construction of moral theory. Yet, because of the fallen estate of man, it was suggested that such an approach to morality needs to be supplemented by and used in conjunction with special revelation. This is the domain of biblical ethics.

The second part of this chapter focused on the nature of the relationship between the law and God. In contrast to the two options for the nature of law presented within the Euthyphro Dilemma, both of which assume a dichotomy between the law and God, this section developed the idea that the law and God are integrally related. As was explored, the law itself is a reflection and revelation of God's moral character. While this is true, however, biblical ethics entails much more than simply keeping the law; for Scripture teaches that Christians are "justified by faith in Christ and not by the works of the law" (Gal 2:16; cf. Phil 3:9). Moreover, Paul instructed the Roman church, "You are not under law but under grace" (Rom 6:14). Passages such as these raise the question of the relationship between the law and the gospel, a question to which this study now turns.

Summary Points

- General revelation can be defined as God's revelation of himself to all peoples, at all times, in all places.
- Historically speaking, theologians have recognized three modes of general revelation:
  - The created order (Ps 19:1–4; Rom 1:18–20)
  - Human conscience (Rom 2:14–15)
  - History or the record of God's providence (Acts 14:17; 17:24–27)
- While general revelation is a valid concept, Protestant ethicists have identified three limitations of employing general revelation (specifically natural law) in ethical theory:
  - The fallen estate of mankind distorts man's ability to receive general revelation.
  - The use of natural law lends itself to the naturalistic fallacy.
  - The lack of clarity of natural law.
- Special revelation is equated with the Bible. In regard to biblical ethics, special revelation consists of the moral standards of God as revealed in Scripture.
- Three perspectives on the nature of law as revealed in special revelation:
  - The authority over law paradigm—The law is right and good simply because God commanded it.
  - The authority under law paradigm—The law is right and good because God commanded what is right and good.
  - The authority is law paradigm—The law is right and good because it reveals the moral character of God who is right and good.

Chapter 3

The Relevancy of the Law

C
hapter 2 of this book covered the nature of the law as it looked at how the law relates to God. The present chapter aims to advance this discussion of biblical ethics by looking at the relevancy of the law, giving specific attention to the question of the relationship between the law and the gospel. The issue of the correlation of the law and the gospel is a perennial favorite topic in Christian circles, spawning numerous publications annually.[1] The purpose of this chapter is not to champion a particular view in the law-gospel debate, although the author's position will be evident. Rather, this chapter seeks to arrive at a better understanding of the law, to present a common definition of the gospel, and to review the major options in the discussion of how the law and the gospel relate, while concurrently demonstrating the importance and relevance of this topic for biblical ethics. Indeed, the relationship between the law and the gospel must be considered by all who participate in the discipline of biblical ethics, for one's answer to this question will set the parameters for the material from which one can engage in moral theory.

---

[1] Examples include: John S. Feinberg, ed., *Continuity and Discontinuity: Perspectives on the Relationship Between the Old and New Testaments* (Wheaton, IL: Crossway, 1988); Daniel P. Fuller, *Gospel and Law, Contrast or Continuum: The Hermeneutics of Dispensationalism and Covenant Theology* (Grand Rapids: Eerdmans, 1980); Ernest C. Reisinger, *The Law and the Gospel* (Phillipsburg, NJ: P&R, 1997); Thomas R. Schreiner, *40 Questions About Christians and Biblical Law* (Grand Rapids: Kregel, 2010); and Wayne G. Strickland, ed., *Five Views on Law and Gospel* (Grand Rapids: Zondervan, 1996).

The question of the relationship between the law and the gospel is a theological issue. Since ethics is applied theology (sometimes called moral theology), throughout history theologians have realized the importance of the law-gospel debate for ethical formation.[2] For example, Martin Luther commented, "He who knows how to distinguish gospel from law should thank God and know that he is a theologian."[3] Similarly, John Newton, author of the classic hymn "Amazing Grace," said, "Clearly to understand the distinction, connection, and harmony between the law and the gospel, and their mutual subservience to illustrate and establish each other, is a singular privilege, and a happy means of preserving the soul from being entangled by errors."[4] Likewise, when commenting on the relationship between the law and the gospel, Spurgeon observed: "There is no point upon which men make greater mistakes than upon the relationship which exists between the law and the gospel. . . . The man who knows the relative positions of the law and of the gospel has the keys of the situation in the matter of doctrine. . . . These are two points which every Christian man should understand."[5]

Surely, then, the discussion of how the law and the gospel relate is an important question; yet, as Spurgeon observed, it is a subject over which Christians have historically disagreed and sometimes erred. For instance, the issue is sometimes described in elementary terms as the relationship between the Testaments. In so doing, some have asserted that since the Old Testament contains more moral laws and duties than does the New Testament, it ought to be

---

[2] For example, see John Murray, *Principles of Conduct: Aspects of Biblical Ethics* (Grand Rapids: Eerdmans, 1957), 181–201.

[3] Cited in Philip Graham Ryken, *Written in Stone: The Ten Commandments and Today's Moral Crisis* (Wheaton, IL: Crossway, 2003), 9.

[4] John Newton, *The Works of the Rev. John Newton* (London: T. Nelson and Sons, 1853), 104.

[5] Charles H. Spurgeon, *The New Park Street Pulpit*, vol. 1 (London: Alabaster & Passmore, 1856), 285; Charles H. Spurgeon, *The Metropolitan Tabernacle*, vol. 28 (London: Alabaster & Passmore, 1882), 277. In a similar fashion Jonathan Edwards wrote, "There is perhaps no part of divinity attended with so much intricacy, and wherein orthodox divines do so much differ as stating the precise agreement and difference between the two dispensations of Moses and Christ." Jonathan Edwards, *The Works of Jonathan Edwards*, vol. 1 (London: Ball, Arnold, 1840), 465. Likewise, in regard to the relationship between law and gospel, Murray notes: "In the degree to which error is entertained at this point, in the same degree is our conception of the gospel perverted. An erroneous conception of the function of law can be of such a character that it completely vitiates our view of the gospel; and an erroneous conception of the antithesis between law and grace can be of such a character that it demolishes both the substructure and superstructure of grace." Murray, *Principles of Conduct*, 181.

viewed as *quantitatively* more important for biblical ethics. Other thinkers, however, have asserted that since the New Testament contains the gospel in its clearest form and is specifically written to the church, it ought to be viewed as *qualitatively* more important for ethical formation. Still others have called for equal treatment of the Testaments, noting the inspired nature of all Scripture and the fact that there is no new moral revelation in the New Testament, only a restatement and refining of the moral norms given in the Old Testament.[6] Obviously, one's position on this topic will influence the formation of one's system of ethics, and perhaps even the moral conclusions that result.

Approaching this issue in a purely exegetical fashion does not resolve or immediately give any direction to this discussion, for Scripture contains many seemingly contradictory passages on the relationship between the law and the gospel. For instance, a sample of verses that appear to teach discontinuity between the law and the gospel includes:

- Luke 16:16: "The Law and the Prophets were until John; since then, the good news of the kingdom of God has been proclaimed, and everyone is strongly urged to enter it."
- John 1:17: "For the law was given through Moses, grace and truth came through Jesus Christ."
- Romans 6:14: "For sin will not rule over you, because you are not under law but under grace."
- Romans 10:4: "For Christ is the end of the law for righteousness to everyone who believes."
- Galatians 5:18: "But if you are led by the Spirit, you are not under the law."

Of course, if all of the biblical passages on law and gospel adopted a discontinuity approach, there would be no law-gospel debate. As was mentioned earlier, however, at first glance Scripture does not appear to be unified in its approach to this topic. For

---

[6] In John's Gospel Jesus stated, "I give you a new command: Love one another. Just as I have loved you, you must also love one another" (John 13:34). Yet here Christ was quoting Lev 19:18. The novelty of Jesus' statement, then, is not the content of his command to love. Rather, the newness to which Jesus refers is the ability of his Spirit-indwelt followers to keep his command to love (cf. Ezek 11:19–20; 36:27; 2 John 5). While no new moral laws are revealed in the New Testament, there is a correction of the Pharisaic interpretation of the law (e.g., "You have heard that it was said. . . . But I tell you . . ." (Matt 5:21–22, 27–28, 33–34, 38–39, 43–44).

example, in contrast to the above citations, verses that seem to teach continuity between the law and the gospel include:

- Romans 3:31: "Do we then cancel the law through faith? Absolutely not! On the contrary, we uphold the law."
- Romans 7:12, 14, 22: "So then, the law is holy, and the commandment is holy and just and good. . . . For we know that the law is spiritual. . . . For in my inner self I joyfully agree with God's law."
- 1 Corinthians 7:19: "Circumcision does not matter and uncircumcision does not matter, but keeping God's commands does."
- Galatians 3:21: "Is the law therefore contrary to God's promises? Absolutely not!"
- 1 Timothy 1:8: "We know that the law is good, provided one uses it legitimately."

The fact that many of the preceding discontinuity and continuity proof-texts occur within some of the same epistles highlights the difficulty in correlating the law and the gospel. For example, to attempt a synthesis of the above verses, in the book of Galatians, Paul writes that the law is not contrary to the gospel (cf. Gal 3:21), but he then proceeds to tell the Galatian churches that if they are led by the Spirit they are not under the law (cf. Gal 5:18). Or, in the book of Romans, Paul teaches the church that faith does not cancel but rather establishes the law (cf. Rom 3:31); yet he then instructs the believers in Rome that they are not under the law (cf. Rom 6:14), a law he later describes as holy, just, good, and spiritual (cf. Rom 7:12, 14). Following this, within the same epistle, Paul announces his own inner joy and agreement with the law (cf. Rom 7:22), which is apparently the same body of legislation he later declares to be ended by Christ for all who believe (cf. Rom 10:4). Assuming the inerrancy and infallibility of Scripture, one is led to the conclusion that Paul must use the term "law" differently within the same writings. One of the challenges in correlating the law and the gospel, then, is to understand the biblical writers' use of the term *law*.

Understanding the Law

IN CHAPTER 2 OF THIS BOOK the term *law* was defined as the moral standards God has revealed to man. While this has been a sufficient working definition up to this point, for the sake of the present discussion on the relevancy of the law, it will prove helpful to investigate how the law is used in Scripture. In seeking to understand the law, especially as it appears in the Old Testament, the majority of Protestant thinkers have employed a rubric that recognizes a threefold division of the law: ceremonial laws, civil laws, and moral laws.[7] While the validity of this rubric will be discussed later, for the sake of the present discussion, simply note that this threefold division does not imply the existence of ontologically separate types or classes of law. Rather, within the Protestant tradition the terms *ceremonial law*, *civil law*, and *moral law* have been used as interpretive categories that identify various manifestations and functions of the law in Scripture. Each of these categories of law reveals the moral standards of God and can be analyzed further.

Categories of Law

THE *CEREMONIAL LAWS* ARE ALSO CALLED religious laws, ritual laws, cultic laws, or the ordinances. Regardless of the terminology employed by various authors, the ceremonial laws are laws given for the functioning of the sacrificial system, including tabernacle/temple operations, religious festivals, and dietary regulations.[8] While there

---

[7] For example, see Calvin, *Institutes* 2.7.1–17, 4.20.14–16. Note that Calvin preferred the terminology moral, ceremonial, and judicial laws. Moreover, on occasion he subsumed the judicial law under the ceremonial law. Martin Luther, too, used a similar division of laws. Cf. Paul Althaus, *The Ethics of Martin Luther* (Philadelphia: Fortress, 1965), 25–35; and Bernhard Lohse, *Martin Luther's Theology: Its Historical and Systematic Development* (Minneapolis: Fortress, 1999), 267–76.

[8] Since man was originally given permission to eat of all of the plants and the animals (cf. Gen 1:29–30; 9:3), many have wondered why some animals were later declared to be unclean in the dietary regulations of the ceremonial law (cf. Lev 11:1–47; Deut 14:3–21). A possible answer is that the laws between clean and unclean animals were designed to emphasize the fallen nature of the created order. To elaborate, the ceremonial law specifies: birds that eat carrion are unclean; all others are clean. Fish with scales or fins are paradigmatic of clean; all others are unclean. Insects or small animals with legs that keep them off the ground are paradigmatic of clean; all others are unclean. Large animals that chew the cud and have parted hoofs are paradigmatic of clean; all others are unclean. This is because chewing cud suggests a greater separation of the food from the cursed ground, and parted hoofs depict greater separation from the ground. Defective, diseased, or injured animals are unclean. In Acts 10:10–16 the unclean animals were labeled as clean in light of Jesus' work on the cross, which will eventually result in the restoration of the created order (cf. Rom 8:19–22; 1 Cor 15:20, 23). Cf. Vern S. Poythress, *The Shadow of Christ in the Law of Moses* (Phillipsburg, NJ: P&R, 1991), 81–82; John Frame, *Doctrine of the Christian Life* (Phillipsburg, NJ: P&R, 2008), 418. All of the clean animals eat plants, not animals. These laws are also reflective of a Jewish hierarchy of the created order that understood minerals are consumed by plants, which are consumed by animals, which are consumed by humans. Cf. Acton Institute,

are numerous ceremonial laws in the Old Testament, a commonality among them is that they all relate to the Israelites' approach to and right standing before God. The ceremonial laws are designed to communicate that God is holy, that man is unclean and unrighteous, and that redemption is on God's terms. In retrospect, it is evident the ceremonial laws prefigure the redemptive work of Jesus, a fact that New Testament authors note was evident to perceptive Jews (cf. John 8:56; Heb 11:13). Moreover, the New Testament is clear that the ceremonial laws were fulfilled—not abrogated—by the advent and work of Christ. In other words Jesus did not nullify the ceremonial laws; rather, he observed and embodied them (cf. John 1:29, 36; 1 Cor 5:7; Col 2:16–17; Heb 10:1–10).

The Old Testament *civil laws* are laws given for the governance of the Hebrew theocracy. Other terms for civil laws are judicial laws, case laws, casuistic laws, cultural laws, or the judgments. As is the case with modern civil laws, biblical civil laws are simply the application of God's moral standards to a particular time and culture.[9] Behind each civil law, then, is a moral law.[10] In fact, as Augustine famously noted, a civil law apart from a moral law is no law at all.[11] Said differently, the civil law is the moral law applied. For example, a memorable Hebrew civil law is, "Whoever strikes his father or his mother must be put to death" (Exod 21:15). Yet this civil law is simply a time-bound, cultural application of the

---

Environmental Stewardship in the Judeo-Christian Tradition (Grand Rapids: Acton Institute, 2007), 22–23.

[9] Reisinger writes, "The precepts of the civil law are all reducible to commandments of the moral law, and especially to those of the second table." Ernest C. Reisinger, *Whatever Happened to the Ten Commandments?* (Carlisle, PA: Banner of Truth, 1999), 3. For more information on the civil law as a manifestation of the moral law see James B. Jordan, *The Law of the Covenant* (Tyler, TX: ICE, 1984), 199–205; Stephen A. Kauffman, "The Structure of Deuteronomic Law," *Maarav* 1, vol. 2 (1978–79): 105–58; Walter Kaiser Jr., *Toward Rediscovering the Old Testament* (Grand Rapids: Zondervan, 1991), 163; Walter Kaiser Jr., *Toward Rediscovering Old Testament Ethics* (Grand Rapids: Zondervan, 1983), 81–137.

[10] This can be seen in the ordering of the civil law in Deuteronomy 6–26, which follows the ordering of the Decalogue. The ordering is as follows: first commandment (Deut 6:1–11:32), second commandment (Deut 12:1–31), third commandment (Deut 13:1–14:21), fourth commandment (Deut 14:22–16:17), fifth commandment (Deut 16:18–18:22), sixth commandment (Deut 19:1–22:8), seventh commandment (Deut 22:9–23:14), eighth commandment (Deut 23:15–24:7), ninth commandment (Deut 24:8–25:4), tenth commandment (Deut 25:5–26:15).

[11] Augustine, *On Free Choice of the Will* 1.5. Note that Martin Luther King Jr. made the same argument in regard to laws that promote segregation in his *Letter from the Birmingham Jail*.

moral duty to honor one's parents (cf. Exod 20:12).[12] So, then, to question whether the command to kill disobedient children applies in modern society is to misunderstand the nature of civil law.[13] While God's moral standards do not change, their application (and penalty for violation) in each time and culture is unique and ever changing. A benefit, then, of studying the civil law is that the civil law shows the breadth of the moral law as well as the different ways in which the moral law has been applied in various ages.

More often than not, the *moral law* is what is in view when theologians use the term *law*. Indeed, that is the case in this book. Moral laws are also referred to as apodictic laws, internal laws, inward laws, standing laws, natural laws, or the commandments. The moral laws are based on, reflect, and demand conformity to God's own moral character. As such, since man is made in God's image, the moral laws are written on men's hearts and are timeless (cf. Rom 2:14–15). As was discussed in the preceding chapter, the moral law was present from creation, well before the giving of the Mosaic law.[14] Oftentimes, however, when conceiving of the moral law, it is both helpful and convenient to think of the Mosaic law—specifically the Decalogue.[15] This is because, as the Shorter Catechism of the *Westminster Confession of Faith* notes, "The moral law is summarily comprehended in the Ten Commandments."[16] In short, then, it can be said that the moral law was present before

---

[12] Another example is the Hebrew civil law, "If you build a new house, make a railing around your roof, so that you don't bring bloodguilt on your house if someone falls from it" (Deut 22:8). This civil law is a time-bound cultural application of the moral duty to respect life (cf. Exod 20:13).

[13] Perhaps a better question might be to ask why the penalties attached to Hebrew civil laws were so harsh. Although this is surely a complex question, some reasons the penalties for violating Hebrew civil laws were so harsh include: (1) to emphasize God's holiness; (2) to emphasize man's sinfulness; (3) to emphasize the fact that sin produces death; (4) because the people of God were still in a nascent state without the visible church; (5) because the nation of Israel was a theocracy; and (6) because the laws depict a restored created order in which there will be no sin.

[14] See chapter 6 of this book for examples of the moral law prior to the giving of the Decalogue at Mount Sinai.

[15] As noted, the moral law is present from creation and is evident throughout the Bible. While the Decalogue is a helpful summary of the moral law, it is possible to sketch out several distinctives of moral law that can assist in identifying moral law elsewhere in Scripture. Distinctives of moral law include: (1) moral law is given theological justification upon first disclosure (cf. Gen 9:5–6; Exod 20:1–2); (2) moral law occurs with an exceptional manner of delivery; (3) moral law is evident prior to the giving of the Mosaic law; (4) moral law is reiterated throughout Scripture; and (5) it is possible to apply moral law universally.

[16] Robert Steel, *The Shorter Catechism with Proofs, Analyses, and Illustrative Anecdotes for Teachers and Parents* (London: T. Nelson, 1885), 132.

Sinai, at Sinai, and after Sinai. Indeed, the moral law is present throughout Scripture. As a revelation of God's character, the moral law is timeless, unchanging, and the standard by which God judges man.

Uses of the Moral Law

ALTHOUGH THERE ARE THREE INTERPRETIVE CATEGORIES of law in Scripture, identifying the category of law present in any given passage is just one task facing the Bible interpreter. A second challenge relates to the use of the moral law in Scripture. In the Protestant tradition theologians have commonly identified three uses of the moral law for Christians (see chart 3.1), the first of which is the *social use*. This is sometimes called the civil use (not to be confused with the interpretive category of civil law) or the political use of the moral law. When functioning in this manner, the law serves as a barricade or a bridle that restrains men from sin—believers and unbelievers alike. For example, after giving the Ten Commandments, Moses explained to gathered Israel that one reason God established the Decalogue was "so that you will fear Him and will not sin" (Exod 20:20). In a similar manner, in his letter to the Galatian churches, Paul rhetorically asked, "Why then was the law given? [Answer:] It was added because of transgressions" (Gal 3:19). So the law can function to corral sin that is ever present in fallen human society. Regarding the social use of the law Calvin wrote:

> The [social use] of the law is this: at least by fear of punishment to restrain certain men who are untouched by any care for what is just and right unless compelled by hearing the dire threats of the law. But they are restrained, not because their inner mind is stirred or affected, but because, being bridled, so to speak, they keep their hands from outward activity, and hold inside the depravity that otherwise they would wantonly have indulged.[17]

A second use of the moral law is the *convictional use*, which is sometimes referred to as the evangelical, proper, or theological use of the moral law. Paul summarized this function of the law when he wrote, "For no one will be justified in His sight by the works

---

[17] Calvin, *Institutes* 2.7.10. Calvin reversed the order of the first and second use of the law, perhaps in an effort to emphasize the grace that is inherent in the theological use of the law.

of the law, because the knowledge of sin comes through the law" (Rom 3:20; cf. 4:15; 5:20; 2 Cor 3:7). When serving in this capacity, then, the law convicts men of sin by becoming a mirror that reflects man's sinful condition in light of God's holiness and moral standards. However, the goal of this use of the law is not solely (or even primarily) to crush men under the weight of their revealed sin; rather, this use of the law entails conviction with the intent of driving men to Christ (cf. Gal 3:24). As Augustine observed, "The usefulness of the law lies in convicting man of his infirmity and moving him to call upon the remedy of grace which is in Christ."[18] Similarly, regarding this use of the law, Luther wrote: "Therefore, we do not abolish the law; but we show its true function and use, namely, that it is a most useful servant impelling us to Christ. . . . [The law's] function and use is not only to disclose the sin and wrath of God but also to drive us to Christ."[19]

The third use of the moral law is the *normative use*, which is also referred to as the didactic or pedagogical use of the law.[20] This use of the law is identified by most Protestant thinkers as the main use of the moral law.[21] When the law functions in this capacity it acts as a lamp to instruct believers in righteousness. Since the law is holy, just, good, and spiritual (cf. Rom 7:12, 14), this use of the law by Christians is not unexpected. Indeed, Paul appealed to the normative use of the law as he wrote to the church in Rome and rhetorically asked, "Do we then cancel the law through faith? [Answer:] Absolutely not! On the contrary, we uphold the law" (Rom 3:31). Clearly, then, the second and third uses of the law—that is, the convictional use and the normative use—complement each other, for the third use of the law cannot take its place until the second use has done its work. In regard to this relationship,

---

[18] Augustine, quoted in Calvin, *Institutes* 2.7.9.

[19] Luther's Works (LW) 26.327.

[20] Note the potential for confusion in terminology, as some writers have referred to the second use of the law as the pedagogical use. This is because of Paul's statement in Gal 3:24, "The law, then, was our guardian [Greek: *paidagōgos*] until Christ, so that we could be justified by faith."

[21] Calvin refers to this as the "principal use" and "proper purpose" of the law. Calvin, *Institutes* 2.7.12. Luther, on the other hand, identified the second use of the law as primary, writing, "The true function and the chief and proper use of the Law is to reveal to man his sin, blindness, misery, wickedness, ignorance, hate and contempt of God, death, hell, judgment, and the well-deserved wrath of God." LW 26.309. Unlike the Anabaptists, however, Luther and Calvin agreed on the first use of the law. Some have claimed Luther denied the third use of the law; however, a review of his writings, as well as Lutheran confessions, does not support this claim.

Description	Metaphor	Scripture Reference	Application
Social or Political Use	Bridle	Exod 20:20; Gal 3:19, 23; 1 Tim 1:8–11	The law restrains men from sin.
Convictional or Theological Use	Mirror	Matt 19:16-26; Rom 3:19–21; 4:15; 5:20; 7:7; 2 Cor 3:7; Gal 3:24	The law convicts men of sin.
Normative or Pedagogical Use	Lamp	Psalm 119; Rom 3:31; 7:12, 14, 22; 8:1–4	The law instructs men in righteousness.

Chart 3.1

Puritan Samuel Bolton wrote, "The law sends us to the gospel, that we may be justified, and the gospel sends us to the law again to enquire what is our duty in being justified."[22]

In sum, understanding the law is an important component in the correlation of the law and the gospel. When the term *law* appears in Scripture, Bible readers must first identify which interpretive category of law is under discussion: the civil law, the ceremonial law, or the moral law. Second, if the moral law is in view, the interpreter must discern how it is being used: the social use, the convictional use, or the normative use. Confusion may enter into a discussion about the relationship between the law and the gospel if the law is misidentified in regard to either category or use. Moreover, given these dynamics, it is understandable how biblical writers may make seemingly contradictory statements about the law within the same epistles. For example, speaking about the convictional use of the moral law, Paul tells believers in Rome, "You are not under law but under grace" (Rom 6:14). Yet, in writing about

---

[22] Samuel Bolton, *The True Bounds of Christian Freedom* (London: Banner of Truth, 1964), 80. In a similar manner, Charles Wesley wrote, "There is the closest connection that can be conceived between law and gospel. On the one hand, the law continually makes way for, and points us to, the gospel; on the other, the gospel continually leads us to a more exact fulfilling of the law." Charles Wesley, *The Sermon on the Mount* (Alachua, FL: Bridge-Logos, 2010), 145. In a related vein, Brian Edwards observes, "Grace and law are only opposites for those who are on the outside of grace. Once we are on the receiving end of grace the law itself becomes grace. It is no longer a tyrant condemning us but a friendly force to keep us in check." Brian Edwards, *The Ten Commandments for Today* (Surrey, UK: DayOne, 2002), 134.

the normative use of the moral law in the same letter, Paul writes: "Do we then cancel the law through faith? Absolutely not! On the contrary, we uphold the law" (Rom 3:31).

Understanding the Gospel

MANY DISCUSSIONS OF THE RELATIONSHIP BETWEEN the law and the gospel include an overview of the categories and uses of the law; yet some do not offer a definition of the gospel. In this study of the relevancy of the law for biblical ethics, however, it will be helpful to have a common understanding of the gospel. Perhaps one of the most concise biblical explanations of the gospel can be found in the book of Mark where the evangelist wrote, "Now after John was arrested, Jesus came into Galilee, proclaiming the gospel of God, and saying, 'The time is fulfilled, and the kingdom of God is at hand; repent and believe in the gospel'" (Mark 1:14–15 ESV; cf. Matt 4:23; 9:35; Luke 4:43). Certainly much could be written about these words, including the fact that Jesus' advent was the fulfillment of many Old Testament prophecies (i.e., "the time is fulfilled").[23] Yet, for the sake of this brief review, note two emphases within Christ's articulation of the gospel message.

First, there is a corporate aspect to the gospel. As Jesus declared, the gospel entails the fact that "the kingdom of God has come near" (Mark 1:15). The kingdom of God is the Lord's sovereign rule and authority over all things. Since Jesus is God, this included Christ's presence in the physical realm during his incarnation. Note that when the Pharisees asked Jesus about the arrival of the kingdom of God, Jesus' response was, "The kingdom of God is not coming with something observable [i.e., a spectacular sign]. . . . For you see, the kingdom of God is among you" (Luke 17:20–21). Furthermore, Jesus taught that the kingdom of God is not idle but is growing like a seed that has been planted (cf. Mark 4:30–32). As was recorded in the Lord's Prayer, a desire for such kingdom growth is to be part of believers' prayer lives (cf. Matt 6:10, "Your kingdom come. Your will be done on earth as it is in heaven"), and its facilitation is a duty of members of the body of Christ as Jesus works in and

---

[23] For example, see: Gen 3:15; 12:3; 18:18; 49:10; Deut 18:15–19; Pss 2:7; 16:10–11; 22:1, 7–8, 14–18; 35:11, 19; 41:9; 68:18; 69:21; 72:10–11; 118:22–23; Isa 7:14; 9:1–7; 28:16; 50:6; Jer 31:15; Dan 9:25–26; Hos 11:1; Mic 5:2; Zech 9:9; 11:12–13; 13:7; and Mal 3:1, among many other passages.

through them. As the kingdom of God grows, then, the gospel gradually counteracts and corrects the effects of sin in the world through the processes of restoration and reconciliation (cf. Rom 8:18–25; 1 Cor 15:1–58). Indeed, the gospel is no less comprehensive than the fall, which affected all areas of life. At Jesus' return, he will destroy sin and death and will physically rule over the kingdom of God (cf. Revelation 20–22). This is the corporate aspect and scope of the gospel.

Second, there is a personal component to the gospel. As was cited above, Jesus preached to his individual hearers, "Repent and believe" (Mark 1:15). Indeed, regeneration of heart, awareness of one's lost condition, repentance of sin, faith in Jesus' substitutionary atonement on the cross, belief in Christ's resurrection, and the consequent imputation of divine righteousness is the core message of the gospel to individuals and is the good news that is repeated throughout the New Testament (cf. Rom 10:9–10; Eph 2:8–9; 2 Cor 5:18–21). For example, the personal aspect of the gospel can be seen clearly as Paul wrote to the Corinthian church:

> Now brothers, I want to clarify for you the gospel I proclaimed to you; you received it and have taken your stand on it. You are also saved by it, if you hold to the message I proclaimed to you—unless you believed for no purpose. For I passed on to you as most important what I also received: that Christ died for our sins according to the Scriptures, that He was buried, that He was raised on the third day according to the Scriptures (1 Cor 15:1–4).[24]

The resurrection of Jesus was more than a display of God's power; it was a sign that Christ's atonement was sufficient to reconcile man to God. Jesus was the firstfruits of salvation (cf. 1 Cor 15:20, 23). This is the personal aspect of the gospel.

The question of the proper relationship between the law and the gospel still remains. At first glance the law and the gospel may seem to be incompatible, or at least difficult to correlate; for the law reveals the moral standards God requires of man, whereas the gospel communicates the gracious work God has accomplished on behalf of man. With this tension in mind, then, and in view of the

---

[24] In this same passage Paul continues his explanation of the gospel to include its corporate aspects, including the destruction of death, the resurrection of the body, and the reign of God over all (cf. 1 Cor 15:1–58).

above summaries of the law and the gospel, this chapter now turns to a discussion of the proper relationship between the law and the gospel.

The Law and the Gospel

ONE VERSE THAT IS USUALLY MENTIONED in studies of the relationship between the law and the gospel is Matt 5:17. In this passage, in the midst of the Sermon on the Mount, Jesus taught, "Don't assume that I came to destroy the Law or the Prophets. I did not come to destroy but to fulfill." This short verse is often cited because it is Jesus' most direct teaching on the relationship between his ministry and the law. Discussions usually focus on the meaning of the Greek word *plēroō*, which is rendered "fulfill" in most English Bible translations of this verse. This term, which occurs ninety-four times in the New Testament, has a range of potential meanings, including: to make full, to complete, to consummate, to perform, to ratify, and to realize, among other possible renderings.[25] The number of meanings of *plēroō* has contributed to the debate over the relationship between the law and the gospel; for depending on one's interpretation of *plēroō*, Matt 5:17 could yield the teaching that Jesus came to do away with the law (i.e., to make full, to complete), or that Jesus came to endorse the law (i.e., to consummate, to ratify). Considered in isolation, then, it does not appear Matt 5:17 can resolve the law-gospel debate.

Many passages in the Bible touch on the relationship between the law and the gospel. As this chapter progresses and these verses are encountered, three observations may be helpful in discerning the meaning of these texts. First, both immediate and distant context must be considered in order to arrive at a proper understanding of any given passage. Since Scripture is unified, context is paramount in Bible interpretation. Second, the Bible does not teach that man's problem is that he has the law; rather, man's problem is that he cannot keep the law he already has. Therefore, one should not necessarily expect Jesus to abolish the law (cf. Matt 5:17, "Don't assume that I came to destroy the Law"); rather, Christ's incarnation focused on remedying man's transgression of the law. The big picture must be kept in view. Third, in exploring the relationship between the

---

[25] Joseph Thayer, *Thayer's Greek-English Lexicon of the New Testament* (1886; repr., Peabody, MA: Hendrickson, 1996), s.v. "πληρόω."

law and the gospel, Bible interpreters must heed Paul's later advice to Timothy, "But avoid foolish debates . . . quarrels, and disputes about the law, for they are unprofitable and worthless" (Titus 3:9). Said differently, while believers should affirm the benefits and discipline of Bible study (cf. Rom 15:4; 1 Cor 10:11; 2 Tim 3:16), the law-gospel debate ought not to fracture Christian fellowship.

Over time, as Christian thinkers have studied the Scripture passages that address the relationship between the law and the gospel, three major views have emerged: a discontinuity approach, a continuity approach, and a semicontinuity approach. In the following pages each of these views will be surveyed. Yet readers should be aware that there are an infinite number of points on the spectrum from continuity to discontinuity; as such, many views and hybrid views have been proposed. In what follows, the positions presented are the three major views that have arisen. Moreover, these approaches to the relationship between the law and the gospel are discussed, more or less, in their pure forms.

A Discontinuity Approach

THOSE WHO HAVE ADOPTED A DISCONTINUITY approach in the discussion of law and gospel have generally held that the New Testament alone is normative for the Christian life. It is common for proponents of this view to juxtapose the law of Moses and the law of Christ. According to this view, the law of Christ (a term used twice by Paul, cf. 1 Cor 9:21; Gal 6:2) consists of the moral teachings of Jesus for the church, while the law of Moses is the moral rule for ethnic Israel. Indeed, it is common for advocates of this approach to make a sharp distinction between Old Testament Israel and the New Testament church. Yet many proponents of this view hold that certain Old Testament laws reiterated in the New Testament have been incorporated into the law of Christ and are thus valid for the church. While this approach is usually defended within the context of a wider theological system, specific support for this view includes the discontinuity verses previously cited, including Rom 6:14–15; 10:4; Gal 5:18, among others. In sum, then, this position sees discontinuity between the law and the gospel.

Historically speaking, a pure discontinuity approach to the relationship between the law and the gospel has not been the majority view of the church. In fact, throughout church history this position has often been associated with unorthodox theology, including the teachings of Marcion and other proponents of anti-Semitism.[26] In more recent times, however, an orthodox version of this view has been espoused within the theological movement known as dispensationalism.[27] For example, ethicist Norman Shields asserts, "The New Testament shows clearly that the law of Moses—moral, ceremonial and civil—was fulfilled in Christ (Matt. 5:17b). It had served its purpose and is not as a body of law binding on Christians except in so far as its moral absolutes were endorsed and re-affirmed by Jesus."[28] Another example of this approach comes from Henry Thiessen, author of one of the most widely read twentieth-century dispensational theology textbooks. In his book Thiessen writes: "The Scriptures teach that in the death of Christ the believer is delivered from the law itself. . . . That this includes the moral law as well as the ceremonial law is evident."[29] One final example of discontinuity theology can be seen in the assertion of one of dispensationalism's most well-known statesmen, Charles Ryrie, as he wrote: "Christ terminated the Law. . . . He terminated the Law and provided a new and living way to God."[30]

---

[26] Cf. Sebastian Moll, *The Arch-Heretic Marcion* (Tübingen: Mohr Siebeck, 2010); and Robert S. Wilson, *Marcion: A Study of a Second-Century Heretic* (New York: AMS, 1980).

[27] Another modern theological movement that has adopted a discontinuity approach to the law/gospel debate is New Covenant Theology. Cf. Tom Wells and Fred Zaspel, *New Covenant Theology: Description, Definition, Defense* (Fredrick, MD: New Covenant Media, 2002); and John G. Reisinger, *Tablets of Stone and the History of Redemption* (Fredrick, MD: New Covenant Media, 2004).

[28] Norman Shields, *Eager to Do What Is Good: What the Bible Teaches about Ethics* (Rossshire: Christian Focus, 2001), 41, 100–101.

[29] Henry C. Thiessen, *Lectures in Systematic Theology*, rev. ed. (Grand Rapids: Eerdmans, 1979), 170.

[30] Charles C. Ryrie, *Basic Theology* (Chicago: Moody, 1999), 348–49. Another example of the discontinuity approach comes from the pen of Lewis Sperry Chafer, founder of Dallas Theological Seminary. Chafer writes: "Since law and grace are opposed to each other at every point, it is impossible for them to co-exist as a ground of acceptance before God or as the rule of life. Of necessity, therefore, the Scriptures of the New Testament which present the facts and scope of grace, both assume and directly teach that the law is done away. Consequently, it is not in force in the present age in any sense whatsoever. This present nullification of the law applies not only to the legal code of the Mosaic system and the law of the kingdom, but to every possible application of the principle of law. . . . That the law, in the widest threefold meaning of the term, is now set aside, is revealed as a fundamental fact in the economy of grace." Lewis Sperry Chafer, *Systematic Theology*, vol. 4 (Dallas: Dallas Seminary Press, 1948), 234. In another work Chafer writes: "It is evident that the law was never addressed to any outside the one nation Israel, and also that, since the death of Christ, no Jew, Gentile, or Christian is now under the law either for justification, or as a rule of life. . . . There is a dangerous and entirely baseless sentiment abroad which assumes that every teaching of Christ must be binding during this age simply because Christ said it." Lewis

Despite the benefits and popularity of a discontinuity approach to law and gospel in some theological circles,[31] this view is not without its limitations. As was previously noted, historically speaking, this position has not been the prevailing view of the church. While a majority vote is not determinative in matters of theology, if the Holy Spirit guides the church in truth (cf. John 14:26; 16:13), it is prudent to examine carefully theological viewpoints that vary from the mainstream. A discontinuity approach to law and gospel certainly falls into this category. It is also worth noting that this position has not been historically stable, even among those who have adopted it. For example, in regard to modern dispensationalism, McQuilkin—himself a dispensationalist—writes, "Few of the leading theologians of the dispensational movement go along with the earlier view [of law and gospel]. Increasingly, dispensational theologians have moved toward the mainstream Christian teaching."[32]

Another major challenge for a discontinuity approach is the view of the nature of law that often accompanies this position. In the previous chapter the importance of the "authority is law" paradigm of the relationship between the law and God was explored. As was

---

Sperry Chafer, *Grace* (Grand Rapids: Zondervan, 1922), 99, 179. Note that many contemporary advocates of dispensationalism would likely repudiate some of the hard-line discontinuity ideas of Ryrie, Chafer, and the like. Toward the end of the twentieth century, many dispensationalists became less rigid in their views of law and gospel, adopting a belief system that became known as progressive dispensationalism. Cf. Craig A. Blaising and Darrell L. Bock, *Progressive Dispensationalism* (Wheaton, IL: BridgePoint, 1993).

[31] Two major benefits of a discontinuity approach are: (1) advocates do not need to wrestle with application questions about Old Testament civil and ceremonial laws; and (2) despite the popularity of a discontinuity view among anti-Semites, theologically speaking, this position has actually served to isolate and protect ethnic Israel. Indeed, the protection of ethnic Israel and the future fulfillment of God's covenant promises to Israel (cf. Rom 11:1–36) is a major emphasis within dispensational theology.

[32] McQuilkin's comments occur in his discussion of the theological views of Lewis Sperry Chafer, a pillar in early twentieth-century dispensationalism. McQuilkin notes: "It is clear that, for Chafer, law as law has been done away with. Neither the Ten Commandments, the Sermon on the Mount, nor even the instructions in the apostolic letters are law for the Christian in the sense of a rule of life or as binding obligations that must be obeyed. . . . Many preachers and lay people continue to follow Chafer's stance on the law and even go beyond him in antinomian teaching, but few of the [modern] leading theologians of the dispensational movement go along with the earlier view. Increasingly, dispensational theologians have moved toward the mainstream Christian teaching in affirming the moral law as God's requirement of Christians." McQuilkin, *Biblical Ethics*, 63–64. For further discussion and resources on this issue, see Robert Saucy, *The Case for Progressive Dispensationalism: The Interface Between Dispensational and Non-Dispensational Theology* (Grand Rapids: Zondervan, 1993), 14–19; and Herbert W. Bateman, ed., *Three Central Issues in Contemporary Dispensationalism: A Comparison of Traditional and Progressive Views* (Grand Rapids: Kregel, 1999).

noted, this paradigm holds that the law is right and true because it is a reflection of God's moral character, which is right and true. Yet, since advocates of the discontinuity approach teach that the law, including the moral law, is no longer binding, they generally do not hold to the "authority is law" paradigm. This is because the law cannot be annulled or discontinuous if it reflects God's unchanging moral character. Consequently, by default, many proponents of a discontinuity approach have adopted an "authority over law" position on the nature of law. As was detailed in the previous chapter, in tying the nature of God's law to his power (rather than to his character) this paradigm often has led to problems, the most common of which is legalism.[33] Not surprisingly, then, a tendency to define ethics as rule-keeping is often seen among advocates of a discontinuity approach to law and gospel.[34] This, in turn, can lead to other problems, including authoritarianism and the tendency to multiply laws, among other moral challenges.[35]

One final limitation facing the discontinuity approach to law and gospel are the many verses in Scripture that testify to the organic unity of the Bible. For example, Rom 15:4 notes, "For whatever was written in the past was written for our instruction," and Paul exhorted Timothy, "All Scripture is inspired by God and is profitable for teaching, for rebuking, for correcting, for training in righteousness" (2 Tim 3:16). Passages such as these,[36] coupled

---

[33] Some advocates of a discontinuity approach who have adopted an "authority over law" paradigm have embraced antinomianism rather than legalism. Logically speaking, in separating the law from God's character, either move is possible, although antinomianism has been less prevalent (in a formal sense). Modern examples include proponents of so-called "easy-believism" and adherents of nonlordship salvation. See the debate between Zane Hodges and John MacArthur as carried out in Zane C. Hodges, *Absolutely Free: A Biblical Reply to Lordship Salvation* (Grand Rapids: Zondervan, 1989); and John MacArthur, *The Gospel According to Jesus: What Is Authentic Faith?* rev. ed. (Grand Rapids: Zondervan, 2008).

[34] Most ethics textbooks come from authors who hold to a continuity or semicontinuity stance. This is because there is little ethical reflection to be done if ethics is reduced to law-keeping. Examples of discontinuity-leaning authors include Geisler, *Christian Ethics*; Feinberg and Feinberg, *Ethics for a Brave New World*; and McQuilkin, *Biblical Ethics*.

[35] It is ironic that a low view of the law tends to lead toward legalism, while a high view of the law has historically made men seekers of grace. Begg observes, "Ironically, legalism seems to breed best where the Law of God is regarded as having no abiding place as a rule of life in the child of God." Alistair Begg, *Pathway to Freedom: How God's Laws Guide Our Lives* (Chicago: Moody, 2003), 32. Similarly, Machen writes, "A low view of law always brings legalism in religion; a high view of law makes a man a seeker after grace." J. Gresham Machen, *What Is Faith?* (New York: Macmillan, 1925), 152.

[36] When Stephen, in the New Testament book of Acts, was accused of teaching against the law (cf. Acts 6:13), he responded by giving a lecture on the unity and continuity of God's plan, including the applicability of the law (cf. Acts 7:2–53). When Paul was later

with the express reiteration of most of the Ten Commandments in the New Testament,[37] are a challenge for the discontinuity position. Indeed, within this approach it seems the law of Christ in the New Testament looks similar to the law of Moses in the Old Testament—an observation that might be expected given that the law of Moses is really the law of God as recorded by Moses.[38]

A Continuity Approach

AT THE OTHER END OF THE spectrum from a discontinuity view of law and gospel is a continuity approach. Advocates of a continuity position teach that the whole body of Old Testament law is binding on Christians. Yet several caveats are usually given. First, proponents of this view hold that the ceremonial laws are not in effect since Jesus fulfilled these laws. Indeed, this caveat is difficult to elude given the teaching about Christ's ministry in the book of Hebrews (cf. Heb 4:14; 9:11). Second, while continuity advocates believe the civil law is still in effect, many hold that certain civil laws are no longer relevant due to changes in architecture, sanitation, and technology. However, the continuity of the majority of the Old Testament civil laws (and their penalties) is paramount to this approach. In fact, followers of this view teach that modern governments ought to implement Old Testament civil laws in order to spread the kingdom of God and hasten the return of Christ. Note that this teaching on the kingdom of God is a component of postmillennial eschatology. Nearly all advocates of the continuity approach are postmillennial in their eschatology; however, not all (or even most) supporters of postmillennial eschatology hold to the continuity view of law and gospel.[39]

Support for the continuity approach comes from the aforementioned continuity proof-texts such as Rom 3:31 and Gal 3:21,

---

charged with the same offense (cf. Acts 21:28), he responded with a similar lecture (cf. Acts 22:1–21).

[37] The fifth through tenth Commandments are approvingly quoted verbatim numerous times in the New Testament. See chapter 6 of this work for further discussion of the enduring nature of the Decalogue.

[38] Even discontinuity advocates like the Feinbergs have noted this. They write: "Laws reflected in the law of Moses and the Law of Christ have much overlap. . . . The Law of Christ is quite similar to the OT law (including the Mosaic Code)." Feinberg and Feinberg, *Ethics for a Brave New World*, 39.

[39] Prior to the twentieth century, postmillennial eschatology was a popular view among Protestant theologians, including Jonathan Edwards, Charles Hodge, and B. B. Warfield, among many others. Yet not one of these thinkers had a continuity view of law and gospel.

among many other passages. Additionally, proponents of this view appeal to positive citations of the Old Testament civil law in the New Testament. For example, at 1 Cor 5:1 Paul condemned the sin of incest, writing, "It is widely reported that there is sexual immorality among you, and the kind of sexual immorality that is not even tolerated among the Gentiles—a man is living with his father's wife." Since incest is not mentioned in the New Testament prior to this point, continuity advocates reason that this must be an endorsement of the Old Testament civil laws that prohibit incest (cf. Lev 18:6–18; 20:11–12, 17, 19–21; Deut 22:30; 27:20, 22–23). Another example comes from 1 Cor 9:9 and 1 Tim 5:18 where Paul approvingly quotes the civil law from Deut 25:4, "Do not muzzle an ox while it treads out grain." These types of citations, along with verses that allude to the unity of the Old Testament law (cf. Gal 3:10; Jas 2:10), are the kind of biblical arguments most often given in support of the continuity position.

While this view may seem foreign to some, the suggestion that the entire Old Testament law is binding on Christians is an idea that goes back to biblical times, albeit in an unorthodox sense. Indeed, this type of view of law and gospel was one of the earliest challenges to Christian orthodoxy. To elaborate, the Judaizers were a New Testament sect that sought to bring believers under the law as a requirement for salvation. Paul frequently wrote against this heresy in his epistles (cf. Gal 1:6–7; 2:3–16; Phil 3:2; Titus 1:10; 3:9), and the teaching of the Judaizers was the cause for the first church council as is recorded in Acts 15:1–29. In a modern, orthodox sense, a continuity approach to law and gospel has been espoused within various movements, including theonomy (theonomic ethics), dominion theology, and Christian reconstructionism. Specific examples of groups with these types of beliefs include the Chalcedon Foundation and the Institute for Christian Economics. Popular authors with a continuity approach to law and gospel include Rousas John Rushdooney, Greg L. Bahnsen, Gary North, David Chilton, and Gary Demar.[40]

---

[40] Rousas John Rushdooney, *By What Standard? An Analysis of the Philosophy of Cornelius Van Til* (Philadelphia: P&R, 1959); *Institutes of Biblical Law* (Philadelphia: P&R, 1973); Greg L. Bahnsen, *Theonomy in Christian Ethics* (Phillipsburg, NJ: P&R, 1984); *By This Standard: The Authority of God's Law Today* (Tyler, TX: Institute for Christian Economics, 1985); *No Other Standard: Theonomy and Its Critics* (Tyler, TX: Institute for Christian Economics, 1991); David Chilton, *Paradise Restored: A Biblical Theology of Dominion* (Fort Worth: Dominion Press, 1997); Gary North and Gary DeMar, *Christian Reconstruction:*

In order to understand the gravity of calling for the application of Old Testament civil laws (and their penalties) in a modern context, it will be helpful to read a somewhat lengthy quotation from continuity advocate Gary North, as he writes about the applicability of Deut 21:18–21, the civil law regarding the execution of a rebellious son. While this law is a lightening rod for the continuity approach, North's comments are nevertheless instructional for understanding this position. In his text *Inheritance and Dominion* North explains:

> The law governing the rebellious adult son was a law supporting family authority. The magnitude of the civil sanction against this son indicates the severity of the crime and the importance of preserving family authority. But this law had social implications as well. It was a law that offered protection to society from an organized criminal class. . . . There was a need for his execution in order to preserve the family's good name and to protect society. Without the willingness of a few parents to take this extreme measure, rebellious adult sons would learn not to fear their parents. These dedicated parents, who placed God's law, family authority, family reputation, covenantal inheritance, and social safety above their own emotional commitment to their son's biological survival, would serve as representatives for the whole society. The actual execution of a rebellious son would reinforce parental authority in many families. These goals have not changed with the coming of the New Covenant. In today's world, the son might be a drug addict rather than a drunken glutton. The point is he must be visibly out of control. . . . There has been one major alteration in the application of this law, however. The New Covenant has increased the responsibility of daughters. Daughters are baptized. They are placed under the covenant's dual sanctions: blessing and cursing. Daughters can inherit if they agree to bear the responsibility of caring for aged parents. To limit the application of this law to sons is illegitimate today. If daughters are rebellious, financially able to

What It Is, What It Isn't (Tyler, TX: Institute for Christian Economics, 1991); Gary North, *Theonomy: An Informed Response* (Tyler, TX: Institute for Christian Economics, 1991); Gary North, *Westminster's Confession: The Abandonment of Van Til's Legacy* (Tyler, TX: Institute for Christian Economics, 1991).

become drunkards and gluttons or crack-cocaine addicts,
and are still living under their parents' household jurisdic-
tion, then there is no judicial reason for them not to come
under this law.[41]

As with a discontinuity approach, a continuity view of the relationship between the law and the gospel is not without its limitations. Perhaps the greatest challenge facing the continuity approach
is its understanding of the nature of the civil law. As was explained
earlier in this chapter, throughout history most theologians have
understood the civil law to be a time-bound, cultural application of
the moral law. Yet, in seeking to apply the Old Testament civil law
in a modern context, followers of a continuity approach seem to
view the civil law as an ontologically separate category of law that
is timeless and cross-cultural. This understanding of the civil law is
not the majority view of the church and is questionable in light of
New Testament teachings on the civil law (see below). Moreover,
even in the Old Testament, the Hebrew civil law was not applied
to Gentile nations. The prophets whom the Lord sent from Israel
to other lands (e.g., Jonah, Obadiah, Nahum) confronted pagans
with their transgression of the moral law, not the Hebrew civil law.
Indeed, the Old Testament law itself contained different provisions
for dealings between fellow Israelites and dealings with Gentiles
(cf. Deut 23:19–20).[42]

A second related limitation of the continuity approach is its
view of the relationship between church and state. While church-
state relations is certainly a debated topic that has generated various
viewpoints throughout history,[43] it seems continuity advocates may
be open to the charge of misunderstanding the roles of church and
state. Although this is surely a complex issue, Scripture is clear that
the church is the custodian of the gospel (cf. 1 Tim 3:15), while the
state has been charged with maintaining public order, among other
civic duties (cf. Rom 13:1–7). In teaching that contemporary, nontheocratic governments should adopt the Old Testament civil laws

[41] Gary North, *Inheritance and Dominion: An Economic Commentary on Deuteronomy*
(Harrisonburg, VA: Dominion Education Ministries, 1999), 813–15.

[42] Deuteronomy 23:19–20 refers to the Old Testament civil law that banned usury
between Jewish brethren but allowed for it in financial transactions between Jews and
Gentiles. For more on this topic, see David W. Jones, *Reforming the Morality of Usury: A
Study of the Differences that Separated the Protestant Reformers* (Lanham, MD: University
Press, 2004).

[43] Cf. H. Richard Niebuhr, *Christ and Culture* (New York: Harper, 1975).

with the goal of spreading the kingdom of God and hastening the return of Christ, followers of a continuity approach seem to be confusing (or perhaps conflating) the role of the state with the role of the church. The kingdom of God spreads by the grace of the gospel, not through the restraint of the civil law.[44]

A Semicontinuity Approach

BOTH THE DISCONTINUITY AND CONTINUITY APPROACH make use of the interpretive categories of civil, ceremonial, and moral laws. As was seen in the quotations from discontinuity advocates, some followers of this approach cite the trifold division of law to teach that they believe all Old Testament laws are not applicable in the modern dispensation. Similarly, continuity advocates appeal to interpretive categories of law; yet they do so in order to teach that the Old Testament moral laws and civil laws (along with their penalties) are valid in the contemporary setting. Despite the use of the civil/ceremonial/moral rubric by other approaches, the trifold division of law is most often associated with a semicontinuity approach. A semicontinuity understanding of the relationship between the law and the gospel holds that only the moral law is applicable to New Testament believers. Advocates of this view hold that the civil law was localized to theocratic Israel and that the ceremonial law has been (and is being) fulfilled by Christ.[45]

In regard to the Old Testament civil law, followers of a semicontinuity approach note that nowhere in the New Testament are Christians told to pursue an earthly theocracy such as was present in the Old Testament. Rather, both the context and the content of the New Testament communicate approval of nontheocratic forms of secular governments. For example, when the Pharisees questioned Jesus about the morality of paying taxes to Rome, Jesus' response

---

[44] Brian Edwards's observation is instructive: "When Christ responded to the challenge of Pilate: 'My kingdom is not of this world. . . . But now my kingdom is from another place' (John 18:36), he was referring not to the location but to the character of his kingdom. He meant that his rule and authority, unlike earthly empires, is essentially spiritual." Edwards, *The Ten Commandments*, 42.

[45] Assuming an eschatological, theocratic reign of Christ on the earth (or new earth) raises the interesting question of whether the Old Testament civil law will again be invoked. Yet, since the Old Testament civil law was a time-bound, cultural application of the moral law, this question is probably best answered in the negative. While Jesus will one day reign on the earth with a theocratic government, given the passage of time and the evolution of culture, it seems that the civil law in the eschatological kingdom will be different from the Old Testament civil law; yet the underlying moral norms will not change.

was not one of condemnation but commendation. Jesus said, "Therefore, give back to Caesar the things that are Caesar's, and to God the things that are God's" (Matt 22:21). In a similar manner Paul demonstrated approval of secular governments, as he urged the Roman Christians to pay their taxes (cf. Rom 13:6–7), reminded Timothy to pray for government leaders (cf. 1 Tim 2:1–2), and instructed Titus to "be submissive to rulers and authorities" (Titus 3:1). Other New Testament passages that speak approvingly of secular governments include Rom 13:1–5 and 1 Pet 2:13–17.

Concerning the Old Testament ceremonial laws, proponents of a semicontinuity approach note that many passages in the New Testament teach these laws have been fulfilled in Christ. For instance, all of the Synoptic Gospels record the supernatural tearing of the temple veil at Jesus' death (cf. Matt 27:51; Mark 15:38; Luke 23:45). According to this view the veil was rent in two, for the sacrificial system was no longer needed after the ultimate sacrifice was made on the altar of Calvary. As the New Testament teaches, Jesus is our Passover Lamb (cf. 1 Cor 5:7) and our high priest (cf. Heb 4:14) who serves in a "greater and more perfect tabernacle not made with hands" (cf. Heb 9:11). Moreover, when the first church council specifically addressed the question of the relevancy of the Old Testament ceremonial law, they ruled it is not applicable to New Testament believers.[46] This teaching is frequently echoed by Paul in his epistles (cf. Rom 14:5; Gal 4:9–11; Col 2:16–17). Additionally, the New Testament teaches the cessation of Old Testament dietary regulations and the purity of all foods (cf. Mark 7:19; Acts 10:9–16).

In regard to the moral law, semicontinuity advocates interpret the many continuity proof-texts cited earlier in this chapter to be references to the application of the moral law. Such passages include Rom 3:31; 7:12, 14, 22; 1 Cor 7:19; Gal 3:21; and 1 Tim

---

[46] In their letter to the churches, James and the other leaders of the church wrote: "For it was the Holy Spirit's decision—and ours—to put no greater burden on you than these necessary things: that you abstain from food offered to idols, from blood, from eating anything that has been strangled, and from sexual immorality. You do well if you keep yourselves from these things" (Acts 15:28–29). A logical question to ask is why the church decided that it would be prudent for believers to avoid: (1) food offered to idols, (2) meat with blood, (3) things that had been strangled, and (4) sexual immorality. While sexual immorality is forbidden in the moral law, it seems the other prohibitions are practical guidelines, not a matter of jurisprudence. While there is certainly room for debate here, perhaps these prohibitions could be explained in that the church leaders did not want Gentile believers to revel in their liberty, causing Jewish Christians to follow and transgress their own consciences (cf. Acts 15:21).

1:8. Followers also find support for a semicontinuity approach by appealing to the "authority is law" paradigm of the nature of law. In other words, if the moral law reflects God's unchanging character, which is right and true, then one would expect the law itself to be unchanging, right, and true. Additionally, proponents of the semicontinuity view argue their position by noting the approving, express quotation of many of the Ten Commandments in the New Testament. Passages in which the Decalogue is explicitly cited include Matt 5:21, 27; 19:17–19; Mark 10:19; Luke 18:20; Rom 7:7; 13:9; Eph 6:2–3; and Jas 2:11.[47]

A semicontinuity approach to law and gospel has been the prevailing view of the church throughout history. According to O'Donovan, this approach, including a trifold distinction in the law, can be seen in the writings of church fathers such as Justin Martyr and Augustine, and it "gained wide acceptance in the patristic period."[48] The distinction between civil, ceremonial, and moral laws may even predate the Christian era, as Montefiore contends, "The [Old Testament] Rabbis, we may say, were familiar with the distinction between ceremonial and moral commands, and on the whole they regarded the 'moral' as more important and more fundamental than the 'ceremonial.'"[49] A semicontinuity approach is also evident in the works of later church thinkers such as Aquinas and Calvin[50] and is the position taken by the majority of contemporary, evangelical ethicists.[51] Note, too, this approach is manifest in many of the historic creeds of the Protestant church, including the *Westminster Confession of Faith*, the *London Baptist Confession*, and the *Philadelphia Confession*.[52]

---

[47] See, also, Matt 15:19; Rom 2:21–24; Col 3:20; 1 Tim 1:9–10.

[48] O. M. T. O'Donovan, "Towards an Interpretation of Biblical Ethics," *Tyndale Bulletin* 27 (1976): 59. O'Donovan cites Justin, *Dial* 44.3 and Augustine, *Speculum* "Quis ignorant," *Patrologiae Latinae* 34, cols. 887–1040.

[49] C. G. Montefiore, *Rabbinic Literature and Gospel Teaching* (New York: Ktav, 1970), 316–17.

[50] Aquinas, *Summa* 1a2ae99, 4; Stephen J. Casselli, "The Threefold Division of the Law in the Thought of Aquinas," *Westminster Theological Journal* 61, no. 2 (Fall 1999): 175–207; Calvin, *Institutes* 2.7.1–2.

[51] For example, Norman L. Geisler, *Christian Ethics: Options and Issues* (Grand Rapids: Baker, 1990), 117; Scott B. Rae, *Moral Choices: An Introduction to Ethics*, 2nd ed. (Grand Rapids: Zondervan, 2000), 21; Robertson McQuilkin, *An Introduction to Biblical Ethics*, 2nd ed. (Wheaton, IL: Tyndale, 1995), 43–53.

[52] Cf. *Westminster Confession of Faith* (1646), 19.1–7; *London Baptist Confession* (1677/1689), 19.1–7; *Philadelphia Confession* (1742), 19.1–7; *New Hampshire Confession* (1833), 12; *Thirty-Nine Articles* (1571), 7; *Methodist Articles of Religion* (1784), 6; *Irish Articles* (1615), 84.

Although a semicontinuity approach has been the main view of the church, and is the position adopted in this book, it is not without its detractors. The most common critique of this view is that the division of the Old Testament law into civil, ceremonial, and moral laws is artificial and was unknown to the original recipients of the law.[53] Several responses to this challenge may be offered. First, as has already been noted, the semicontinuity approach is not unique in its appeal to a trifold division of the law. All of the main views of the relationship between law and gospel employ the civil/ceremonial/moral distinction. Second, it must not be overlooked that the trifold division of the law is not an ontological division of the law; rather, it is an interpretive rubric. As Kaiser notes, "The threefold distinction is not intended to be an account of the way Israel had to regard her own law, rather it is only a catalogue of its constitute elements."[54] Finally, it should be noted that just because the name of a literary genre, interpretive concept, or subject is not found in Scripture does not make it invalid (e.g., narrative, poetry, literary seam, Trinity, rapture, etc.).

Conclusion

THE RELEVANCY OF THE LAW IS an important topic for biblical ethics, for one's view of the law will set the parameters for the material from which one may engage in moral theory. By examining the law and the gospel, as well as the relationship between the two, this chapter has sought to show that the moral law is essential for biblical ethics. Indeed, the moral law as revealed within the Word of God, which is the source of moral authority for biblical ethics, is that from which ethical norms are drawn. The moral law of God does not change from Genesis to Revelation, is the standard by which men are judged, and provides the framework for the practice of biblical ethics.

---

[53] For example, Geisler writes, "The whole division of commands into civil, ceremonial, and moral is postbiblical, questionable, and probably of late Christian origin (possibly the thirteenth century)." Geisler, *Christian Ethics*, 92. As the previous discussion has shown, however, Geisler is plainly wrong in his undocumented assertion. It is interesting, too, that later in his text (p. 117) Geisler himself appeals to the trifold distinction in the law to support his graded absolutist position on conflicting moral absolutes.

[54] Kaiser, *Toward Old Testament Ethics*, 46.

Summary Points

- The relationship between the law and the gospel is one of the central components of biblical ethics.
- The law is comprised of the moral standards God has revealed to humans. It can be described in three basic categories:
  - Ceremonial laws are given for the functioning of the sacrificial system, including tabernacle/temple operations, religious feasts, and dietary regulations.
  - Civil laws are given for the governance of the Hebrew theocracy.
  - Moral laws are based on, reflect, and demand conformity to God's moral character and are summarized in the Ten Commandments.
- Three basic uses of the law are identified in the Protestant tradition:
  - Social use—When functioning in this manner, the law serves as a barricade or a bridle that restrains men from sin.
  - Convictional use—When serving in this capacity, the law convicts men of sin by becoming a mirror that reflects man's sinful condition in light of God's holiness and moral standards.
  - Normative use—When the law functions in this capacity, it acts as a lamp to enlighten believers in righteousness. This use of the law is identified by most Protestant thinkers as the main use of the moral law.
- Three considerations for conducting a study of scriptural evidence for the law/gospel question:
  - Both immediate and distant context must be considered in discerning the meaning of texts.
  - The Bible does not teach that man's problem is that he has the law; rather, man's problem is that he cannot keep the law he has.
  - The law-gospel debate ought not to fracture Christian fellowship.
- There are three basic approaches to the law/gospel question:
  - Discontinuity approach—Adherents of this position generally hold that the New Testament alone is normative for the Christian life.

- ○ Continuity approach—Advocates of this position teach that the whole body of Old Testament law is binding upon Christians, with the exception of the ceremonial law and those civil laws that have become technologically outdated (e.g., due to changes in sanitation and architecture).
- ○ Semicontinuity approach—Proponents of this view hold that only the moral law is applicable to New Testament believers; the civil law was localized to theocratic Israel, and the ceremonial law has been (and is being) fulfilled by Christ.

Chapter 4

The Coherency of the Law

Over the previous two chapters the nature and the relevancy of the law were explored. In these chapters it was argued that the nature of the law is that it reflects God's own moral character. It was shown that the law does not exist apart from God but rather is a revelation of the Lord's own being. In regard to the relevancy of the law, the law and the gospel are not to be juxtaposed, for they work in concert. While it could rightly be argued that the law and the gospel differ in regard to quality and scope of revelation (cf. Heb 7:22; 8:6), the quantity revealed is the same—that is, both the law and the gospel reveal the character of God, effectually emphasize man's lost condition and need of a Savior, and instruct God's people in covenant faithfulness. As such, the law and the gospel work in harmony, not in opposition. Said differently, for the unregenerate man, the moral law reveals what he cannot do without the gospel; for the redeemed man, the moral law reveals what he must do in light of the gospel.

Having looked at how the law relates to God, as well as at the issue of how the law relates to the gospel, a logical area for exploration is the nature of the relationship between the various parts of the moral law—that is, the issue of the internal coherency of the law, or the question of how the law relates to itself. While this may seem to be an esoteric issue, it is a foundational matter for biblical ethics.[1]

---

[1] Commenting on the importance of this issue for Christian ethics, Thielicke writes, "We have observed that he who thinks through [the coherency of the law] is . . . forced to betray

Luck observes, "Plural (absolute) rules + their conflict in application = an incoherent (and therefore unacceptable) system."[2] Similarly, the Feinbergs identify this as an important topic, for the prospect of incoherency within the moral law raises "crucial concerns for people confronted with concrete decisions."[3] Indeed, if moral absolutes can conflict with one another, then both in principle and in practice there must be a means for resolving such conflict in order to avoid moral paralysis. Sider warns, "There is no easy ethical calculus to solve such [moral] conflicts."[4] Nevertheless, as ethicists have considered this issue over time, several viewpoints have emerged. Following the general trajectory set by Geisler,[5] this chapter will review five perspectives on the internal coherency of the moral law, focusing specifically on possible options for dealing with conflicting moral absolutes or what are sometimes referred to as ethical dilemmas.[6] For each view that is presented, the approach will be explained, proponents will be identified, strengths will be mentioned, and weaknesses (if any) will be explored. This chapter will conclude by applying several of the described approaches to the biblical narrative of Rahab and the Hebrew spies as recorded in Josh 2:1–24.

Conflicting Moral Absolutes

AS THIS SURVEY OF APPROACHES TO conflicting moral absolutes is begun, three caveats are in order. First, while the issue of the coherency of the law is an important and oft-discussed topic in moral

---

almost all of his dogmatic and ethical secrets: his doctrine of justification, his concepts of the world, of history, and of the Law, and his views on the nature of sin and on natural law." Helmut Thielicke, "The Borderline Situation of Extreme Conflict," in *Readings in Christian Ethics*, vol. 1, ed. David K. Clark and Robert V. Rakestraw (Grand Rapids: Baker, 1994), 128n3.

[2] William F. Luck, "Moral Conflicts and Evangelical Ethics," *Grace Theological Journal* 8 (Spring 1987): 20.

[3] John S. Feinberg and Paul D. Feinberg, *Ethics for a Brave New World* (Wheaton, IL: Crossway, 1993), 29. The *Westminster Dictionary of Christian Ethics* notes, "If several rules are defended as absolute, it is necessary to work out the boundaries of those rules in order to avoid conflict." *The Westminster Dictionary of Christian Ethics* (1986), s.v. "norms."

[4] *Baker's Dictionary of Christian Ethics* (1973), s.v. "conflict of duties, interest."

[5] Cf. Norman L. Geisler, *Christian Ethics: Options and Issues* (Grand Rapids: Baker, 1990), 29–132. While Geisler identifies six perspectives on moral absolutes, his categories of antinomianism and generalism are needlessly separate.

[6] The phrase "possible options" is used in light of Cambridge ethicist A. C. Ewing's warning, "No philosopher has succeeded in producing adequate general rules for dealing with conflicts of duties, possibly because this is intrinsically impossible." *The Westminster Dictionary of Christian Ethics* (1986), s.v. "conflict of duties."

literature, ethical dilemmas (in the sense of conflicting moral norms) are exceptional, not normative.[7] This topic, then, is addressed not because of its frequency of occurrence but because of its importance within the discipline of biblical ethics. Second, the possibility of moral laws colliding, resulting in an incoherent system of ethics, assumes the belief in more than one moral norm. Ethical systems that do not affirm multiple moral absolutes do not resolve this question; rather, they avoid it. Yet such perspectives still bear upon the coherency of the moral law and are included in the discussion that follows. Third, since the first two viewpoints that follow do not affirm the existence of multiple moral absolutes, historically they have not been viewed as normative, viable options for Christians. Among other reasons this is so because the Bible contains many axiomatic moral norms. These views are included here for the sake of comprehensiveness and, as Geisler notes, "Since they challenge Christian ethics, they must be addressed."[8]

Antinomianism

ANTINOMIANISM IS A FORM OF ETHICAL relativism that practically denies there are any divine, universal moral absolutes.[9] The word *antinomianism* was coined by Protestant Reformer Martin Luther and literally means "against the law." As was previously noted, since antinomianism denies the existence of objective moral law or rejects

---

[7] Jones observes: "Now there is something to be said for keeping borderline cases in perspective. Ethics courses structured around hard cases easily give the impression that the moral life is just one big quandary, that there are no easy answers to any of its questions." David Clyde Jones, *Biblical Christian Ethics* (Grand Rapids: Baker, 1994), 126. Seasoned ethicist Robertson McQuilkin makes the telling observation, "I personally have never experienced a moral dilemma that was not resolved by biblical definition and choosing to trust God with the consequences." Robertson McQuilkin, *An Introduction to Biblical Ethics*, 2nd ed. (Wheaton, IL: Tyndale, 1995), 148. For a contrary perspective, see John Warwick Montgomery, who writes, "Christian morality fully realizes the difficulty of moral decisions, and frequently a Christian finds himself in a position where it is necessary to make a decision where moral principles must be violated in favor of other moral principles." John Warwick Montgomery, *The Suicide of Christian Theology* (Minneapolis: Bethany Fellowship, 1970), 69. Similarly, R. A. Hig writes, "Conflicts of moral duty occur. . . . Human beings are then obligated to rank one duty higher than the other, to disobey one rule in order to obey another." *New Dictionary of Christian Ethics and Pastoral Theology* (1995), s.v. "absolutes."

[8] Geisler, *Christian Ethics*, 29.

[9] Beginning with Luther, the term *antinomian* has been used by some to refer to individuals who reject the role of the moral law in the Christian life. Others have used the term to describe the view that there are no universal divine moral absolutes. In regard to biblical ethics, both of these approaches produce the same outcome—that is, a denial of the regulative use of the law—either because the law does not exist or because its application is denied.

their application, this is not a normative Christian view and ought not to be confused with the previously reviewed discontinuity approach to law and gospel (see chap. 3).[10] In a sense, the term *antinomianism* is a misnomer, for most antinomians are not literally against the law; they are just without the law since they deny a regulative role for the moral law. Obviously, since there are no moral absolutes within an antinomian ethical system, conflict between moral norms cannot occur. For advocates of antinomianism, then, the coherency of the law is mostly a nonissue, as there are no laws within this approach that can be at odds and thus result in an incoherent system of ethics.

In pre-Christian and non-Christian ethical systems, denial or rejection of the regulative role of the moral law is fairly widespread. Indeed, there are many views that fall into these categories that could be cited as examples of antinomianism. In a formal or academic sense, though, antinomianism is not nearly as common as it is in practice. Examples in the time of the early church include the Epicureans who elevated pleasure at the expense of moral absolutes, and certain varieties of Gnostic thinkers who elevated spiritual unity and knowledge at the expense of earthly morality. More recent secular examples of antinomianism include utilitarian thinkers such as Jeremy Bentham and John Stuart Mill,[11] existentialists such as Jean-Paul Sartre,[12] nihilists such as Friedrich Nietzsche,[13] and emotivists such as A. J. Ayer.[14] While there certainly are different nuances and emphases between and among these individuals, a common denominator is a rejection of objective (especially divine) moral law and an elevation of some type of self-generated morality.

---

[10] *The Westminster Dictionary of Christian Ethics* seems to confuse or perhaps conflate antinomianism with discontinuity approaches to law and gospel. In this dictionary *antinomianism* is defined as, "The view that, for the Christian, faith has abolished the law so that one is no longer subject to it." *The Westminster Dictionary of Christian Ethics* (1986), s.v. "antinomianism." The Feinbergs, both of whom advocate a discontinuity view of law and gospel, emphasize they are not antinomians as they write, "We conclude that rejecting the Mosaic Code as binding today is not antinomianism." Feinberg and Feinberg, *Ethics for a Brave New World*, 38.

[11] Jeremy Bentham, *Introduction to the Principles of Morals and Legislation* (New York: Hafner, 1965); John Stuart Mill, *The Utilitarians* (Garden City, NY: Doubleday, 1961).

[12] Jean-Paul Sartre, *Being and Nothingness*, trans. Hazel E. Barnes (New York: Philosophical Library, 1956).

[13] Friedrich Nietzsche, *The Birth of Tragedy and the Genealogy of Morals*, trans. Francis Golffing (Garden City, NY: Doubleday, 1956).

[14] A. J. Ayer, *Freedom and Morality and Other Essays* (New York: Oxford University Press, 1984).

While antinomianism is not a normative Christian view, it has nevertheless been manifest from time to time within the church. For example, in Scripture the apostle Paul dealt with a stripe of antinomianism in the Corinthian church that resulted in sexual immorality (cf. 1 Corinthians 5–6). In Rome some who either misunderstood or purposely distorted the doctrine of justification by faith alone believed Paul to have taught, "Let us do what is evil so that good may come" (Rom 3:8; cf. 6:1–2). In the early church Augustine addressed a faction of Carthaginian antinomians in his *Against Adversaries of the Law and the Prophets.*[15] Likewise, during the Reformation, some who misunderstood the doctrine of justification by faith alone embraced antinomianism. An example of such teaching can be seen in the lengthy debate between Johannes Agricola, Philip Melanchthon, and Martin Luther.[16] Moreover, in Protestant theology antinomianism has occasionally appeared among certain sects of Anabaptists, High Calvinists, Puritans, and Wesleyans.[17]

Antinomianism is certainly not without its benefits, including its stress on individual moral responsibility and its emphasis on the emotive and relational aspects of ethics.[18] Yet antinomianism also has a number of significant drawbacks. For example, a major philosophical challenge facing antinomianism is that it appears to be a self-defeating idea. To elaborate, it is logically impossible for antinomians to claim that there are no moral absolutes without making an absolute moral claim. As Geisler observes: "One cannot deny all value without presupposing some value. . . . Moral absolutes cannot be denied unless they are implied."[19] Another critique of antinomianism is that even if it were possible to actualize it, the use and value of antinomianism is questionable in light of man's need for absolutes in order to function and to exist. Indeed, by default, humans create and use moral norms; therefore, to deny their existence seems both irrational and illogical. Additionally, as was previously mentioned, for Christians a problem with antinomianism is that the Bible contains many moral norms. To embrace

---

[15] For a review of this work see, *Augustine Through the Ages: An Encyclopedia* (1999), s.v. "adversarium legis et prophetarum, contra."

[16] From more information about this debate, see Timothy Wengert, *Law and Gospel: Philip Melanchthon's Debate with John Agricola of Eisleben over Poenitentia* (Grand Rapids: Baker, 1997).

[17] *New Dictionary of Christian Ethics and Pastoral Theology* (1995), s.v. "antinomianism."

[18] Geisler, *Christian Ethics*, 34–35.

[19] Ibid., 39–40.

antinomianism, then, would seem to be damaging to the authority
and the content of Scripture.

Situationalism

SITUATIONALISM, WHICH IS ALSO CALLED SITUATIONAL or contextual
ethics, is an approach to morality that attempts to avoid the pitfalls of both antinomianism and legalism. Situationalism affirms
the existence of one universal, moral absolute—that is, the duty to
love others. Joseph Fletcher, the classic proponent of this approach
to morality, explains, "Christian ethics or moral theology is not a
scheme of living according to a code but a continuous effort to relate
love to a world of relativities through a casuistry obedient to love;
its constant task is to work out the strategy and tactics of love."[20] In
short, then, this approach could be summarized with the sentence,
"Do the most loving thing." According to this view of ethics, when
the duty to love others is upheld, morality is served.

Situationalism does not, however, just emphasize an existential
or ontological duty to keep moral norms with a heart motivated
by love. On the contrary, situationalism claims that the only universal moral norm is to love. As such, situationalists are opposed
to a plurality of moral norms as well as to concrete ethical systems
comprised of fixed moral norms. This is because, for the situationalist, moral acts are determined by the individual and will vary by
situation—hence, the name "situational ethics." So, according to
situationalism, two people in the exact same situation may make
different choices and both be correct; or, the same person in the
same situation twice could make differing choices each time and be
correct both times.[21] The key is for the individual to do the most
loving thing in a given situation, not to follow any preconceived
system of moral standards. Fletcher writes: "Any [fixed] ethical system is unchristian. . . . Jesus had no [system of] ethics. . . . In situation ethics even the most revered principles may be thrown aside
if they conflict in any concrete case with love. . . . Christian situation ethics reduces love from a statutory system of rules to the love

---

[20] Joseph Fletcher, *Situation Ethics: The New Morality* (Philadelphia: Westminster, 1966),
158.

[21] In his critique, McQuilkin explains the essence of situationalism: "The decision as to
what is right or wrong, good or bad, is relative to the situation at hand. . . . There is no
set of rules. You must decide for yourself as you face each decision: What would love do?"
McQuilkin, *Biblical Ethics*, 134, 137.

canon alone."[22] Since situationalism affirms only one moral norm, conflict between norms cannot occur.

As mentioned previously, the spokesman for situational ethics is Joseph Fletcher. Indeed, Fletcher's book *Situation Ethics: The New Morality* popularized this approach to ethical reasoning, bringing it from the academy to the masses. Yet shades of situationalism can be seen in other thinkers, too, both before and after Fletcher. For example, other names that have been associated in moral literature with a situational-type approach to ethics, whether fairly or not, include Rudolf Bultmann, Emil Brunner, John Dewey, Paul Lehmann, H. Richard Niebuhr, Reinhold Niebuhr, John A. T. Robinson, Friedrich Nietzsche, and Paul Tillich.[23]

On account of its ostensible simplicity and elevation of love, a situational type approach to ethics may appear winsome, if not compatible with a system of biblical ethics.[24] Situationalism, however, has several significant limitations. For example, situationalism does not appear to have a firm basis for its exaltation of love. It is inconsistent for the situationalist to appeal to Scripture to exalt the norm of love, for the Bible contains many moral norms. This critique would especially apply to a Christian situationalist. The choice to elevate love, then, seems arbitrary. A related problem is the ability of situationalism to define love apart from Scripture. Davis calls this the "fundamental difficulty" of situational ethics,[25] and McQuilkin observes that "by divorcing love from law, the situationalist empties it of concrete meaning."[26] Situationalism specifies that each individual gets to define love. Yet, given the Bible's

---

[22] Fletcher, *Situation Ethics*, 12, 33, 69.

[23] *Baker's Dictionary of Christian Ethics* (1973), s.v. "situational ethics;" Geisler, *Christian Ethics*, 43. *New Dictionary of Christian Ethics and Pastoral Theology* (1995), s.v. "situation ethics;" *The Westminster Dictionary of Christian Ethics* (1986), s.v. "situation ethics."

[24] A logical area for exploration is the difference between situational ethics and biblical ethics. McQuilkin notes: "The Bible itself demonstrates a form of situationism in which normally wrong behavior becomes right under certain circumstances. . . . Again, there is a type of response in the Bible that might be called situation ethics of a sort." McQuilkin, *Biblical Ethics*, 133, 137. Indeed, the system of situational ethics is similar to biblical ethics in that it recognizes morality is concerned with more than just conduct. The major difference, however, is the source of moral authority. To elaborate, situationalism differs from biblical ethics in that within biblical ethics the right thing to do is determined by God and will not vary by situation or agent. In situational ethics the right thing to do is determined by the agent; thus, it varies from agent to agent and from situation to situation.

[25] John Jefferson Davis, *Evangelical Ethics: Issues Facing the Church Today*, 3rd ed. (Phillipsburg, NJ: P&R, 2004), 19.

[26] McQuilkin, *Biblical Ethics*, 140. Scripture passages that connect love and law include John 14:15; Rom 13:10; Jas 2:8; 1 John 5:1–4.

teaching on unregenerate man's ability to love, this appears to be problematic at best (cf. Rom 3:10–18; 7:18–19). Moreover, since such a definition of love will inevitably vary between individuals, it is not really a moral norm at all. It seems, then, that situationalism can be fundamentally reduced to a utilitarian form of antinomianism, a charge Fletcher seems to admit.[27] Therefore, the previous critiques of antinomianism can be applied to situationalism.

Conflicting Absolutism

A POPULAR CHRISTIAN APPROACH TO NAVIGATING moral dilemmas is *conflicting absolutism*, alternatively known as ideal absolutism, tragic morality, or a lesser-evil view of moral conflict. This position holds that there are many universal moral absolutes. As its name implies, this approach teaches that moral norms can and do come into real conflict both in theory and in practice. When such a clash of norms occurs, conflicting absolutism teaches that man must choose sinfully to break one of the moral norms in tension—hopefully opting for the lesser of two evils—and then repent and seek forgiveness. John Warwick Montgomery, a leading contemporary proponent of conflicting absolutism, explains:

> The Christian morality fully realizes the difficulty of moral decision [making], and frequently a Christian finds himself in a position where it is necessary to make a decision where moral principles must be violated in favor of other moral principles, but he never vindicates himself in this situation. He decides in terms of the lesser of evils or the greater of goods, and this drives him to the Cross to ask forgiveness for the human situation in which this kind of complication and ambiguity exists.[28]

In addition to Montgomery, other major advocates of conflicting absolutism include Helmut Thielicke, J. I. Packer, Dietrich

---

[27] Fletcher writes: "Let's say plainly that *agape* is utility; love is well-being; the Christian who does not individualize or sentimentalize love *is* a utilitarian. . . . [What] remains as a difference between the Christian and most utilitarians is only the language used." Fletcher, *Situation Ethics*, 332. Geisler observes that situationalism "is not distinguishable from antinomianism." Geisler, *Christian Ethics*, 44. Gordon Clark writes, "[Situationalism] is simply the utilitarian calculus applied to love." *Baker's Dictionary of Christian Ethics* (1973), s.v. "situational ethics."

[28] Montgomery, *The Suicide of Christian Theology*, 69.

Bonhoeffer, and Erwin Lutzer.[29] Interestingly, in the Protestant tradition this approach is most often (although not solely) seen among those who have adopted or been influenced by Lutheran theology. It has been suggested that this phenomena is due in part to Martin Luther's doctrine of the two kingdoms.[30] Lutheran scholar Bernhard Lohse explains: "The intent behind the differentiation between the two kingdoms or two governments, both of which exist side by side in Luther, is to distinguish human existence 'before God' (*coram Deo*) and 'before the world' (*coram mundo*). . . . They are especially to serve the purpose that the spiritual remain spiritual and the temporal temporal."[31]

So, whether it was Luther's intent or not, the dualistic nature of this doctrine has produced, or at least allowed for, paradoxes in certain areas of Lutheran moral theology,[32] one of which is conflicting absolutism. An example from Luther's own thought where this tension can be detected comes from a letter to his colleague Philip Melanchton. Here Luther wrote:

---

[29] J. I. Packer, "Situations and Principles," in *Law, Morality, and the Bible*, ed. Bruce Kaye and Gordon Wenham (Downers Grove, IL: InterVarsity, 1978), 164–65; Erwin W. Lutzer, *The Morality Gap* (Chicago: Moody, 1972); John W. Montgomery and Joseph Fletcher, *Situation Ethics: True or False* (Minneapolis: Bethany Fellowship, 1972), 46; Helmut Thielicke, *Theological Ethics: Foundations*, vol. 1 (Grand Rapids: Eerdmans, 1979), 578–631. Note that some ethicists have traced the origins of conflicting absolutism back to the tragedies of ancient Greek drama. Cf. Geisler, *Christian Ethics*, 98; Jones, *Biblical Christian Ethics*, 132.

[30] Geisler, *Christian Ethics*, 98. Note that the term "two kingdoms doctrine" does not actually appear in Luther's work but was evidently coined by Karl Barth to describe this aspect in Luther's thought. Cf. Bernhard Lohse, *Martin Luther's Theology: Its Historical and Systematic Development* (Minneapolis: Augsburg, 1999), 154.

[31] Lohse, *Martin Luther's Theology*, 315. Observe Luther's own words about the two kingdoms in his 1525 *Open Letter on the Harsh Book Against the Peasants*, "There are two kingdoms, one the kingdom of God, the other the kingdom of the world. . . . God's kingdom is a kingdom of grace and mercy . . . but the kingdom of the world is a kingdom of wrath and severity. . . . Now he who would confuse these two kingdoms—as our false fanatics do—would put wrath into God's kingdom and mercy into the world's kingdom; and that is the same as putting the devil in heaven and God in hell." LW 4.265–66.

[32] In his classic work *Christ and Culture*, H. Richard Niebuhr writes of the tension such theology produces, stating, "Man is seen as subject to two moralities, and as a citizen of two worlds that are not only discontinuous with each other but largely opposed. In the polarity and tension of Christ and culture life must be lived precariously and sinfully. . . . [Luther] seems to have a double attitude toward reason and philosophy, toward business and trade, toward religious organizations and rites, as well as toward state and politics. . . . Luther divided life into compartments, or taught that the Christian right hand should not know what a man's worldly left hand was doing." H. Richard Niebuhr, *Christ and Culture* (New York: Harper & Row, 1951), 43, 171.

If you are a preacher of grace, then preach a true, not a fictitious grace; if grace is true, you must bear a true and not a fictitious sin. God does not save people who are only fictitious sinners. Be a sinner and sin boldly, but believe and rejoice in Christ even more boldly. For he is victorious over sin, death, and the world. As long as we are here we have to sin. This life is not the dwelling place of righteousness but, as Peter says (2 Pet 3:13), we look for a new heavens and a new earth in which righteousness dwells. . . . Pray boldly—you too are a mighty sinner.[33]

Advocates of conflicting absolutism support this view by appealing to Scripture passages that address the fallen condition of the world as well as the inevitability of personal sin (cf. Ps 51:5; Rom 3:23). As Geisler notes, the fact that the world is fallen and that moral conflicts will occur is "a central assumption of [conflicting absolutism]."[34] This is one of the strengths and attractions of conflicting absolutism—that is, an emphasis on the fallen estate of man, the holiness of God, the unbending nature of moral absolutes, and man's need to repent when he transgresses the law.[35] Yet proponents of this approach are careful to note that unavoidable sinful choices have their root in the corruption of man, not in the design of God. Another benefit of conflicting absolutism is its simplicity when faced with complex moral situations. Indeed, conflicting absolutism can ease the process of dealing with difficult ethical scenarios by teaching that sometimes there is no sin-free option, for sin is inevitable in a fallen world.[36] In such cases man is to sin freely, repent, and then seek forgiveness.

Additional support for conflicting absolutism comes from examples in Scripture that advocates of this view claim demonstrate real conflict between moral norms. Without commenting (at this point) as to the quality of these examples, key passages

---

[33] LW 48.281–82. Note, however, that Luther's point here was not to encourage sin. Rather, it was to emphasize man's lost condition and, more importantly, the boldness of God's grace.

[34] Geisler, *Christian Ethics*, 97; cf. Jones, *Biblical Christian Ethics*, 132.

[35] John Frame, *The Doctrine of the Christian Life* (Phillipsburg, NJ: P&R, 2008), 233; Jones, *Biblical Christian Ethics*, 132.

[36] Frame writes, "We should try to understand, however, why the theory of tragic moral choice is so plausible to many. The main reason, I think, is that many moral decisions are very difficult to make. Sometimes it is hard to find the way of escape, and people are tempted to think that such a way does not exist." Frame, *Doctrine of the Christian Life*, 233.

cited in the moral literature in support of conflicting absolutism include: Abraham and Sarah's lie before Pharaoh and Abimelech (cf. Gen 12:10–20; 20:2–18), the Hebrew midwives' lie to Pharaoh concerning the birth of male babies (cf. Exod 1:15–20), Rahab's lie about the location of the spies (cf. Josh 2:1–14), Samson's divinely approved suicide (Judg 16:30), Michal's lie about David's whereabouts (cf. 1 Sam 19:14), David's lie about his mission (cf. 1 Sam 21:2), Samuel's lie about his intentions (cf. 1 Sam 16:1–5), Daniel's companions' defiance of the governing authorities (Dan 3:8–30), and the apostles' disobedience of the religious rulers (Acts 4:13–22).

Despite the appeal of conflicting absolutism, this approach to resolving moral dilemmas is not without its problems. In fact, Frame asserts that this view is "morally confused," even claiming it is "[not] compatible with Scripture,"[37] and Geisler calls it "morally absurd."[38] A major challenge for conflicting absolutism is the Christological implications that stem from the position. To elaborate, this approach seems to make Jesus' incarnation either less authentic or artificially engineered, for Christ never sinned. Scripture is clear that Jesus was fully God and fully man yet was without sin (cf. Heb 2:14–18; 4:15; 1 Pet 2:22; 1 John 3:5). Yet, since conflicting absolutism teaches that in certain scenarios man must sin, it seems that during his incarnation Jesus must have been supernaturally preserved from situations in which he would have to sin. Yet, if this is true, in what significant sense can it be said that Christ "has been tested in every way as we are" (Heb 4:15)? It seems conflicting absolutism must hold that Jesus' incarnation was fundamentally different from that of other men in that he never experienced real moral conflict. If so, Jones writes that conflicting absolutism "renders the example of Jesus meaningless . . . [in that he] was not tested in all points like us."[39]

A second problem with conflicting absolutism is its view of the nature of law. Given that there is no conflict within the Godhead

---

[37] Ibid., 231.

[38] Geisler, *Christian Ethics*, 103.

[39] Jones, *Biblical Christian Ethics*, 132. Lutzer's response to this critique, which Geisler labels "the antecedent sin defense," is common among advocates of conflicting absolutism. Lutzer claims the event of having to choose between conflicting moral absolutes is always the result of previous sinful choices. Since Jesus never sinned, he never faced a moral dilemma. Yet the teaching that all moral conflicts are the result of others' sins seems suspect. Cf. Lutzer, *The Morality Gap*, 112; Geisler, *Christian Ethics*, 107–8.

(cf. John 17:22) if the law reflects the moral character of God, it is difficult to understand how the law could conflict with itself. While proponents of conflicting absolutism may appeal to the fallen estate of the created order in support of their view, the fall of man did not ontologically affect God or his law. Only man and the creation were cursed. It would seem, then, that advocates of this position cannot adopt the "authority is law" paradigm of the nature of law (see chap. 2). Moreover, it is also worth noting that God formally gave his law to mankind *after* the fall. Therefore, in light of divine injunctions to keep the law (cf. John 14:15, 21; 15:10; 1 John 5:2–3), it seems reasonable to expect that redeemed man could in fact do so. While no one will perfectly keep the law, to deny this possibility may have the effect of minimizing personal holiness and creating a moral duty to sin on some occasions. Moreover, it would seem to make God unjust if he allows mankind to exist in an environment in which sinning is inevitable and yet still holds man accountable for such necessary transgressions of the law.[40]

A third challenge for conflicting absolutism is that the Bible expressly forbids doing evil that good may result (cf. Rom 3:8; 6:1, 15) and clearly teaches, "No temptation has overtaken you except what is common to humanity. God is faithful, and He will not allow you to be tempted beyond what you are able, but with the temptation He will also provide a way of escape so that you are able to bear it" (1 Cor 10:13; cf. 2 Pet 2:9). Furthermore, the Bible nowhere explicitly addresses the issue of conflicting moral absolutes—a surprising omission given that moral dilemmas, if possible, would likely be some of the greatest trials a Christian could face. Indeed, the burden of Scripture is on doing what is right—that is, simply keeping moral norms—not upon committing a lesser evil in the name of avoiding a greater sin. Perhaps, then, conflicting absolutism is open to the charge of being overly simplistic in that when faced with moral dilemmas, it fails to look for a way of escape.

---

[40] Jones writes: "The idea of being compelled by (providentially governed) circumstances to choose the lesser of two moral evils, that is, the lesser of two sins, is highly problematic on Christian assumptions. It impugns the integrity of the Lawgiver by supposing he has issued conflicting commands, yet holds us responsible for obeying both of them." Jones, *Biblical Christian Ethics*, 132.

Graded Absolutism

A VIEW OF RESOLVING MORAL CONFLICTS that gained popularity in the late twentieth century is known as *graded absolutism*. This approach has also been called ethical hierarchicalism, contextual absolutism, and qualified absolutism. In short, graded absolutism teaches there are many universal moral norms that can and do conflict. In this sense graded absolutism is similar to conflicting absolutism. Yet graded absolutism differs from other approaches to moral dilemmas, including conflicting absolutism, in its claim that all ethical norms can be arranged in a hierarchy of merit. According to graded absolutism, when moral conflict occurs, resolution can be achieved by breaking a lower moral norm in order to keep a higher moral norm. Yet the hallmark of graded absolutism is its teaching that when a lower moral norm is broken in order to resolve a moral conflict, no sin has been committed. In this way graded absolutism differs from conflicting absolutism since it does not focus on sinfully committing a lesser evil but on righteously keeping the greater good. Norman Geisler, the modern architect of graded absolutism, summarizes this approach to moral dilemmas:

> The essential principles of graded absolutism are: There are many moral principles rooted in the absolute moral character of God; there are higher and lower moral duties— for example, love for God is a greater duty than love for people; These moral laws sometimes come into unavoidable moral conflict; In such conflicts we are obligated to follow the higher moral law; When we follow the higher moral law we are not held responsible for not keeping the lower one.[41]

Although shades of graded absolutism can be detected in earlier thinkers such as W. D. Ross,[42] and while other contemporary

---

[41] Norman L. Geisler, *Options in Christian Ethics* (Grand Rapids: Baker, 1981), 132. Geisler gives a similar definition in an earlier work: "Ethical hierarchicalism is so named because it maintains a hierarchical arrangement or ordering of ethical norms based on the relative scale of value they represent. It implies a pyramid of normative values which in and of themselves are objectively binding upon men. But when any two or more of these values happen to conflict, a person is exempted from his otherwise binding obligation to a lower norm in view of the pre-emptory obligation of the higher norm." Norman L. Geisler, *Ethics: Alternatives and Issues* (Grand Rapids: Zondervan, 1971), 114.

[42] Cf. W. D. Ross, *The Right and the Good* (Oxford: Clarendon, 1930); W. D. Ross, *Foundations of Ethics* (Oxford: Clarendon, 1939).

ethicists have adopted graded absolutism—including John Jefferson Davis, John Feinberg, and Paul Feinberg,[43]—Geisler crafted and popularized the approach as it is known in modern evangelical ethics. Interestingly, Geisler shuns credit as the innovator of this view, claiming that it is rooted in the Reformed tradition.[44] Yet his examples of Augustine and Charles Hodge as past advocates of graded absolutism are not convincing and are tenuous at best, a fact Geisler himself seems to concede.[45]

General support for graded absolutism comes from the apparent unavoidability of moral conflicts, both in Scripture and in real life, coupled with the divine expectation of holiness (cf. Matt 5:48). Geisler remarks: "It is both unrealistic and unbiblical to assume that moral obligations never conflict. Real life reveals this kind of conflict daily in hospitals, courtrooms, and battlefields. . . . It is naïve to assume that these kinds of situations never happen."[46] Scriptural examples of moral conflict cited by advocates of this approach are identical to those mentioned earlier in support of conflicting absolutism, including, for example, the Hebrew midwives, the Rahab narrative, and the like. Therefore, in view of the divine imperatives to keep God's laws, as well as the aforementioned shortfalls of conflicting absolutism, graded absolutists reason that there must be a way to navigate real moral conflict without creating a necessity to sin in order to avoid moral paralysis and incoherency of the law.

Obviously, the aspect of graded absolutism on which the entire system depends is the idea of a hierarchy of moral norms. Proponents of graded absolutism generally admit there is not an

---

[43] Davis, *Evangelical Ethics*, 20–22; Feinberg and Feinberg, *Ethics for a Brave New World*, 30–32. Another name associated with graded absolutism is Stephen Charles Mott, *Biblical Ethics and Social Change* (New York: Oxford University Press, 1982), 154–60.

[44] Geisler, *Ethics*, 113.

[45] Geisler admits that Augustine held "the unqualified absolutist position on the issue of lying" and that his views were only "similar to those of graded absolutism." Moreover, Geisler notes that Hodge's view was "a form of graded absolutism" and that it only has the "essential elements" of the approach. Geisler, *Ethics*, 113–14, 116. Presumably following Geisler, both Davis and the *New Dictionary of Pastoral Theology and Christian Ethics* cite Hodge as a proponent of graded absolutism. Davis, *Evangelical Ethics*, 21; *New Dictionary of Christian Ethics and Pastoral Theology* (1995), s.v. "norms." A reading of Hodge's exposition of the ninth commandment, which is the portion of his *Systematic Theology* cited by Geisler, shows that while Hodge's language is undefined in places, he was clearly a non-conflicting absolutist. For example, Hodge writes, "The question now under consideration is not whether it is ever right to do wrong, which is a solecism; nor is the question whether it is ever right to lie; but rather what constitutes a lie." Charles Hodge, *Systematic Theology*, vol. 3 (Grand Rapids: Eerdmans, 1873), 442.

[46] Geisler, *Christian Ethics*, 94.

explicit hierarchy of moral absolutes disclosed in Scripture; yet they claim such a hierarchy, or what Geisler calls a "pyramid of values,"[47] can be readily discerned and constructed through various allusions in the Bible. Examples of such veiled references include: Jesus' reference to the "least of these commandments" (Matt 5:19); Jesus' citation of "the greatest and most important command" (Matt 22:38); Jesus' reference to "the more important matters of the law" (Matt 23:23); Jesus' reference to he who has committed "the greater sin" (John 19:11); and Paul's claim that "the greatest of these is love" (1 Cor 13:13). Advocates of graded absolutism also cite the idea of degrees of punishment in hell (cf. Luke 10:12–14) and rewards in heaven (cf. 1 Cor 3:12–15) as evidence of there being a hierarchy of moral norms; for, they reason, there must be a hierarchy of norms in order to produce a gradation of punishments and rewards.[48]

That graded absolutism is attractive to some modern evangelical ethicists is not surprising, for this approach appears to offer a way to resolve real moral conflict without requiring personal sin. Yet graded absolutism is not without its limitations. For example, many have found the idea of a graded hierarchy of moral norms to be problematic if not entirely unbiblical. While the aforementioned proof-texts for a hierarchy of absolutes may indicate that all moral norms are not to be weighed equally in application, these passages do not provide a working hierarchy of moral absolutes.[49] In view of this lack of an explicit hierarchy of moral norms, Jones comments, "As a method, Geisler's hierarchicalism is too open-ended. Such a theory requires that one know which value is intrinsically higher in the conflict situation."[50] Similarly, John and Paul Feinberg, who themselves are advocates of graded absolutism, admit that they are not "certain that if one did construct a hierarchy, it

---

[47] Ibid., 124.

[48] Ibid., 116.

[49] In his first ethics textbook, Geisler suggested the following hierarchical calculus: Persons are more valuable than things. An infinite person is more valuable than finite person(s). A complete person is more valuable than an incomplete person. An actual person is of more value than a potential person. Potential persons are more valuable than actual things. Many persons are more valuable than few persons. Personal acts that promote personhood are better than those that do not. Geisler, *Ethics*, 115–21. For reasons that are unclear, Geisler seems to have abandoned this calculus, as he suggests a different one in his later ethics textbook. Geisler's more recent hierarchical calculus is: Love for God over love for man. Obey God over government and mercy over veracity. Geisler, *Christian Ethics*, 121–22.

[50] Jones, *Biblical Christian Ethics*, 136.

would be applicable to every situation, regardless of the factors involved in each case."[51] Of course, without a working hierarchy of moral norms, graded absolutism ceases to be a viable system of resolving moral conflict.

A second related challenge for graded absolutism is that even if a fixed hierarchy of ethical absolutes could be established from Scripture, proponents of this approach would still need to demonstrate that conflict between higher and lower moral norms actually occurs. The examples of moral conflict cited by advocates of both conflicting and graded absolutism are not described in Scripture as involving moral conflict. Indeed, as was mentioned previously, the Bible does not contain any univocal examples of conflict between moral norms, nor is there any teaching in Scripture on how to resolve such hypothetical moral conflict. Furthermore, even if advocates of graded absolutism could establish a hierarchy of moral norms from Scripture and show that real conflict between higher and lower moral norms can occur, they would still need to demonstrate that the Lord sanctions breaking lower moral norms as a means of resolving such conflict.

A third limitation of graded absolutism is that in teaching that it is not sinful to break a lower moral norm, albeit at the expense of keeping a higher moral norm, this approach appears to trivialize the concept of moral absolutes. Indeed, in explaining this concept, it seems that at times advocates of graded absolutism are playing a word game or using, as Luck notes, "linguistic mirrors."[52] For example, Geisler writes: "Not all absolutes are absolutely absolute. Some are only relatively absolute, that is, absolute relative to their particular area. . . . Lower norms are not universal in the broadest sense of the word. . . . That is, lower ethical norms cannot be universally universal but only locally universal. They are valid on their particular relationship but not on all relationships."[53] In another place Geisler attempts to clarify this concept, writing, "There are

---

[51] Feinberg and Feinberg, *Ethics for a Brave New World*, 32.

[52] Luck continues: "There simply is no such thing as a nonbinding yet applicable moral rule. Obligation is part of the denotative meaning of a rule or law. A rule is a statement of obligation. Remove the obligation and you are left with a string of words or at most a descriptive sentence, but not a moral rule." Luck, "Moral Conflicts and Evangelical Ethics," 22.

[53] Geisler, *Ethics*, 132. Rakestraw accurately observes that these statements betray the anthropocentric nature of graded absolutism. He writes that graded absolutism "fatally weakens the binding character of God's ethical norms and, in practice, shifts the locus of authority from the divine lawgiver to the moral agent." Robert V. Rakestraw, "Ethical

no exceptions to absolute moral laws, only exemptions from obeying them."[54] Needless to say, to claim that moral norms are not absolutely absolute, nor universally universal, and that there are exemptions to obeying moral laws, but no exceptions to keeping them, Geisler leaves himself open both to misunderstanding and to criticism.

One final limitation of graded absolutism is that this approach seems to have problems dealing with verses in Scripture that specify breaking one point of the moral law makes one guilty of violating the entire law. For example, Paul taught, "Everyone who does not continue doing everything written in the book of the law is cursed" (Gal 3:10; cf. Deut 27:26; Rom 3:19); and James wrote, "For whoever keeps the entire law, yet fails in one point, is guilty of breaking it all" (Jas 2:10). Rather than teaching that it is permissible to violate one part of the law in view of a greater good, these passages seem to indicate that there is an organic unity of the entire moral law that cannot be violated. A related challenge for graded absolutism is the so-called vice lists in Scripture that seem to present all laws as being equal in essence (cf. Matt 15:19; Gal 5:19–21; 1 Pet 4:3–4). Indeed, many more passages in Scripture present the law as being equal than veiled allusions to a hierarchy of moral norms. So, while this approach is creative in its desire to affirm the reality of conflicting moral absolutes, as well as man's duty to avoid sin, there may yet be a better solution to resolving moral dilemmas.

Nonconflicting Absolutism

A THIRD CHRISTIAN APPROACH TO DEALING with moral conflict is known as *nonconflicting absolutism*. This view, which Jones accurately observes is "the classic Christian approach,"[55] has also been called unqualified absolutism, case analysis, and casuistical divinity. As with both conflicting and graded absolutism, nonconflicting absolutism holds that there are many universal and absolute moral norms. However, as its name implies, nonconflicting absolutism differs from other approaches in its teaching that conflict between moral norms cannot

Choices: A Case for Non-conflicting Absolutism," in *Readings in Christian Ethics*, vol. 1, ed. David K. Clark and Robert V. Rakestraw (Grand Rapids: Baker, 1994), 123.

[54] Geisler, *Christian Ethics*, 129.

[55] Jones, *Biblical Christian Ethics*, 140. Curiously, Geisler claims that nonconflicting absolutism is rooted in the Anabaptist tradition; yet there does not appear to be any historical evidence or proponents to support this, nor does Geisler offer any proof. Cf. Geisler, *Ethics*, 113.

and does not occur. In other words, nonconflicting absolutism holds that there will never be a case where moral norms collide, resulting in the need to break one moral norm in order to keep another, or vice versa. Rakestraw summarizes this approach well, "Divinely-given moral absolutes never truly conflict, although there are occasions when they appear to conflict. Non-conflicting absolutism holds that there will never be a situation in which obedience to one absolute will entail disobedience to or the setting-aside of another absolute."[56]

In the preceding citation Rakestraw makes the important observation that sometimes moral norms will appear to collide. Yet, nonconflicting absolutists hold that such conflict is only apparent—the result of either misperception of circumstances, misunderstanding of moral norms, or both; however, true conflict between moral norms does not occur. Advocates of nonconflicting absolutism teach that in order to avoid confusion, as well as the appearance of conflict, in ethical analysis it is important that moral norms be defined and viewed biblically. O'Donovan writes, "If we are to obey any rule, we must understand the scope and meaning of its terms; and that applies no less to God-given rules such as those in the Decalogue."[57] Similarly, Jones comments:

> Analysis of how the commandments apply in typical cases begins with careful consideration of the commandments themselves. Absolutes in the sense of objective, universal, exceptionless moral norms can only be formulated by attending carefully to the whole teaching of Scripture in a given area. Many of the dilemmas posed in the evangelical literature on moral conflicts are readily resolvable on this basic principle.[58]

---

[56] Rakestraw, "Ethical Choices," 119.

[57] Oliver O'Donovan, "Christian Moral Reasoning," in *New Dictionary of Christian Ethics and Pastoral Theology*, ed. David J. Atkinson and David H. Field (Downers Grove, IL: InterVarsity, 1995), 125. O'Donovan further explains, "When we deliberate about our moral rules, we aim to make them less general and more specific, i.e., to give them the clarity and precision that they need in relation to distinct kinds of circumstances." Ibid.

[58] Jones, *Biblical Christian Ethics*, 140. Similarly, McQuilkin writes: "The Bible itself, giving the command, must be allowed to define the limits of that command. . . . When we define the ethical choice in biblical terms . . . most dilemmas are solved." McQuilkin, *Biblical Ethics*, 148. Likewise, Frame observes: "Some alleged examples of tragic moral choice are really questions of priority within the divine law. . . . Others have to do with questions of interpretation." Frame, *Doctrine of the Christian Life*, 233. Rakestraw, too, notes: "Non-conflicting absolutists pay close attention to the definition and scriptural basis of each moral absolute. . . . [So-called exceptions] are always within the absolute itself!

This call for careful consideration and defining of moral norms is not a plea for what Kierkegaard called a "teleological suspension of the ethical,"[59] nor is it an attempt to recognize what Ross called "*prima facie* duties,"[60] nor still is it to engage in what Geisler critically labeled "stipulative redefinition."[61] Rather, it is a call for critical, biblical analysis of moral dilemmas and the norms contained therein. To illustrate, if a father were to ask his son to steal a pack of cigarettes from a local convenience store, there is the veneer of moral conflict between the duty to obey parents and the law that prohibits stealing. Yet, upon further reflection, there is no real moral conflict here for, as Paul notes, the fifth commandment does not entail blind obedience; rather, it requires obedience in "the Lord" (Eph 6:1). Similarly, if a soldier were ordered by his commanding officer to kill an enemy in a time of war, there would be no actual moral conflict between the duty to submit to authority and the commandment that prohibits killing. This is because the sixth commandment does not prohibit killing *per se*; rather, it forbids murder—that is, the intentional, lawless, and malicious taking of human life. As such, there is a difference between cold-blooded murder and killing in a time of war.

As was noted previously, nonconflicting absolutism is the classic Christian position on dealing with moral dilemmas. Yet, as Rakestraw rightly observes: "It is very difficult to find a clear, systematic, evangelical presentation of non-conflicting absolutism by an advocate of the position. Non-conflicting absolutism is most often assumed rather than argued."[62] This being true, cogent presentations and examples of nonconflicting absolutism can be found in classic Christian thinkers such as Augustine and Charles Hodge (*contra* Geisler) and in modern ethicists including John Frame, David Clyde Jones, William F. Luck, Robertson McQuilkin,

---

They are part of the absolute and are therefore not exceptions to the absolute." Rakestraw, "Ethical Choices," 119–20.

[59] Soren Kierkegaard, *Fear and Trembling* (New York: Class House, 2009), 47–60.

[60] W. D. Ross coined the phrase "*prima facie* duty" in reference to an act that must be done because it is first mentioned, promised, or required, even if it is wrong. The term Ross uses to describe this confusing concept, *prima facie* duty, has been used by others to describe a duty that appears valid on first view yet is not required upon consideration. However, this is not Ross's definition of the concept. Cf. W. D. Ross, *The Right and the Good* (Oxford: Clarendon, 1930); W. D. Ross, *Foundations of Ethics* (Oxford: Clarendon, 1939).

[61] Geisler, *Christian Ethics*, 92.

[62] Rakestraw, "Ethical Choices," 118n1.

John Murray, and Robert Rakestraw, among others.[63] Moreover, as Rakestraw alludes to, nonconflicting absolutism is the assumed view of most ethics texts in the evangelical Protestant tradition.

One of the greatest arguments in favor of nonconflicting absolutism is a natural reading of the Bible. As was noted earlier, there are no univocal examples of moral conflict in Scripture. While proponents of both conflicting and graded absolutism cite alleged examples of moral conflict in the Bible, none of these proof-texts are presented as moral conflicts in the narrative of Scripture itself— either in their appearance or in their resolution. Indeed, it seems clear that the focus of the Bible is not on conflict between moral norms but on conflict between believers and moral norms, including the temptation to sin. In the face of such conflict, Christians have promises such as "No temptation has overtaken you except what is common to humanity. God is faithful, and He will not allow you to be tempted beyond what you are able, but with the temptation He will also provide a way of escape so that you are able to bear it" (1 Cor 10:13); and "The Lord knows how to rescue the godly from trials" (2 Pet 2:9). Additionally, believers have the example and help of Jesus, who was "tested in every way as we are, yet without sin" (Heb 4:15).[64]

Another important argument in favor of nonconflicting absolutism is the nature of moral norms themselves. If moral norms are based on and reveal the moral character of God (see the "authority is law" paradigm in chapter 2), given the fact that there is no conflict within the Godhead (cf. John 17:22), it would seem logically impossible for moral norms to collide—this despite the fact that the world is fallen, for the moral law itself was not affected by the fall. Said differently, if God is absolute and noncontradictory, then his moral norms ought to be absolute and noncontradictory.

---

[63] Cf. Augustine, *On Lying*; Hodge, *Systematic Theology*, 437–63; Frame, *Doctrine of the Christian Life*, 230–34; Jones, *Biblical Christian Ethics*, 138–44; Luck, "Moral Conflicts and Evangelical Ethics," 19–34; McQuilkin, *Biblical Ethics*, 148–50; John Murray, *Principles of Conduct* (Grand Rapids: Eerdmans, 1957); Robert V. Rakestraw, "Ethical Choices: A Case for Non-Conflicting Absolutism," *Criswell Theological Review* 2 (Spring 1988): 239–67.

[64] Geisler's objection to the biblical teaching that moral conflict is only apparent and that the Lord will provide a way of escape are troublesome. He either misunderstands this tenet of nonconflicting absolutism or the biblical teaching upon which it is based. Geisler writes: "God does not always intervene and spare all the faithful from moral dilemmas. There is no evidence for this premise of unqualified absolutism either inside or outside the Bible. . . . God may sometimes in his mercy desire to intervene, but there is no reason to believe he must (or will) always do so." Geisler, *Christian Ethics*, 93.

Rakestraw explains: "The very definition and nature of absolutes argues for non-conflicting absolutism. . . . The character of God argues for non-conflicting absolutism. If God has given numerous moral absolutes, some of which [supposedly] conflict at times, it appears that there is conflict within the mind and moral will of God!"[65]

Of course, not all ethicists embrace nonconflicting absolutism, despite the preceding arguments and evidence, as well as the historicity of the position. Indeed, some have argued that, when taken at face value, real-life experience and scriptural examples prove nonconflicting absolutism to be untrue.[66] However, as has been discussed, nonconflicting absolutists respond that such conflict is only apparent, the result of a misperception of circumstances, a misunderstanding of moral norms, or both.

Another charge that has been leveled against nonconflicting absolutism is that it focuses too much on defining moral norms to the neglect of the individuals involved in moral events. In so doing, Geisler believes nonconflicting absolutism is tantamount to legalism. He writes, "Another difficulty with unqualified absolutism is that it often tends toward legalism by neglecting the spirit of the law in order to avoid breaking the letter of the law."[67] Yet it seems Geisler has either misunderstood nonconflicting absolutism or begged the question, for proponents of nonconflicting absolutism would argue their approach does the exact opposite of what Geisler claims. That is, nonconflicting absolutism focuses on discerning the true spirit of the law in order to understand better and define the letter of the law and thus avoid a skewed or legalistic approach to morality. In so doing, nonconflicting absolutism attempts to avoid creating a moral duty to sin, like conflicting absolutism, or trivializing the concept of absolute, like graded absolutism.[68]

---

[65] Rakestraw, "Ethical Choices," 122–23.

[66] Geisler, *Christian Ethics*, 94.

[67] Ibid., 95.

[68] Rakestraw writes: "This is not to say that non-conflicting absolutism is unconcerned with results or ends, or that we value some abstract rule or principle above the lives and real concerns of human beings, but that the moral guidelines of the living God, when followed fully and consistently, will produce the greatest good for those following them. Non-conflicting absolutism is concerned with results, but never at the cost of disregarding God's absolutes." Rakestraw, "Ethical Choices," 121.

A Biblical Test Case: Rahab and the Spies

PERHAPS THE PRECEDING APPROACHES TO DEALING with moral conflict can best be understood by way of application to a biblical example. The account of Rahab's concealment of the Hebrew spies is one of the most well-known examples of apparent moral conflict in Scripture. This narrative is cited in almost all Christian treatments of moral dilemmas, regardless of the favored approach of a given volume. Since antinomianism and situationalism do not recognize moral conflict within their respective systems, only conflicting absolutism, graded absolutism, and nonconflicting absolutism need review and consideration. For the sake of better understanding these three approaches to moral conflict, each view's interpretation of the account of Rahab and the spies will be given in what follows without comment or critique.

The details of the Rahab narrative, recorded in Josh 2:1–24; 6:17, 23–25, are familiar: Rahab, a harlot residing in the city of Jericho, lodges two Hebrew spies who have been sent by Joshua to scout out the city. When word of the foreigners' presence reaches the king of Jericho, Rahab voluntarily hides the men and then deceives the inquiring authorities about the spies' whereabouts. Consequently, when Israel later captures Jericho, Rahab and her family are spared. After these events Rahab is only mentioned three times in Scripture, all in the New Testament: Matt 1:5; Heb 11:31; and Jas 2:25. The apparent moral dilemma in the Rahab narrative is that when the king of Jericho asked Rahab to turn over the spies, she was faced with two logical options: either assist the authorities and facilitate the spies' capture and murder or assist the spies by lying to the authorities. Given these options, it seems as though there was not a way for Rahab not to sin.

Advocates of *conflicting absolutism* read the Rahab narrative as describing a legitimate moral conflict between the laws prohibiting murder and lying—that is, the sixth commandment and the ninth commandment. Since most would view lying to be a lesser evil than murder, followers of this approach understand the text to teach that Rahab acted wisely as she fulfilled her moral duty to sin by lying about the spies' presence. While the text does not record Rahab's repentance for this sin, conflicting absolutists would understand Rahab to have later repented of her willing yet unavoidable deception. J. I. Packer, a conflicting absolutist, writes:

When one sets out to be truthful, new problems appear. . . . In such exceptional cases [of moral conflict] as we have mentioned, all courses of action have something evil in them, and an outright lie, like that of Rahab (Joshua 2:4–5; note the commendation of her in James 2:25) may actually be the best way, the least evil, and the truest expression of love to all the parties involved. Yet a lie, even when prompted by love, loyalty, and an escapable recognition that if telling it is bad, not telling it would be worse, remains an evil thing. . . . But the lie as such, however necessary it appears, is bad, not good, and the right-minded man knows this. Rightly will he seek fresh cleansing in the blood of Christ and settle for living the only way anyone can live with our holy God—by the forgiveness of sins.[69]

As with conflicting absolutism, proponents of *graded absolutism* view the Rahab narrative as containing real moral conflict. Davis, a graded absolutist, asserts, "After Rahab the harlot received the Israelite spies, she was met with a choice between telling the truth and preserving life."[70] Geisler concurs, noting, "The point here is that the conflict was genuine and both obligations were moral ones."[71] So, graded absolutists view the apparent moral conflict in the Rahab narrative to be real; yet unlike conflicting absolutists, their solution is not to commit the lesser evil and then to repent. Rather, graded absolutists understand the text to teach that in order to assist the spies Rahab innocently deceived the authorities and kept the greater good. According to graded absolutists Rahab's deception was not sinful, for the truth norm ceased to be normative in this scenario as it was trumped by the higher norm of protecting life. Davis writes:

When Rahab the harlot (Josh. 2:1–7), for example, spoke falsehood to protect the Israelite spies, was she choosing the "lesser of two evils," or a course of action acceptable to God? . . . Her course of action was acceptable to God. In the New Testament, Rahab is cited as an example of faith for receiving the spies and sending them out another way

---

[69] J. I. Packer, *Keeping the Ten Commandments* (Wheaton, IL: Crossway, 2007), 97–99.
[70] Davis, *Evangelical Ethics*, 18.
[71] Geisler, *Christian Ethics*, 118.

(James 2:25). Nowhere in Scripture is Rahab condemned for her action. On this construction Rahab fulfilled the moral absolute that applied. . . . Her actions, rather than being the lesser of two evils, were actually good.[72]

Nonconflicting absolutists arrive at the same conclusion as do graded absolutists—that is, Rahab did not sin in her deception—albeit via a different route. Whereas graded absolutists hold that Rahab's breaking of the truth norm was not a sin since it was committed in view of a greater good, nonconflicting absolutists teach that Rahab's deception was not a violation of a moral absolute at all. Frame, a nonconflicting absolutist, gives a general definition of lying as he asks, "What, then, is a lie? I would say that a lie is a word or act that intentionally deceives a neighbor in order to hurt him. . . . The sin of false witness is that of distorting the facts in such a way as to harm one's neighbor."[73] In view of this definition of lying, nonconflicting absolutists hold that Rahab did not break the truth norm by deceiving the authorities, for she did not lie for her own glory or expressly to harm the authorities. Rather, Rahab herself explains her own actions in view of her fear of the Lord (cf. Josh 2:9, 11). Moreover, advocates of this approach note that not only is Rahab not condemned for her words and actions in the text, but she is commended for them at Heb 11:31 and Jas 2:25. Rae writes, "[Rahab] is included in God's 'hall of faith' in Hebrews 11 . . . she is praised for her act of faith in providing a safe refuge for the spies. Clearly, part of providing that refuge was deceiving the authorities who were after the spies."[74]

---

[72] Davis, *Evangelical Ethics*, 21–22. Geisler's comments are similar. He writes: "The Bible indicates that there are occasions when intentionally falsifying (lying) is justifiable. Rahab intentionally deceived to save the lives of Israel's spies and was immortalized in the spiritual 'hall of fame' (Heb. 11). It should be noted that first, nowhere does the Bible condemn her for this deception; second, her falsehood was an integral part of the act of mercy she showed in saving the spies' lives; and third, the Bible says, 'Rahab . . . shall be spared, because she hid the spies we sent' (Josh. 6:17). But the real concealment was accomplished by deceiving the authorities at her door. It seems that God blessed her because of it, not in spite of it. Hence, her 'lie' was an integral part of her faith for which she was commended of God (Heb. 11:31; James 2:25)." Geisler, *Christian Ethics*, 122.

[73] Frame, *Doctrine of the Christian Life*, 830–35. J. I. Packer, a conflicting absolutist, similarly defines lying as "false witness against your neighbor—that is, as we said, prideful lying designed to do him down and exalt yourself at his expense." Packer, *Keeping the Ten Commandments*, 98.

[74] Rae, *Moral Choices*, 34. Frame notes, "With regard to Rahab . . . what Scripture commends is precisely her concealment, her creating a false impression in the minds of the Jericho officials." Frame, *Doctrine of the Christian Life*, 837. Jones notes: "Certainly concealing the

Conclusion

THIS CHAPTER HAS SOUGHT TO DEMONSTRATE that the coherency of the law is an important topic for biblical ethics and has investigated various options for dealing with apparent moral conflict. The prospect of moral norms colliding raises crucial questions for biblical ethics as it seeks to apply God's Word to all areas of life. In investigating ways of dealing with moral conflict, this chapter has suggested Christians have historically held to one of three main approaches: conflicting absolutism, graded absolutism, and nonconflicting absolutism. While there is certainly room at the table of moral discussion for each of these perspectives, this chapter found nonconflicting absolutism to be the least problematic option of the three.

Summary Points

- Antinomianism—Literally means "against-the-law;" there are no applicable moral absolutes in an antinomian system; therefore, conflict between moral norms cannot occur.
  - Strengths—Stress on individual moral responsibility; emphasis on emotive and relational aspects of ethics.
  - Weaknesses—Self-defeating as it makes morally absolute claim there are no moral absolutes; denies the fact that humans create and use moral norms.
- Situationalism—Affirms the existence of one universal, moral absolute—the duty to love others.
  - Strengths—Appears to be winsome due to the centrality of love.
  - Weaknesses—Love is declared to be central arbitrarily; inconsistent with the many moral norms of Scripture; relies on individual decision to determine what is most loving.
- Conflicting absolutism—Many universal moral norms conflict so that someone must sin in certain situations.

---

spies from the king of Jericho (treason from his point of view) is approved. Although it is not specifically mentioned in the New Testament retrospectives that extol Rahab's faith, the misdirection of the king's men would seem to be integral to the welcome and protection for which she is commended (Heb. 11:31; James 2:25)." Jones, *Biblical Christian Ethics*, 150. McQuilkin writes: "These spies were hidden, in good spy-thriller fashion, by an ancestor of Jesus, Rahab. At that point she began the act of deception, not when she uttered words that further deceived the home troops. For this act she was commended and rewarded by God (Heb. 11:31)." McQuilkin, *Biblical Ethics*, 440.

- o Strengths—Emphasizes the fallenness of man, the holiness of God, the unbending nature of moral absolutes, and the need for repentance; simplicity when complex moral situations arise: sin, repent, and seek forgiveness.
- o Weaknesses—Makes Jesus' incarnation less authentic or artificially engineered since Christ was fully human and divine but did not sin; conflicting absolutes would reflect conflict within the Godhead since the moral law is a reflection of God's character; Scripture appears inconsistent with this position (cf. Rom 3:8; 1 Cor 10:13).

- Graded absolutism—Many universal moral norms can and do conflict, but ethical norms are hierarchical; thus, one can obey the higher norm while breaking the lower norm without sin.
  - o Strengths—Acknowledges the apparent unavoidability of moral conflicts; allows for resolving moral conflict without sin.
  - o Weaknesses—No basis exists for a hierarchy of moral norms; does not demonstrate that conflict actually exists between higher and lower norms; teaches that it is not sinful to break a lower norm; Scripture teaches that if an individual violates one part of the law, he violates the whole (cf. Gal 3:10; Deut 27:26; Jas 2:10).

- Nonconflicting absolutism—Many universal moral norms cannot and do not conflict.
  - o Strengths—Scripture provides no indication of conflicting moral absolutes or how to resolve them. Since moral norms are based on God's character, by definition they cannot conflict. Also, the classic evangelical approach.
  - o Weaknesses—Real-life situations seem to result in conflicting moral norms; can seem to focus more on the norms than the people involved in the situation.

Chapter 5

The Structure of the Law

The previous three chapters have reviewed various aspects of the law, which is at the heart of biblical ethics. Chapter 2 studied the nature of the law as it focused on the relationship between the law and God. Chapter 3 looked at the relevancy of the law as it focused on the relationship between the law and the gospel. Chapter 4 considered the coherency of the law as it looked at the interrelationship between various laws. The present chapter, which will bring the foundational section of this book to a close, will review the structure of the law as it focuses on the relationship between the law and man. The purpose of this chapter is to explore the framework of biblical ethics and to suggest a methodology by which believers can use the law in the process of moral decision making. Of course, no model of ethics can mechanically generate answers to moral questions apart from serious moral reflection. Yet an understanding of the nature, relevancy, and coherency of the law, coupled with knowledge of the structure of the law, can provide believers with the basic materials needed in order to engage in the work of biblical ethics.

In their discussion of the Bible and ethical methodology, Clark and Rakestraw observe, "It is surprising how little attention ethicists have given to the methodological question of how Scripture actually functions in relation to Christian ethics."[1] This observation, which

[1] David K. Clark and Robert V. Rakestraw, eds., *Readings in Christian Ethics*, vol. 1 (Grand Rapids: Baker, 1994), 180.

appears to be accurate,[2] is interesting; for while knowledge of the Bible can be personally edifying in isolation, the inability to apply Scripture to moral issues in a consistent and competent manner makes one's understanding of God's law merely academic. Clearly believers need a method by which they can engage in moral evaluation. However, participating in the discipline of biblical ethics is not always an easy task, for while moral issues are unavoidable, they are often indefinite, complex, or both. In regard to ethical analysis, Rae writes, "The process of making a moral decision can be as important as the decision itself, and many ethical decisions that people face are so complex that it is easy to exhaust oneself talking around the problem."[3] Yet, with an understanding of how the law relates to man, believers can competently bring their knowledge of God's law to bear upon the complicated moral issues that continually face mankind.

Ethical Methodology

CHAPTER 1 OF THIS BOOK NOTED that in evaluating a moral event, evangelical ethicists have traditionally weighed at least three factors: conduct, character, and goals.[4] These key components of ethical methodology were referred to as the three parts of morality. As will be explored over the following pages, when arranged in relational order between man and God, the three parts of morality provide

[2] A survey of Christian and biblical ethics textbooks reveals few attempts to identify an explicit method, model, process, or structure for engaging in moral evaluation. Most texts seem to assume a methodology without specifically identifying one. Examples of methodologies can be found in J. Douma, *Responsible Conduct*, trans. Nelson D. Kloosterman (Phillipsburg, NJ: P&R, 2003), 367–90; Oliver O'Donovan, "Christian Moral Reasoning," in *New Dictionary of Christian Ethics and Pastoral Theology*, ed. David J. Atkinson and David H. Field (Downers Grove, IL: InterVarsity, 1995), 122–27; and Scott B. Rae, *Moral Choices: An Introduction to Ethics*, 2nd ed. (Grand Rapids: Zondervan, 2000), 104–6.

[3] Rae, *Moral Choices*, 104. Rae continues: "What makes many moral dilemmas so difficult is that the Scriptures do not always [directly] address an issue. . . . There is often disagreement about which biblical principles are applicable to the specific issue under discussion." Ibid. In a similar vein, Frame comments: "Although Scripture is sufficient as a source of God's words concerning our ethical life, it does not speak directly to every situation, especially to situations that are distinctive to modern life. . . . But although there are many subjects that Scripture does not explicitly mention, it speaks of everything implicitly." John Frame, *The Doctrine of the Christian Life* (Phillipsburg, NJ: P&R, 2008), 356, 152. While some complex moral issues are exceptional, such topics ought not to be considered outside of a model of ethics; rather, they ought to confirm it.

[4] Two additional parts of morality that are often, although not always, components of moral decision making include the observers of the event (cf. Rom 14:15, 21; 1 Cor 10:28–29) and one's own convictions (cf. Rom 14:23; Jas 4:17).

a framework or a structure that can be used in the process of making moral decisions (see chart 5.1). Before this structure is explored, however, two caveats are in order. First, the framework described below ought not to be viewed as a magical formula that will instantly provide moral guidance in any and every situation. As was previously observed, on account of their complexity, ethical issues often require careful consideration and critical analysis before one can arrive at moral conclusions. Second, since the three parts of morality are equal components of moral events and are ontologically interrelated, their connection is not nearly as linear or as chronological as may be implied by the methodology and diagram that follow. Indeed, other helpful structures of biblical ethics have been suggested elsewhere.[5] Yet, regardless of the framework employed, the essential elements of biblical ethics ought to remain the same.

The Goal of Biblical Ethics

IF THE NATURE OF THE LAW is that it reflects and reveals God's own moral character (see chap. 2), it is logical to begin a look at the structure of the law with God himself. As was noted in chapter 1 of this book, the *summum bonum* of biblical ethics is the glorification of God. This speaks to the teleological aspect of biblical ethics as it emphasizes the design and necessary end of moral events, which is to love and to glorify God. This forward-looking goal is not inconsistent with the deontological, divine command basis of biblical ethics; rather, it gives purpose and direction to the discipline of biblical ethics.

Scripture teaches all that the Lord does is for his own glory. This can be seen by tracing God's plan of redemption throughout the Bible. For example, Scripture notes God created the world for his glory (Prov 16:4; Col 1:16–18); God elected his people before the foundation of the world for his own glory (Eph 1:5–6); God created man for his own glory (Isa 43:7); God chose Israel for his own glory (Isa 49:3); God delivered Israel from Egypt for his own glory (Ps 106:7–8); God restored Israel after their exile for his own glory (Isa 48:9–11); God sent his Son into the world that Gentiles might glorify him for his mercy (Rom 15:8–9); God sent the Holy

---

[5] For example, see the triangle structure of biblical ethics suggested by many, including T. B. Maston, *Biblical Ethics* (Macon, GA: Mercer University Press, 1982), 18; and Frame, *The Doctrine of the Christian Life*, 34–36. See, also, the concentric circle structure in Timothy Tow, *The Law of Moses and of Jesus* (Singapore: Christian Life Publishers, 1986), 111.

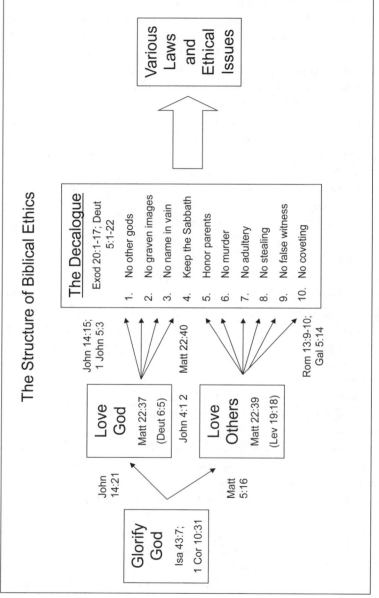

The Structure of Biblical Ethics

Glorify God
Isa 43:7;
1 Cor 10:31

John 14:21

Matt 5:16

Love God
Matt 22:37
(Deut 6:5)
John 4:1 2

Love Others
Matt 22:39
(Lev 19:18)

John 14:15;
1 John 5:3

Matt 22:40

Rom 13:9-10;
Gal 5:14

The Decalogue
Exod 20:1-17; Deut 5:1-22

1. No other gods
2. No graven images
3. No name in vain
4. Keep the Sabbath
5. Honor parents
6. No murder
7. No adultery
8. No stealing
9. No false witness
10. No coveting

Various Laws and Ethical Issues

Chart 5.1

Spirit to glorify his Son (John 16:14); God commands his people to do all things for his own glory (1 Cor 10:31; 1 Pet 4:11); God will send his Son a second time into the world to receive the glory due him (Phil 2:9–10; 2 Thess 1:10); and in the end times God will fill the earth with the knowledge of his own glory (Hab 2:14).

As has been previously noted, the goal of biblical ethics must be to love and to glorify God. Yet how do believers demonstrate their love for God and bring glory to his name in the context of moral decision making? Two Scripture passages provide direction. In John 14:21 Jesus taught his disciples, "The one who has My commands and keeps them is the one who loves Me," and at Matt 5:16, in his Sermon on the Mount, Christ instructed his listeners, "In the same way, let your light shine before men, so that they may see your good works and give glory to your Father in heaven." A primary way, then, that believers can love and glorify God is to keep his commands and to perform the good works prescribed therein. On this topic Frame writes, "God's ultimate purpose is his own glory (1 Cor 10:31). But God has more specific goals as well: the filling and subduing of the earth (Gen 1:28), the evangelization and nurture of people of all nations (Matt 28:19–20), and the success of his kingdom (Matt 6:33)."[6] Indeed, the Lord commands believers to fulfill and to participate in these purposes, for doing so brings glory to God. This is the goal of biblical ethics. Therefore, when faced with an ethical challenge, believers must give consideration to the question, "What path, choice, or answer would bring the most glory to God?"

Character and Biblical Ethics

THE IDEA OF GLORIFYING AND LOVING God by keeping his commandments can be refined, though; for while equal in essence, not all commandments in Scripture are of equal importance. To elaborate, in Matt 22:34–40 a discussion between Jesus and a religious lawyer about law keeping is recorded:

---

[6] Frame, *The Doctrine of the Christian Life*, 33. In his writing on ethical methodology, O'Donovan similarly writes: "Reflection, if it is to provide a ground for deliberation [i.e., conduct], must describe the elements of teleological order which make deliberation intelligible and necessary. . . . God's purposes interpret the teleological structures of the world." O'Donovan, "Christian Moral Reasoning," 123.

When the Pharisees heard that He had silenced the
Sadducees, they came together. And one of them, an
expert in the law, asked a question to test Him: "Teacher,
which command in the law is the greatest?" He said to
him, "Love the Lord your God with all your heart, with all
your soul, and with all your mind. This is the greatest and
most important commandment. The second is like it: Love
your neighbor as yourself. All the Law and the Prophets
depend on these two commands."

So while the Bible contains a variety of divine laws, commands,
and injunctions, Jesus identified the two greatest commandments
as loving God and loving others. Note that in doing so, Jesus
merely quoted Deut 6:5 and Lev 19:18; thus, Christ's directives to
love God and to love neighbor are not new commands. Man has
always been expected and required to love God and to love others.
Moreover, the concepts of law and love ought not to be juxtaposed,
for, as Jesus taught, love is commanded by the law.[7]

In the contemporary milieu, love is usually thought of as an
emotion; yet most often in biblical usage love is a willful choice
that stems from right character. In his classic text on biblical ethics,
Murray notes, "We must not forget that love to God with all our
heart and soul and strength and mind, and love to our neighbor
as ourselves, are themselves commandments."[8] Unlike emotions,
then, obedience to commandments can be chosen. Indeed, moral
choices that manifest love for God and love for fellowman ought
to be desired by followers of Christ, for such love is Christlike.
Kevan observes, "The joyfully rendered obedience of love, however,
is a quite different thing [than legalism] and is of the very essence
of Christian life."[9] To choose to love, then, even at great personal
cost, is an incarnational type of love and is worthy of moral praise.
Commenting on the place of love in moral decision making, Frame

---

[7] Frame makes the interesting observation: "Love and law are the same content, considered from two different angles. . . . The difference between them is in focus or emphasis. Law
focuses on the acts we are to perform, while love focuses on the heart motives of these acts."
Frame, *The Doctrine of the Christian Life*, 196. After citing 1 John 5:3; John 14:21; 15:10,
Murray makes a similar observation as he writes, "To say the very least, the witness of our
Lord and the testimony of John are to the effect that there is indispensible complementation;
love will be operative in the keeping of God's commandments." John Murray, *Principles of
Conduct: Aspects of Biblical Ethics* (Grand Rapids: Eerdmans, 1957), 183.

[8] Murray, *Principles of Conduct*, 23.

[9] Ernest Kevan, *Moral Law* (Phillipsburg, NJ: P&R, 1991), 2.

writes, "Love is the great commandment, the greatest command-ment, the highest virtue, the mark of the believer, the center of biblical ethics."[10]

Loving God and loving neighbor are more than just Christian duties. They describe the disposition of someone with right moral character. This part of morality speaks to the essential nature of believers. In regard to Christian character, Frame writes: "Here the focus is inward, examining our heart's relationship to God. It deals with our regeneration [and] our sanctification."[11] Moreover, loving God and loving others are essentially connected; for as the apostle John wrote, "We have this command from Him: The one who loves God must also love his brother" (1 John 4:21). This is because, as *The Westminster Dictionary of Christian Ethics* observes, "Christian love of neighbor is nothing less than God's own agape love flowing through human hearts."[12] This, then, is the proper order and connection between love of God and love of neighbor: love of God leads to love of neighbor. Regarding this bond, Rooker writes: "Social concern stems from and must be rooted in the religious conscience. Hence a profession of belief in God and the observance of religious ritual are undermined, if not negated, if they are not accompanied by proper treatment of one's fellow man."[13]

Yet, like other aspects of sanctification, a mature, loving heart is not automatically bestowed in full form at the moment of conver-sion. Rather, character marked by love for God and love of oth-ers needs to be actively sought after, cultivated, and monitored throughout the Christian life. Said differently, while character is eternal, it must be developed over time. In the process of making a moral decision, believers ought to consider their motives and ask the question, "Am I acting out of love for God and love for neigh-bor?" Such introspection and concern for keeping the divine com-mands to love God and to love others is the hallmark of Christian character and brings glory to the Lord.

---

[10] Frame, *The Doctrine of the Christian Life*, 193.

[11] Ibid., 34.

[12] *The Westminster Dictionary of Christian Ethics* (1986), s.v. "love."

[13] Mark F. Rooker, *The Ten Commandments: Ethics for the Twenty-First Century* (Nashville: B&H Academic, 2010), 21.

The Conduct of Biblical Ethics

IN THE AFOREMENTIONED NARRATIVE BETWEEN JESUS and a religious lawyer about the greatest commandment (cf. Matt 22:34–40), after prescribing love for God and love of neighbor, Christ concluded his teaching with the assertion, "All the Law and the Prophets depend on these two commands" (Matt 22:40). The phrase "Law and the Prophets" is a common Jewish idiom for the entire Old Testament (cf. Matt 5:17; 7:12; 11:13; Luke 16:16; 24:44; Acts 24:14; 28:23; Rom 3:21),[14] yet the phrase is often used in reference to the moral commands of Scripture (e.g., Matt 7:12, "Therefore, whatever you want others to do for you, do also the same for them—this is the Law and the Prophets").[15] Ethically speaking, the heart of the Old Testament is the Ten Commandments, for they are a summary of the moral law (Exod 20:1–17; Deut 5:1–22). Therefore, in responding to the Jewish lawyer's moral inquiry, Jesus taught that the Decalogue can be summarized by love for God and love of neighbor; or, conversely, that love for God and love of others is fleshed out within the Ten Commandments. In one sense this connection is not surprising, for as Murray notes, "The Ten Commandments, it will surely be admitted, furnish the core of the biblical ethic."[16] Yet, how is love for God and love of others embodied by the Decalogue? How do the two greatest commandments relate to Christian living?

First, consider the command to love God. As has already been touched upon, the Bible is clear in connecting love for God with keeping his commandments. Believers do not love God because they keep his commandments; rather, believers keep God's commandments because they love God. Jesus taught, "If you love Me, you will keep My commands" (John 14:15), and John instructed the early church, "For this is what love for God is: to keep His commands" (1 John 5:3). In focusing on the first four of the Ten Commandments, what is oftentimes referred to as the first table of

---

[14] Blomberg makes an observation that is fairly standard in commentaries on the Gospels: "Both the Law and the Prophets together and the Law by itself were standard Jewish ways of referring to the entire Hebrew Scriptures." Craig Blomberg, *Matthew* (Nashville: Broadman, 1992), 103.

[15] Gurtner and Nolland write, "It is crucial to see that the expression 'the Law and the prophets' is understood as a canon or integrity-formula that summarizes God's revelation that has taken place so far." Daniel M. Gurtner and John Nolland, *Built upon the Rock: Studies in the Gospel of Matthew* (Grand Rapids: Eerdmans, 2008), 103.

[16] Murray, *Principles of Conduct*, 7.

the law, this connection comes into focus, for the first four commandments illuminate various ways in which believers manifest love for God. The first table of the law will be explored in more detail in chapter 7 of this book; yet, for the time being, note the following: the first commandment addresses *internal* love for God; the second commandment addresses *external* love for God; the third commandment addresses *verbal* love for God; and the fourth commandment addresses *temporal* love for God.

Second, consider the command to love others. Many have observed that the first table of the law is vertical in orientation as it focuses on believers' relationship with God, while the second table of the law (i.e., the fifth through tenth commandments) is horizontal in orientation as it focuses on relationships among believers. Although the second table of the law will be examined more closely in chapter 8 of this text, for the sake of the present discussion, consider the areas addressed by the second table of the law. Each commandment in this part of the Decalogue identifies a facet of human relations where love for others must be maintained. The fifth commandment addresses the sanctity of *human authority*; the sixth commandment addresses the sanctity of *human life*; the seventh commandment addresses the sanctity of *relational intimacy*; the eighth commandment addresses the sanctity of *material stewardship*; the ninth commandment addresses the sanctity of *truth*; and the tenth commandment addresses the sanctity of proper *motives*. Note Paul's reiteration of Jesus' teaching on the second table of the law, "The commandments: Do not commit adultery, do not murder, do not steal, do not covet, and whatever other commandment—all are summed up by this: Love your neighbor as yourself. Love does no wrong to a neighbor. Love, therefore, is the fulfillment of the law" (Rom 13:9–10; cf. Gal 5:14).

When faced with a moral decision, then, believers ought to ask themselves the question, "What moral norm(s) apply in this situation?" The Decalogue is helpful in answering this question; yet as was mentioned in chapter 3 of this book and will be explored further in the following chapters, the Ten Commandments are only a summary of the moral law. The moral law existed prior to Sinai, at Sinai, and is present throughout Scripture. So, while using the Decalogue as a guide is helpful, other means of gaining knowledge of the moral law may assist believers in the process of moral decision making. For example, knowledge of the moral law can be gained by considering biblical examples and directives, by investigating the underpinnings of the civil law, by studying the history of moral doctrine, by listening to ethical advice from other mature Christians (including counsel and preaching), and even by considering the natural law (see chap. 2).[17] O'Donovan describes this process, writing, "Particular moral judgments, or 'decisions,' involve bringing the particular instance under a generic moral principle or rule that has been grasped independently."[18] Note, however, Scripture is the source of moral authority behind each of these avenues of moral guidance.[19]

To synthesize the ethical methodology described above, within biblical ethics moral decision making does not begin with an isolated analysis of the ethical issue at hand. Rather, biblical ethics incorporates the three parts of morality. In practice, working from conduct, to character, to goals is most expedient and practical (i.e., work from right to left on chart 5.1). This is so because, as has been discussed, of the three parts of morality, conduct is the most easily quantified, prescribed, and measured.

The process of engaging in biblical ethics can be summarized as follows. When faced with a moral scenario, the first question that should be asked is, "What ethical norm(s) apply in this situation?" Much of the work in biblical ethics occurs at this stage in the process of moral decision making, for identifying what moral

---

[17] Milne observes, "New Testament writers appeal to other supplementary sources of moral wisdom such as nature (1 Cor. 11:14), Christ's example (Phil. 2:5–8), church tradition (1 Cor. 14:33–34), the gospel (1 Cor. 6:14–15), and experience (2 Tim. 2:20–21)." Douglas Milne, "The Relationship Between the Law and Love," in *Love Rules: The Ten Commandments for the 21st Century*, ed. Stuart Bonnington and Joan Milne (Carlisle, PA: Banner of Truth, 2004), 16.

[18] O'Donovan, "Christian Moral Reasoning," 126. Similarly, Frame writes, "Most applications of Scripture require extrabiblical data, and they lead to conclusions that may not be stated explicitly in Scripture." Frame, *The Doctrine of the Christian Life*, 200.

[19] It has become common in contemporary Christian circles to look beyond Scripture for moral revelation. For example, some believers make moral decisions based on so-called "open" or "closed doors," having a personal peace, or impressions and intuition, among other means. Certainly in Scripture God did speak through extrabiblical modes of revelation, including prophets (cf. Heb 1:1–2), Urim and Thummim (cf. Exod 28:30; Lev 8:8), casting of lots (cf. Lev 16:8; Acts 1:26), dreams and visions (cf. Gen 37:5–11; Dan 7:1–8:27), various supernatural signs (cf. Exod 3:1–22; Judg 6:36–40), angels (cf. Matt 1:20–21; Luke 1:26–38), and even audible communication from the Lord (cf. John 20:14–18). Yet Christians are nowhere told to seek or to use such means in the church age. Moreover, given the subjective nature of many modes of extrabiblical revelation, the above means must be judged to be vastly inferior when compared to the objective, inerrant, sufficient, written Word of God.

norms are in play can be a challenging task. However, identifying the relevant moral norms is essential for it will set the parameters of the moral discussion. Once the applicable moral norms are identified, a second question that must be addressed is, "Am I acting out of love of God and love for neighbor?" Of course, believers must remember it is easy to manifest the right norm with the wrong motive and thus break the moral law. Finally, the last step in the process of moral decision making is to answer the question, "What path, choice, or answer would bring the most glory to God?" The right path is to keep the moral law out of a love for God and neighbor with the intent of bringing glory to God.

Biblical Ethics in Practice

PERHAPS THE BEST WAY TO UNDERSTAND the ethical methodology described above is by way of example. Certainly there are ethical issues that require little moral analysis, for the teaching of Scripture is explicit and clear on many subjects. Examples of such topics include murder, adultery, theft, and homosexuality, among many others. Reaching a moral conclusion that follows the moral law, manifests love, and glorifies God is not difficult in regard to these issues. Yet many other subjects are not directly addressed in Scripture about which ethical questions arise. Take, for example, the practice of cremation.[20]

The ethics of cremation is an interesting topic for discussion, for it is a subject on which the Bible gives little explicit moral guidance.[21] The lack of specific, biblical teaching on cremation notwithstanding, in increasing numbers many contemporary believers and unbelievers alike are requesting and facilitating the practice.[22] At the same time, throughout history, the nearly unanimous position of those in the Judeo-Christian tradition has been that cremation

---

[20] Cf. David W. Jones, "To Bury or to Burn? Towards an Ethic of Cremation," *Journal of the Evangelical Theological Society* 53, no. 2 (June 2010): 335–47.

[21] Only three passages in Scripture mention cremation, and each instance is a passing reference, not a direct teaching (cf. 1 Sam 31:11–12; Amos 2:1–3; 6:8–11).

[22] In 2002, the Cremation Association of North America (CANA) reported 676,890 cremations conducted in the United States, which amounts to 27.78 percent of all interments. By 2006 the cremation rate had risen to 33.61 percent. By way of comparison, in 1970 there were 88,096 cremations in the United States, or 4.59 percent of all deaths. CANA estimates that cremations will reach 58.89 percent in the United States by the year 2025. Douglas J. Davies and Lewis H. Mates, eds., *Encyclopedia of Cremation* (Aldershot, UK: Ashgate, 2005), 450, 456.

ought to be avoided. So, the question remains, what is a correct biblical ethic of cremation?

Given the ethical methodology described above, in handling the deceased, the first question that must be addressed is, "What ethical norm(s) apply in this situation?" An appeal to the moral law as embodied in the Ten Commandments does not provide immediate moral guidance, for the Decalogue does not explicitly address burial or cremation. Yet, as will be explored further in chapter 8 of this text, the eighth commandment addresses the subject of material stewardship. While the moral norm manifested in the eighth commandment is stated negatively—that is, "Do not steal" (Exod 20:15)—it could be stated positively as, "Respect material goods" or "Properly steward physical possessions." As was mentioned earlier, in applying this moral norm to interment procedures, those in the Judeo-Christian tradition have historically understood this commandment to teach that burial is the best way to handle the body of the deceased. As John wrote, "The custom of the Jews is to bury" (John 19:40 NKJV). This was the nearly unanimous practice and view of the church from biblical times until the middle of the nineteenth century.[23] Believers reasoned that burial best reflects proper stewardship of the body, visibly depicts the gospel message, and most clearly communicates the hope of future bodily resurrection.

Turning to the analysis of character, Scripture is clear that love of God and love for others (even deceased others) is expected of Christians and is a mark of Christlike character (cf. John 11:1–44). In deciding between cremation and burial, then, the question that must be asked is, "Which method of interment best demonstrates love of God and love for neighbor?" Certainly the friends and family of the deceased could be considered "neighbors" who ought to be loved in the midst of the interment process. Yet, assuming a holistic view of human beings, it could also be argued that the body of the deceased itself needs to be respected and shown neighbor-love by those deciding the interment procedure. To elaborate, in view of doctrines such as the dignity of the human body and the future bodily resurrection,[24] Christians should view the body, as

---

[23] Davies and Mates, eds., *Encyclopedia of Cremation*, 353–58.

[24] The dignity of the human body can be supported by such biblical teachings as God's "very good" (Gen 1:31) creation of the human body, man being an image bearer of God (Gen 1:26–27), the incarnation of Christ (Heb 2:14), and the redemption of man's body

Meilaender notes, as "more than a prosthesis used by the real self."[25] If the body is more than just a temporary shell that is inhabited for a season—indeed, if man is a holistic being made up of a body/soul/spirit complex—then even a body that is currently separated from a soul/spirit needs to be shown respect. Just as the soul/spirit is renewed at conversion (cf. 2 Cor 5:17), so the physical body will be renewed at the end of the age (cf. 1 John 3:2). Such moral reasoning may begin to give moral direction to the ethics of cremation.

Finally, in handling the body of the deceased, the third question that must be addressed is, "What method of interment would bring the most glory to God?" The main options available to most people are cremation and burial. For a variety of reasons, those faced with this decision may lean more toward one option or the other, yet rarely is the glory of God cited as a rationale for a chosen method of interment. Rather, funerary choices are usually made based on utilitarian concerns such as expense, environmental issues, and ease of arrangement, among many other rationales.[26] While pragmatic factors such as these are not inappropriate to consider, in the process of making a moral decision the cheapest or easiest option is not always the path that brings the most glory to God.

Certainly not all will agree with the historical view of the church that cremation should be avoided. Yet, in view of the ethical methodology described above, it should be clear that the church built this position on biblical and theological moorings. Indeed, given that cremation was common in the Greco-Roman world,[27]

(Rom 8:23). The future bodily resurrection is taught in passages such as 1 Cor 15:35–49 and Phil 3:20–21. Note, too, that in Scripture buried corpses are referred to as persons, often by name, not as things or former persons (cf. Mark 15:45–46; John 11:43). Moreover, the most prevalent word used in the New Testament to describe the death of a believer is "sleep," a term employed by both Jesus (cf. Matt 9:24; Mark 5:39; Luke 8:52; John 11:11) and Paul (1 Cor 11:30; 15:6, 18, 20, 51; 1 Thess 4:13–16).

[25] Gilbert Meilaender, "Broken Bodies Redeemed: Bioethics and the Troublesome Union of Body and Soul," *Touchstone* 20, no. 1 (January/February 2007): 35.

[26] Norman L. Geisler and Douglas E. Potter, "From Ashes to Ashes: Is Burial the Only Christian Option?" *Research Journal* 20 (July–Sept, 1998): 31. Other practical reasons for cremation often cited in the field literature include: request of the deceased, fear of being buried alive, ease of storage and/or transportation, and the therapeutic value for mourners. Interestingly, and perhaps accurately, in his book on cremation, Stephen Prothero argues that the greatest reason cremation is practiced in the United States is style or worldview. Cf. Stephen Prothero, *Purified by Fire: A History of Cremation in America* (Berkley, CA: University of California Press, 2002). Santmire makes the same argument as does Prothero in H. Paul Santmire, "Nothing More Beautiful than Death," *Christian Century* 100, no. 38 (December 14, 1983): 1155.

[27] William E. Phipps, *Cremation Concerns* (Springfield, IL: Charles G. Thomas, 1988), 9–16. See also, Paul E. Irion, *Cremation* (Philadelphia: Fortress, 1968); and Arthur D. Nock,

the church's preference for burial is not an example of utilitarian ethics or cultural accommodation. This being said, certainly not all deaths will afford loved ones an opportunity to choose the method of interment. Factors such as the location and manner of death and nation-specific legal parameters, as well as the resources of the surviving family, will bear upon funerary practices and decisions. Yet, if given a choice, contemporary believers who are open to cremation would be wise to consider the practice carefully and evaluate it in light of Scripture.[28]

Conclusion

THIS CHAPTER SUGGESTED THAT THE MORAL law can be applied to ethical issues by appealing to the three parts of morality: conduct, character, and goals. When arranged between God and man—or more specifically, between God and the moral issues that confront man—the three parts of morality create a framework that can be used in the process of moral decision making. While this ethical methodology does not automatically generate answers to moral questions, it does provide believers with a viable approach to biblical ethics. Certainly many ethical issues are more complex than the example of cremation given in this chapter, while others are less complicated. Regardless of the complexity of moral issues, applying the moral law, displaying love, and glorifying God will lead to a right moral decision.

"Cremation and Burial in the Roman Empire," *Harvard Theological Review* 25, no. 4 (1932): 321–59.

[28] Recent treatments of cremation by well-known evangelicals include Timothy George, "Good Question: Cremation Confusion," *Christianity Today* (May 21, 2002): 66; Norman L. Geisler and Douglas E. Potter, "From Ashes to Ashes: Is Burial the Only Christian Option?" *Research Journal* 20 (July–September 1998): 28–35; Russell D. Moore, "Grave Signs," *Touchstone* 20, no. 1 (January/February 2007): 24–27; Hank Hanegraaff, *Resurrection: The Capstone in the Arch of Christianity* (Nashville: Word, 2000), 129–32. Other examples of popular treatment of cremation by lesser known evangelicals include: A. Graybill Brubaker, "On Cremation for Christians," *Brethren in Christ History and Life* 28, no. 1 (April 2005): 220–24; Samuel M. Brubaker, "Toward a Christian Perspective on Cremation," *Brethren in Christ History and Life* 28, no. 1 (April 2005): 225–30; Steven A. Kreloff, "The Biblical Perspective of Cremation," *Journal of Modern Ministry* 2, no. 3 (Fall 2005): 9–26; Alvin J. Schmidt, *Dust to Dust, Ashes to Ashes: A Biblical and Christian Examination of Cremation* (Salisbury, MA: Regina Orthodox, 2005); Carroll E. Simcox, *Is Cremation Christian?* (Cincinnati: Forward Movement, 2006); and, in a somewhat dated article, Robert L. Rayburn, "The Christian and Cremation," *Baptist Bulletin* 33, no. 6 (November 1968): 12–13.

Summary Points

- The Goal of Biblical Ethics
  - The *summum bonum* of biblical ethics is the glorification of God.
  - In the process of moral decision making, believers should ask themselves the question, "What path would bring the most glory to God?"
- Character and Biblical Ethics
  - An attitude of love reflects the character and commands of God and is central to biblical ethics.
  - Loving God and loving neighbor are more than Christian duties; they describe the disposition of someone with right moral character.
  - Character is eternal but must be developed over time.
  - When making a moral decision, believers ought to consider their motives and ask the question, "Am I acting out of love for God and love for neighbor?"
- The Conduct of Biblical Ethics
  - Loving God—The Bible is clear in connecting love for God with keeping his commandments. Believers keep God's commandments because they love him.
  - Loving others—Believers love others by remaining in a right relationship with others by obeying God's laws.
  - When making moral decisions, believers ought to ask themselves, "What moral norm(s) apply in this situation?"

Chapter 6

The Giving of the Law

The preceding chapter concluded the foundational section of this book by investigating the structure of the law and suggesting a method for engaging in biblical ethics. Within this ethical methodology an understanding of the content of the moral law is essential for moral decision making. While the moral law is present throughout Scripture, it is most clearly summarized in the Decalogue, commonly referred to as the Ten Commandments. As was noted, the Decalogue is composed of two theological tables, the first of which addresses the love of God and the second of which details love of neighbor. By way of delivery, the Ten Commandments were given by God twice (cf. Exod 31:18; 34:28) and are listed twice in the Pentateuch (cf. Exod 20:1–17; Deut 5:6–21). This formal, summary giving of the moral law is important, for it is God's first specific verbal revelation of himself to his gathered people. With the goal of helping the reader better understand the scope, content, and significance of the moral law, chapters 6–8 of this text will explore the Decalogue. The present chapter focuses on the giving of the law.

The Delivery of the Law

IN THE SCRIPTURAL NARRATIVE THE PROCEEDINGS surrounding the giving of the Ten Commandments are purposefully dramatic in order to highlight the importance of the event, both for the original recipients of the law and to later readers. One easily overlooked aspect of the giving of the moral law is that God commanded his people to become ceremonially clean before the law was formally delivered. Scripture reports that the Lord commanded Moses: "Go to the people and consecrate them today and tomorrow. They must wash their clothes and be prepared by the third day, for on the third day the LORD will come down on Mount Sinai in the sight of all the people" (Exod 19:10–11). The ceremonial cleansing prescribed here, which included the cordoning off of Mount Sinai from man and animal (cf. Exod 19:12–13, 23) as well as the consecration of the priests (cf. Exod 19:22), is unusual in Scripture apart from activities related to tabernacle/temple operations. This divine command for ceremonial cleansing of body and clothing emphasizes the holiness of God and highlights the nature of the moral law, which is a revelation of God's own moral character. Additionally, ceremonial cleansing foreshadows the end or goal of the law, which is a heart "sprinkled clean from an evil conscience and our bodies washed in pure water" (Heb 10:22; cf. Eph 5:26). Indeed, at the end of the ages, believers are described as those who have "washed their robes and made them white in the blood of the Lamb" (Rev 7:14).

The giving of the law was also preceded by smoke, thunder, lightning, fire, and trumpet blasts from heaven. The biblical narrative reports, "On the third day, when morning came, there was thunder and lightning, a thick cloud on the mountain, and a loud trumpet sound, so that all the people in the camp shuddered" (Exod 19:16; cf. 24:17; Judg 5:5). In the New Testament the writer of the book of Hebrews comments on the spectacular events surrounding the giving of the moral law. After mentioning blazing fire, darkness, gloom, storm, the blast of a trumpet, and the sound of words, the writer of Hebrews notes: "Those who heard it begged that not another word be spoken to them, for they could not bear what was commanded. . . . The appearance was so terrifying that Moses said, 'I am terrified and trembling'" (Heb 12:19–21; cf. Deut 9:19). This response of the people and of Moses ought to be understood not only as a reaction to the supernatural events they had witnessed but also as a response to the content of the Ten Commandments, which reveal man's sinful estate (cf. Rom 3:19–20). Observe that the writer of Hebrews specifies the people did not ask for the supernatural events to cease but rather for no more words to be spoken.

The trumpet blasts from heaven that accompanied the bestowal of the Decalogue are an interesting phenomenon. These divine trumpet blasts are specifically mentioned three times in the account of the giving of the law (cf. Exod 19:16, 19; 20:18), as well as in the previously cited passage from the book of Hebrews (12:19). The sounding of trumpets, or rams' horns, is occasionally mentioned in Scripture, as trumpets were used for signaling purposes in various religious ceremonies, in times of war, and in other military-related events (cf. Num 10:1–10; Josh 6:13). Yet, as Brian Edwards observes, the sounding of a trumpet at Mount Sinai is unique, for "there are only two occasions in the Bible where we read of the trumpet sounding from heaven."[1] These two occasions are at Mount Sinai and at the return of Christ (cf. 1 Cor 15:52; 1 Thess 4:16; Revelation 8–11). The fact that divine trumpet blasts accompany the arrival of both the written Word of God and the living Word of God (cf. John 1:1, 14) is a testimony to the divine character of each.

Scripture teaches Moses received the moral law from God in the midst of a multitude of angels. In the exodus narrative an angel led and protected the people during their flight and pilgrimage (cf. Exod 23:20, 23; 33:2); however, what is not clear in the Old Testament is that Moses actually received the Ten Commandments in the midst of, or perhaps even from, an angel. This information comes later, in the New Testament, in Stephen's premartyrdom address to the Jewish council. In his message Stephen referred to Moses as "the one who was in the congregation in the wilderness together with the angel who spoke to him on Mount Sinai, and with our ancestors. He received living oracles to give to us" (Acts 7:38). Furthermore, Stephen charged the Jewish leaders with disobeying the Decalogue saying, "You received the law under the direction of angels and yet have not kept it" (Acts 7:53). Likewise, in his epistle to the Galatians, Paul notes, "The law was put into effect through angels by means of a mediator" (Gal 3:19), and the author of the book of Hebrews claims, "The message spoken through angels [is] legally binding" (Heb 2:2).

The fact angels were present at the giving of the moral law is not surprising, for the Bible teaches that angels continually dwell in

---

[1] Brian Edwards, *The Ten Commandments for Today* (Surrey, UK: DayOne, 2002), 26.

God's presence and worship him (cf. Isa 6:1–3; Rev 4:6–11). In the book of Psalms, the presence of angels at Mount Sinai is even mentioned as David writes, "God's chariots are tens of thousands [of angels], thousands and thousands; the Lord is among them in the sanctuary as He was at Sinai" (Ps 68:17; cf. Deut 33:2). Observe, however, that despite the fact that angels continually dwell in God's presence, the appearance of gatherings of angels on earth, even in the presence of God, is relatively rare in Scripture. Noteworthy terrestrial gatherings of angels in the Bible occur at the giving of the Ten Commandments, at the birth of Christ (cf. Luke 2:13–14), and at Jesus' second coming (cf. Matt 25:31).[2] As with the divine trumpet blasts cited earlier, these earthly angelic assemblies testify to the divine nature and similarities between the written Word of God and the living Word of God. When both the moral law and Christ are revealed to mankind, angels are present.

Another easily overlooked yet important aspect of the bestowal of the moral law is that the Ten Commandments were spoken directly by the voice of God, not by a mediator. They were audibly dictated by God and do not involve human judgment as to framing, style, or content. Near the end of the exodus event, after restating the moral law, Moses reminded the people, "The LORD spoke these commands in a loud voice to your entire assembly from the fire, cloud, and thick darkness on the mountain" (Deut 5:22). Although it is common for believers to refer to the entire Bible as the Word of God, God rarely speaks directly in Scripture,[3] for the Lord usually speaks indirectly through a prophet or an apostle. Even more remarkable, though, is that the Decalogue was written down directly by God himself. Scripture reports: "When [God] finished speaking with Moses on Mount Sinai, He gave him the two tablets of the testimony, stone tablets inscribed by the finger of God. . . . The tablets were the work of God, and the writing was God's writing, engraved on the tablets" (Exod 31:18; 32:16; cf. 34:1, 28; Deut 5:22; 10:2). The fact that God himself recorded the

---

[2] Other notable angelic gatherings are usually related to the help angels provide to God's people, which is one of their main duties (cf. Heb 1:14). For example, angels protected Elisha and his servant (cf. 2 Kgs 6:17), ministered to Jesus after his temptation in the wilderness (cf. Matt 4:11), and comforted the apostles after Jesus' ascension (cf. Acts 1:11). Additionally, Jesus indicated that he could have summoned a company of angels to deliver him from crucifixion if he so desired (cf. Matt 26:53).

[3] Noteworthy instances of the Lord speaking directly in Scripture include Jesus' baptism (cf. Matt 3:17), Jesus' transfiguration (cf. Matt 17:5), and Paul's journey on the road to Damascus (cf. Acts 9:5–6).

Ten Commandments is reiterated at least six times in Scripture and is significant in that the moral law is the only part of the Bible written directly by God. This alone ought to draw believers' attention to the Ten Commandments.

To summarize the preceding discussion: Scripture is clear that the Decalogue was both spoken and recorded by God in the presence of a multitude of angels and accompanied by heavenly trumpet blasts. Additionally, however, note that the Bible teaches the Lord wrote the Ten Commandments on two tablets of stone. Engraving in stone was relatively rare in biblical times, as parchment or vellum was usually used. Stone was likely chosen in the recording of the Decalogue as a sign or depiction of the permanence of the moral law (cf. Exod 31:18; 34:1; Deut 4:13; 9:10–11; 10:1). While the two stone tablets are frequently mentioned in the Pentateuch, Scripture is silent as to how the law was divided in written form between the two tablets. Over time, three general views about the recording of the law have emerged.

First, in Jewish and Christian art, each stone tablet is usually depicted as containing five of the commandments. Such an arrangement is a logical division of the law and is convenient for artistic balance.[4] Moreover, as Rooker has noted, this organization of the law has been argued for in light of the fact, "The phrase 'YHWH (your God)' appears in each of the first five commandments, whereas in the second pentad the Tetragrammaton (Yahweh; LORD) does not occur at all."[5] According to this view, then, in the recording of the law the commandments that cited God's name were kept separate from the commandments that lacked an explicit reference to YHWH.

A second view of the division of the law suggests that the first four commandments were written on one tablet of stone, and the last six commandments were engraved on the second tablet. This

---

[4] An interesting side note relating to the artistic presentation of the Ten Commandments is that Moses is often depicted as returning from the top of Mount Sinai with horns on his head. This stems from a mistranslation of Exod 34:29 by Jerome in the Latin Vulgate. Translated into English Jerome rendered this passage as follows, "When Moses came down from Mount Sinai bearing two tablets of the testimony, he did not realize that horns were on his face from speaking with God" (Exod 34:29). Properly translated, Jerome's "horns were on his face" should be rendered "his face shone" (cf. 2 Cor 3:7–9).

[5] Mark F. Rooker, *The Ten Commandments: Ethics for the Twenty-First Century* (Nashville: B&H Academic, 2010), 13. Note that Rooker must be appealing to the Jewish enumeration of the Decalogue, as in traditional Protestant enumeration YHWH does not occur in the first commandment (Exod 20:3), but it does appear in the prologue (Exod 20:2).

arrangement is often mentioned in commentaries and in other works of Bible scholars, as it is more of a theological division of the law. As was discussed in the preceding chapter of this book, the moral law can be divided into two tables (not tablets) in that the first four commandments deal with man's relationship to God and the last six deal with man's relationship to his neighbor. Yet this theological division into two tables is not necessarily the way in which the law was recorded on the two tablets of stone.

A third view of the arrangement of the written law understands the Ten Commandments to be equivalent to an ancient Near East suzerain-vassal treaty in which each party would usually receive a copy of the agreement.[6] According to this view each of the stone tablets would have contained the entire Decalogue, one copy for God and one copy for mankind. Yet in the end since Scripture does not specify the exact breakdown of the law in written form between the two tablets of stone, it is impossible to know the division of the commandments with certainty. However, one detail reported by Moses about the tablets of stone that ought not to be overlooked is, "They were inscribed on both sides—inscribed front and back" (Exod 32:15).

Once the law was given to Israel, it was placed within the ark of the covenant (cf. Exod 25:16, 21; 40:20; Deut 10:5). Rooker observes, "The placement of the tablets of the Ten Commandments inside the most holy article of the tabernacle/temple furniture, the ark of the covenant, indicates how special they were."[7] In one sense it is not surprising that the Decalogue was placed within the ark of the covenant, for God commanded Moses, "You are to place them [i.e., the Ten Commandments] in the ark" (Deut 10:2), and the ark was built for this purpose. Such placement of the Decalogue testifies to the divine nature of the moral law. Said differently, since the moral law reflects God's character, it was kept in the ark of the covenant, the place where God's presence dwelt.[8]

---

[6] Cf. Michael Horton, *The Law of Perfect Freedom: Relating to God and Others Through the Ten Commandments* (Chicago: Moody, 1993), 108; and Rooker, *The Ten Commandments*, 15–19.

[7] Rooker, *The Ten Commandments*, 5.

[8] At God's command a sample of manna was later placed within the ark of the covenant (cf. Exod 16:33), stored in a "golden jar" (Heb 9:4). Additionally, at the Lord's direction, Aaron's rod that budded was placed within the ark. Some 500 years later, during the time of Solomon, Scripture reports, "Nothing was in the ark except the two stone tablets that Moses had put there at Horeb, where the LORD made a covenant with the Israelites when they

The Essence of the Law

CHAPTERS 2 AND 3 OF THIS work explored the nature and relevancy of the moral law in some detail. In these chapters it was noted that the Decalogue ought not to be viewed as the beginning of the moral law but rather as a summary or codification of the moral law. With this understanding of the essence of the Ten Commandments, Reisinger writes: "They . . . go back to creation and are authoritative for all people in every time and place. They are a fixed, objective standard of righteousness."[9] Therefore, despite the fact that the Decalogue was given to Israel more than 3,000 years ago, to conclude that the moral law does not apply in the modern context is to confuse address with application. Indeed, being a reflection of God's moral character, the norms codified in the Ten Commandments are universally applicable and are demonstrable in the biblical record both before and after God's people gathered at Sinai.

For example, the fourth commandment can be seen in God's pre-Sinai instructions to the Jews concerning their collection of manna, which they were to refrain from on the Sabbath (cf. Exod 16:22–26). The fifth commandment can be seen in Ham's being cursed for dishonoring his father by not covering Noah's nakedness upon seeing him in a drunken state (cf. Gen 9:18–27). The sixth commandment can be seen in the Lord's confrontation of Cain for killing his brother Abel (cf. Gen 4:6–15), as well as in God's instructions to Noah after the flood (cf. Gen 9:5–6). The seventh commandment can be seen in the account of the destruction of Sodom and Gomorrah (cf. Gen 19:1–29), as well as in the Judah and Tamar narrative (cf. Gen 38:1–40) and in the destruction of Shechem on account of the rape of Dinah (cf. Gen 34:1–26). The eighth commandment can be seen in Rachel being described as a thief for stealing her father's household gods before fleeing to Canaan with her husband Jacob (cf. Gen 31:19–32). The ninth commandment can be seen in Abraham's being depicted as a liar, on more than one occasion, for telling a half-truth regarding his relationship with his wife Sarah (cf. Gen 12:10–20; 20:1–18). The tenth commandment can be seen in Lot's wife being depicted as covetous when she turned to see the destruction of the city of

came out of the land of Egypt" (1 Kgs 8:9). The disappearance of the jar of manna and the rod that budded is not explained. Note the reference to the ark in Rev 11:19.

[9] Ernest C. Reisinger, *Whatever Happened to the Ten Commandments?* (Carlisle, PA: Banner of Truth, 1999), 1.

Sodom, longing for the pleasures left behind (cf. Gen 19:17–26; Luke 17:19–32).

The New Testament, too, testifies to the universal and enduring nature of the Ten Commandments. Indeed, the fifth through tenth commandments are approvingly quoted verbatim numerous times in the New Testament. For example, Jesus quotes the fifth commandment in Matt 15:4 and Mark 7:10. Jesus quotes the sixth and seventh commandments in the Sermon on the Mount at Matt 5:21, 27. Jesus quotes the fifth through ninth commandments in Matt 19:17–19; Mark 10:19; and Luke 18:20. Paul quotes the tenth commandment in Rom 7:7. Paul quotes the sixth through tenth commandments in Rom 13:9. Paul quotes the fifth commandment in Eph 6:2–3. James quotes the sixth and seventh commandments at Jas 2:11. Other New Testament passages that allude to and approve of the Ten Commandments include Matt 15:19; Rom 2:21–24; Col 3:20; and 1 Tim 1:9–10, among many others.

As the New Testament passages mentioned above highlight, the Ten Commandments are not simply rules but are categories of moral responsibility. Reisinger writes, "Though the commandments themselves are brief, their scope is vast and the whole of Scripture is a commentary on them."[10] This is perhaps most clearly seen in the Sermon on the Mount where Jesus teaches that the sixth commandment does not just prohibit murder but also hatred (cf. Matt 5:21–26) and that the seventh commandment does not merely prohibit adultery but also lust (cf. Matt 5:27–30). Indeed, as Jesus alluded, each of the Ten Commandments represents a broad area of moral accountability. Viewed in this light, all ethical issues can be addressed by the moral law. Moreover, while it is tempting to view the Decalogue as a list of negative rules that restrict personal liberty, keeping the moral law actually enables true freedom—that is, the ability to freely worship God apart from the entanglements of sin (cf. Rom 8:12; Jas 1:25; 2:12).

A topic that often arises in conjunction with studies of the Decalogue is the question of whether the moral law was ever meant to be a means of salvation. Certainly there was an expectation that God's people would keep the moral law. Before restating the Ten Commandments Moses even instructed Israel: "Listen to the statutes and ordinances I am proclaiming as you hear them today.

---

[10] Reisinger, *Whatever Happened to the Ten Commandments?* 2.

Learn and follow them carefully" (Deut 5:1). Yet, going beyond the expectation of obedience, a number of passages in the Pentateuch appear to teach that salvation is possible through law-keeping. For example, in Lev 18:5 God said, "Keep My statutes and ordinances; a person will live if he does them. I am Yahweh," and at Deut 4:1 Moses instructed the people, "Now, Israel, listen to the statutes and ordinances I am teaching you to follow, so that you may live." Likewise in the New Testament Paul observed, "For Moses writes about the righteousness that is from the law: The one who does these things will live by them" (Rom 10:5), and again, "But the law is not based on faith; instead, the one who does these things will live by them" (Gal 3:12).

Despite the proof-texts cited above, a thorough reading of Scripture reveals that the moral law was never given as a means of salvation, nor was salvation ever possible through law-keeping. The passages cited above are teaching about sanctification not justification. Note Paul's repeated teaching in his sermons and epistles about the impossibility of being justified through the law:

> Everyone who believes in [Jesus] is justified from everything that could not be justified from through the law of Moses. . . . For no one will be justified in His sight by the works of the law. . . . We . . . know that no one is justified by the works of the law. . . . by the works of the law no human being will be justified. . . . No one is justified before God by the law. . . . If a law had been given that was able to give life, then righteousness would certainly be by the law. (Acts 13:39; Rom 3:20; Gal 2:16; 3:11, 21)

Clearly, then, in these passages Paul teaches that the moral law was never given as a means of salvation, for salvation has always been by faith alone.[11] In fact, as Paul notes, salvation was not even hypothetically possible though law-keeping, for as was cited above, "If a law had been given that was able to give life, then righteousness would certainly be by the law" (Gal 3:21). The Ten Commandments were given in order to promote public order, to

---

[11] Numerous Old Testament passages communicate that God never desired legalistic law-keeping and ceremonial obedience (cf. 1 Sam 15:22; Ps 51:16–19; Jer 7:21–24; Isa 1:11–20; Hos 6:6; Mic 6:6–8). Indeed, as Habakkuk taught, "The righteous one will live by his faith" (Hab 2:4). The New Testament teaches that the gospel was clearly communicated in the Old Testament (cf. Gal 3:8; Heb 4:2).

demonstrate peoples' need for a Savior (cf. Rom 3:19–20; 2 Cor 3:6–8),[12] and to instruct believers in holy living.[13]

The Enumeration of the Law

IN STUDYING THE MORAL LAW IT is important to note that not all theological traditions have enumerated the Decalogue in the same manner. All theological traditions have agreed there are ten commandments, for Scripture clearly reports, "Moses was there with the LORD 40 days and 40 nights. . . . He wrote the Ten Commandments, the words of the covenant, on the tablets." (Exod 34:28; cf. Deut 4:13). Yet, since the commandments themselves are not numbered, there has been disagreement among the various faith traditions as to the proper identification and enumeration of the laws that comprise the Decalogue.

Using the Reformed Protestant tradition employed in this book as a baseline, the different numbering systems will be summarized below (see chart 6.1). Consider first the Jewish interpretive tradition, which identifies what most Christians consider to be the prologue as the first commandment. This verse reads, "I am the LORD your God, who brought you out of the land of Egypt, out of the place of slavery" (Exod 20:2). While this passage appears to lack an explicit imperative, since this verse contains the name of God (i.e.,

---

[12] While the liberated, gathered Israelites at Mount Sinai were a picture or object lesson of salvation, for the most part they were unregenerate. This is clear not only from their actions during the exodus event but also from later biblical commentary. For example, Moses spoke to the people, "You have seen with your own eyes everything the LORD did in Egypt to Pharaoh, to all his officials, and to his entire land. You saw with your own eyes the great trials and those great signs and wonders. Yet to this day the LORD has not given you a mind to understand, eyes to see, or ears to hear" (Deut 29:2–4). Similarly, summarizing the exodus event, the psalmist wrote: "Therefore, the LORD heard and became furious; then fire broke out against Jacob, and anger flared up against Israel because they did not believe God or rely on His salvation. . . . God's anger flared up against them, and He killed some of their best men. He struck down Israel's choice young men. Despite all this, they kept sinning and did not believe His wonderful works" (Ps 78:21–22, 31–32). The writer of Hebrews, noted, "But the message they heard [i.e., the gospel] did not benefit them, since they were not united with those who heard it in faith" (Heb 4:2). Note, too, Stephen's charge against the Jewish religious leaders prior to his martyrdom, "You stiff-necked people with uncircumcised hearts and ears! You are always resisting the Holy Spirit; as your ancestors did, so do you" (Acts 7:51). See also Num 14:11; Deut 32:5; 1 Cor 10:5.

[13] Although salvation through law-keeping is impossible, Scripture teaches that law-keeping ought not to be burdensome for Spirit-indwelt believers. Note Jesus' teaching, "Come to Me, all of you who are weary and burdened, and I will give you rest. All of you, take up My yoke and learn from Me, because I am gentle and humble in heart, and you will find rest for yourselves. For My yoke is easy and My burden is light" (Matt 11:28–30). Similarly, John wrote, "For this is what love for God is: to keep His commands. Now His commands are not a burden" (1 John 5:3).

YHWH), the Jews viewed it to contain an implicit commandment to worship and to obey God.[14] Moreover, in identifying Exod 20:2 as a separate commandment, the Jewish numbering system emphasized the fact that the Decalogue begins with and stems from God's own moral character. However, since Jewish scholars labeled the prologue as the first commandment, they then combined the first and second commandments into one imperative in order to avoid having eleven commandments.

Akin to Jewish enumeration, the Roman Catholic and Lutheran numbering systems combine the first and second commandments into one imperative. Yet, since these approaches do not consider the prologue to be a commandment, they then divide the tenth commandment into two commandments in order to avoid having only nine commandments. A minor difference between these two approaches is that the Roman Catholic tradition follows the word order of Deut 5:21, whereas Lutherans follow the wording in Exod 20:17. This results in the ninth and tenth commandments,

Commandment	Reformed, Anglican, & Orthodox	Jewish	Roman Catholic	Lutheran
I am the Lord your God	—	1	—	—
No other gods before me	1	2	1	1
No making of carved images	2			
No misusing God's name	3	3	2	2
Remember the Sabbath day	4	4	3	3
Honor your parents	5	5	4	4
No murder	6	6	5	5
No adultery	7	7	6	6
No stealing	8	8	7	7
No bearing false witness	9	9	8	8
No coveting another's wife	10	10	9	10
No coveting another's property			10	9

Chart 6.1

[14] For more on the Jewish reverence for and reluctance to pronounce YHWH, but instead substituting the vowel pointing of "Adonai" upon the word "YHWH" resulting in the impossible "Jehovah," see J. Weingren, *A Practical Grammar for Classical Hebrew*, 2nd ed. (New York: Oxford University Press, 1959), 23.

which Reformed Protestants consider to be one commandment, being inverted between the Roman Catholic and Lutheran numbering systems.

While the differences between Reformed Protestant, Jewish, Roman Catholic, and Lutheran enumeration of the Ten Commandments may seem trivial, these differences are potentially significant for both practical and theological reasons. For example, practically speaking, a simple reference to the seventh commandment would bring to mind the prohibition against adultery for a Reformed Protestant, while it would remind a Roman Catholic of the imperative not to steal. Obviously there is potential for confusion here, both in dialogue and in academic study. Furthermore, it is interesting to note that within the Jewish numbering system, there is not a separate commandment against idolatry. Interestingly, idolatry was a constant plague on the people of Israel in the Old Testament. Similarly, within the Roman Catholic numbering system there are actually two commandments against adultery. Perhaps not coincidentally, ideas such as suspicion of sexuality and the prohibition of marriage among the clergy (in order to avoid the possibility of adultery) have been emphasized within the Roman Catholic tradition. This is not to say other factors have not influenced these ideas; however, the enumeration of the Decalogue has certainly contributed to such theological emphases. Indeed, it seems the differing numbering systems among the faiths have made a theological impact.

Interpreting the Law

As was previously discussed, the Ten Commandments are more than simple rules. Jesus indicated in his Sermon on the Mount that each commandment is a placeholder or a representative for an entire category of moral responsibility. As this study now turns toward the Decalogue, it will be helpful to delineate several principles for interpreting the Ten Commandments with this is mind.

First, the Ten Commandments must be interpreted *internally*— that is, they are not to be applied only to external conduct but also to the thoughts, motives, and intentions of the heart, for as Paul taught, "The law is spiritual" (Rom 7:14). Concerning this principle, Reisinger writes:

The commandments demand both external and internal obedience. Addressing the will and the heart, as well as actions, they require more than merely outward conformity. They also require inward affection. The commandments forbid not only evil acts but evil desires and inclinations. They go to the mind—including the will and affections—thereby calling for obedience from the whole man.[15]

To overlook this principle is to run the risk of interpreting the moral law legalistically. To understand this principle is to realize that the Decalogue prohibits murder and hate, adultery and lust, stealing and envy, and so on.

Second, the Ten Commandments must be interpreted *contextually*—that is, they must be understood according to the explanation assigned to them by later biblical revelation. Again, Reisinger is helpful here as he writes, "The Decalogue must be understood as all Scripture must be understood: according to the explanation and application that the Prophets, Christ, and the apostles have given it."[16] As has been noted, the moral law is the backbone for the time-bound, culture-specific, civil law in the Old Testament, and the Ten Commandments are cited repeatedly throughout both Testaments. These citations and uses of the moral law are helpful in interpreting the breadth and depth of the norms summarized in the Decalogue.

Third, the Ten Commandments must be interpreted *wholly*—that is, the negative prohibitions in the law include positive duties, and the positive duties in the law include negative prohibitions. For example, the seventh commandment prohibits murder; yet, it also entails the duty to protect innocent human life. Interestingly, eight of the Ten Commandments are stated negatively. Perhaps this can be explained in that throughout Scripture man is commanded to do what he is not inclined to do and prohibited from doing what he is inclined to do.[17] The negative formulation of the Ten Commandments, then, assumes men are murderers, adulterers,

---

[15] Ernest C. Reisinger, *The Law and the Gospel* (Phillipsburg, NJ: P&R, 1997), 71.

[16] Ibid.

[17] Frame writes, "Why is the Decalogue so largely negative? All of the commandments except the fourth and fifth are stated as prohibitions, and the fourth contains much negative language. It is, of course, a matter of emphasis. . . . The negative focus reflects the reality of

thieves, liars, etc. The Decalogue addresses man's fallen estate, while at the same time providing moral guidance. Viewed in this light, the moral law can be understood as a manifestation of God's grace to fallen mankind. As Ryken observes, "We have such a strong propensity to do what is displeasing to God . . . thus we need to be told to stop."[18] Additionally, as some have noted, the negative formulation of the Ten Commandments can be explained in that it is easier to prohibit certain acts than it is to detail the vast freedoms the law creates for redeemed man.[19]

Fourth, the Ten Commandments must be interpreted per *synecdoche*—that is, when a specific sin is mentioned, the commandment intends to cover an entire range of related sins. The *Oxford English Dictionary* defines *synecdoche* as, "A figure [of speech] by which a more comprehensive term is used for a less comprehensive or vice versa; as a whole for part or part for whole, genus for species or species for genus."[20] Although the term does not occur in the New Testament, *synecdoche* can be etymologically traced back to a Greek word meaning "to take with something else." So each of the Ten Commandments is much broader than might be apparent at first glance.

Finally, the Ten Commandments must be interpreted with *charity*—that is, the motivation behind keeping the moral law must be love for God and love of neighbor. This was discussed in some detail in the previous chapter as Jesus' teaching at Matt 22:37–40 was reviewed. An unfortunate result of a legalistic interpretation

---

sin and temptation." John Frame, *The Doctrine of the Christian Life* (Phillipsburg, NJ: P&R, 2008), 413–14.

[18] Philip Graham Ryken, *Written in Stone: The Ten Commandments and Today's Moral Crisis* (Wheaton, IL: Crossway, 2003), 46. Douma writes, "We may deduce from the negative prohibitions that man is a sinner inclined to transgress the law. In the law we have a mirror in which we look to see ourselves as we really are: you shall not kill, because you are a murderer; you shall not commit adultery, because you really are an adulterer!" J. Douma, *The Ten Commandments: Manual for the Christian Life*, trans. Nelson D. Kloosterman (Phillipsburg, NJ: P&R, 1996), 10. Similarly, Edwards observes, "Eight out of the ten Commandments are negative because God knows that sin inevitably brings us into conflict with the will of God, so he needs to start by telling us what we must not do." Edwards, *The Ten Commandments*, 75. Note, too, that the fallen human mind remembers negative things more easily than positive.

[19] In regard to the negative formulation of the Ten Commandments, Douma writes: "A rule that prohibits one particular thing still permits many others. In the Garden of Eden, eating from one particular tree was forbidden, but Adam and Eve were permitted to eat from all the other trees. The gates of freedom provide a permanent opening in a wall that you may not climb over." Douma, *The Ten Commandments*, 11.

[20] *Oxford English Dictionary*, 2nd ed. (1989), s.v. "synecdoche."

of the moral law is improper motivations for obeying the law, including fear and guilt (because of lawbreaking) or love of self and pride (because of law-keeping). Moreover, a legalistic view of the Ten Commandments often leads to a lack of love for lawbreaking neighbors. Such a perspective betrays an incorrect understanding of the Decalogue, for, as Paul noted, "Love, therefore, is the fulfillment of the law" (Rom 13:10). Love for God and love of neighbor, with a desire to glorify the Lord, must be the motivation behind all obedience to the moral law.

The Prologue

THE PROLOGUE TO THE TEN COMMANDMENTS reads, "I am the LORD your God, who brought you out of the land of Egypt, out of the place of slavery" (Exod 20:2). In this verse—the Lord's first verbal revelation of himself to his gathered people—God does not attempt to prove his own existence, justify his authority, or even command obedience to the laws that would follow. Rather, beginning in history, the Lord identifies himself by what he had done for Israel—namely, deliver them from Egypt.[21] Additionally, using his covenant name (i.e., LORD or Yahweh), God refers to himself as "the LORD your God," which he also does in the third, fourth, and fifth commandments (cf. Exod 20:5, 7, 10, 12). By revealing himself in this manner, the Lord was showing that he is a personal, relational, and historical God, as well as the Redeemer of his people. As Redeemer, obedience to the commands that followed was both natural and expected. Rooker writes: "The liberation of Israel from bondage to Pharaoh gave the Lord the sovereign right to establish rules for His people that should in turn characterize their behavior. . . . This deliverance was a presupposition throughout all the demands of the law."[22]

God begins the revelation of the Ten Commandments by revealing himself and by stating the reality of his lordship. In beginning the Decalogue this way, God was declaring that he is the source of all moral authority. Indeed, mankind has the ability to disobey God

---

[21] In the New Testament, Peter takes a similar approach in identifying God to believers. Peter writes, "For you know that you were redeemed from your empty way of life inherited from the fathers, not with perishable things like silver or gold, but with the precious blood of Christ, like that of a lamb without defect or blemish" (1 Pet 1:18–19). Horton refers to 1 Pet 1:18–19 as a "New Testament reiteration of the Old Testament preamble (to the Decalogue)." Horton, *The Law of Perfect Freedom*, 30–31.

[22] Rooker, *The Ten Commandments*, 19.

but not the right to disobey God. Because of his lordship, one day every knee will bow before God and every tongue will confess and glorify the name of the Lord (cf. Phil 2:10; Rev 5:13). Concerning the prologue to the Ten Commandments, Reisinger writes:

> This indicates that the Decalogue is a law of God's own making and disclosing, which stems from his own nature and dealings with his people. He asserts his own authority and presents himself as the sole object of the worship and service which he requires. This is because he is the "I AM," self-existent and all-determining, and as the Lord he is also the Redeemer. He who made all things brought his people out of Egypt, and so they belong to him. . . . The significance of this prologue cannot be overstated. The Ten Commandments were of God's making, of God's speaking—a law stemming from God's nature.[23]

One way to think of the prologue to the Ten Commandments is that it is essentially a summary of all that had happened in the book of Exodus to this point. As Ryken observes, "God summarizes the whole epic adventure of the exodus in two short phrases: 'who brought you out of the land of Egypt, [and] out of the house of slavery.'"[24] Yet the exodus event itself was more than just a historical occurrence. The liberation of Israel from Egypt through the shed blood of the Passover lamb was metaphorical and prophetic of the liberation of humanity from sin through the shed blood of "Christ our Passover" (1 Cor 5:7; cf. Jer 16:14–15; Luke 4:18; John 1:29, 36; Rev 7:9; 14:1). Viewed in this light, it becomes evident that the Ten Commandments begin with grace; for God graciously freed his people from slavery and then gave them the law; he did not give them the law in order to free them from slavery.[25]

Therefore, the Ten Commandments are not a form of bondage but are a result of freedom from bondage and will produce liberty (cf. Deut 30:11–14). Indeed, God was telling his people that the

---

[23] Reisinger, *Whatever Happened to the Ten Commandments*, 2; Reisinger, *The Law and the Gospel*, 70. In light of this view of the prologue, Edwards concluded, "The fulfillment of Exodus 20:2 is to love Christ with all our heart." Edwards, *The Ten Commandments*, 77.

[24] Ryken, *Written in Stone*, 28.

[25] Ryken writes, "The Ten Commandments do not begin with the law, but with the gospel." Ibid., 27.

goal of the law was to produce freedom, not captivity. This is why James can refer to the moral law as "the perfect law of freedom" (Jas 1:25; cf. 2:12). With this reminder of freedom from slavery, God commences the Ten Commandments.

Conclusion

IN PREPARATION FOR A STUDY OF the Ten Commandments, this chapter has explored the events surrounding the giving of the moral law as well as several issues that have arisen in the study of the Decalogue. While this material may seem to be tangential at first glance, this chapter has shown the importance of the giving of the law. The Lord could have delivered the written law in many different ways; yet he chose to do so in a manner that emphasized his character and the holy nature of the law. A straightforward reading of the events leading up to the giving of the law, as well as the prologue to the Ten Commandments, should leave the reader in joyful anticipation of the words of life that follow.

Summary Points

- Delivery of the Law
  - Scripture is purposefully dramatic to highlight the importance of the giving of the Law.
  - There are various views on the form of the recording of the Decalogue.
- Essence of the Law
  - Since the Decalogue is a reflection of God's moral character, the norms codified in the Ten Commandments are universally applicable and demonstrable both before and after their issuance on Mount Sinai.
  - The moral law was never intended for salvation; it was intended for sanctification, not justification.
- The Enumeration of the Law
  - All theological traditions have ten commandments.
  - The Reformed Protestant, Jewish, Roman Catholic, and Lutheran traditions differ on the enumeration of the laws within the Decalogue.

- o These differences have practical and theological significance.
- Interpreting the Law
  - o Internally: The Decalogue applies to thoughts, motives, and intentions, not just external actions.
  - o Contextually: The Decalogue must be understood by explanations provided by later biblical revelation.
  - o Wholly: The negative prohibitions in the law include positive duties, and the positive duties contain negative prohibitions.
  - o Per synecdoche: When a specific sin is mentioned, the commandment is intended to cover an entire range of related sin.
  - o With charity: The motivation behind keeping the moral law must be love for God and love for neighbor.
- The Prologue
  - o By revealing himself in the prologue, God was showing himself as personal, relational, and as the Redeemer of his people.
  - o By beginning the Decalogue in this way, God declares that he is the source of all moral authority.
  - o The prologue of the Ten Commandments is essentially a summary of all that happened in the book of Exodus up to that point.

Chapter 7

The First Table of the Law

W hen asked by an unnamed Pharisee to identify the greatest commandment in the law, Jesus replied by quoting Deut 6:5, "Love the LORD your God with all your heart, with all your soul, and with all your mind" (Matt 22:37). As was discussed in chapter 5 of this work, in citing this verse rather than one of the Ten Commandments, Jesus was emphasizing the importance of the entire first table of the Decalogue— that is, the first four of the Ten Commandments. The first four laws of the Decalogue instruct God's people in various aspects of manifesting and cultivating love for the Lord. To elaborate, the first commandment emphasizes *internal* love for God, as it identifies the object of worship. The second commandment emphasizes *external* love for God, as it identifies the manner of worship. The third commandment emphasizes *verbal* love for God, as it identifies the language of worship. The fourth commandment emphasizes *temporal* love for God, as it identifies the time of worship. In this chapter each of these commandments will be explored in some detail in order to show the breadth, depth, and moral implications of the first table of the law.

The First Commandment

THE FIRST COMMANDMENT IS SEEMINGLY STRAIGHTFORWARD, as God instructed his people, "Do not have other gods besides Me" (Exod

20:3). This section will show that although this commandment is brief in form, it is significant in content, as well as being elementary for moral living. J. I. Packer refers to the first commandment as "the fundamental commandment, first in importance as well as in order, and basic to every other. . . . True religion starts with accepting it as one's rule of life."[1] On the surface, the first commandment appears simple and easy to keep, as most Christians would claim the Lord as their God and deny the worship or harboring of other gods. Nevertheless, Brian Edwards correctly asserts that while the first commandment "is the most significant of all the Commandments, it is the one that we most consistently break."[2] Indeed, with a fuller understanding of the first commandment, as well as the sinful depths of the human heart, it becomes evident that the first precept of the Decalogue is more difficult to keep than might appear. False gods constantly vie for man's attention and worship.

The God-Man Relationship

IN SEEKING TO DEFINE THE RELATIONSHIP between God and man, which is the focus of this commandment, there are four conceptually possible arrangements for the God-man relationship: The first conceptual option is known as universalism. This approach teaches that all men are in a saving relationship with God. Concerning ethical norms, as was briefly discussed in chapter 1 of this book, it is indeed true that God's moral standards apply universally to all of mankind.[3] However, the focus of universalism is not the ecumenical application of God's moral law; rather, it is the assertion of the right standing of all men before God. In light of the sin and immorality of mankind, however, advocates of this position are forced to lower or to deny God's moral standards in order to support the idea of universal salvation. Since God's moral standards are a revelation of his character, by altering divine moral standards, proponents of universalism ultimately end up rejecting the God with whom they seek to affirm a relationship. As Frame notes, it is the "rejection of the personal God of Scripture [that] inevitably brings universalism: either all are saved

---

[1] J. I. Packer, *Keeping the Ten Commandments* (Wheaton, IL: Crossway, 2007), 47. Similarly, Ryken observes, "This is the fundamental commandment, the one that comes before all the others and lays the foundation for them." Philip Graham Ryken, *Written in Stone: The Ten Commandments and Today's Moral Crisis* (Wheaton, IL: Crossway, 2003), 57.

[2] Brian Edwards, *The Ten Commandments for Today* (Surrey, UK: DayOne, 2002), 75.

[3] *The Westminster Dictionary of Christian Ethics* (1986), s.v. "universalizability of moral judgments."

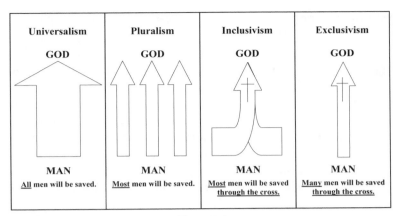

Universalism	Pluralism	Inclusivism	Exclusivism
GOD	GOD	GOD	GOD
MAN	MAN	MAN	MAN
<u>All</u> men will be saved.	<u>Most</u> men will be saved.	<u>Most</u> men will be saved through the cross.	<u>Many</u> men will be saved through the cross.

Chart 7.1

or all are lost."[4] Ultimately, then, universalism results in the worship of a false god of man's own making, thereby breaking the first commandment.

A second conceptual option for the structure of the relationship between God and man is pluralism. Pluralism teaches there are many ways for man to be in a right relationship with God. *The Westminster Dictionary of Christian Ethics* defines *pluralism* as the belief that "there is no single, true, objective way of combining values into a rationally grounded, coherent whole. . . . It is, rather, a matter of individual citizens pursuing a conception of the good in their own way."[5] Similarly, the *New Dictionary of Christian Ethics and Pastoral Theology* notes pluralism's belief that "there is no fundamentally moral superiority between different religions, thus none can claim to have a monopoly on truth or what is moral."[6] In short, pluralism teaches that God's identity and moral standards are not as important to the God-man relationship as is the fact that man is sincerely pursuing a relationship with God. Said differently, whether the path is Christian, Muslim, Hindu, or some other option, pluralism holds that the specific path is not as important as is the fact that man is on a path to God. While it may be politically correct and socially acceptable to affirm that there are many ways to God, Ryken correctly observes, "The pluralistic approach to religion is a direct attack on the first commandment, in which

---

[4] John M. Frame, *The Doctrine of the Christian Life* (Phillipsburg, NJ: P&R, 2008), 899.

[5] *The Westminster Dictionary of Christian Ethics* (1986), s.v. "pluralism."

[6] *New Dictionary of Christian Ethics and Pastoral Theology* (1995), s.v. "pluralism."

we are commanded to worship God alone."[7] Pluralism, therefore, is not compatible with Scripture.

A third conceptual option for the relationship between God and man is inclusivism. This approach teaches there is only one way for man to be in a right relationship with God, which from a Christian perspective is the cross of Christ. Yet, unlike the exclusivist position that will be explored shortly, inclusivism holds that the application of Jesus' atonement is much wider than many people may realize.[8] In fact, inclusivism even posits the idea of there being so-called anonymous Christians—that is, individuals who have been reconciled to God through the cross of Christ apart from their own knowledge or even consent. For example, an inclusivist might say that a sincere Muslim worshipper of Allah, who is basing his salvation on keeping the five pillars of Islam, may actually be a Christian who just has the name of God and method of salvation wrong. Obviously, inclusivism is at odds with the Decalogue, for the first commandment assumes volitional observance, not unwitting inclusion based on earnestness or coincidence.

The fourth conceptual option, and the one which most faithfully communicates the biblical structure of the God-man relationship, is known as exclusivism. This approach teaches that only one God exists and there is one way for man to be reconciled to God—that is, the cross of Christ. Indeed, behind the command, "Do not have other gods besides Me" (Exod 20:3) is the assumption that there is only one way for man to be reconciled to God. Passages supporting the exclusivist position include, "I, I am Yahweh, and there is no other Savior but Me" (Isa 43:11). "Jesus told him, 'I am the way, the truth, and the life. No one comes to the Father except through Me'" (John 14:6). "There is salvation in no one else, for there is no other name under heaven given to people, and we must be saved by it" (Acts 4:12). And, "For there is one God and one mediator between God and humanity, Christ Jesus, Himself" (1 Tim 2:5). It should be noted, however, as Edwards observes, "Exclusivism and certainty on our part do not imply aggression and intolerance."[9] In

---

[7] Ryken, *Written in Stone*, 68.

[8] For an example of a text advocating a form of inclusivism, see Clark H. Pinnock, *A Wideness in God's Mercy: The Finality of Jesus Christ in a World of Religions* (Grand Rapids: Zondervan, 1992).

[9] Edwards, *The Ten Commandments*, 65.

other words, just because the exclusivist view affirms one God, one morality, and one way of salvation does not mean it is intolerant of other views in the marketplace of ideas.

Idols and False Gods

IT IS ONE THING TO AFFIRM the exclusive worship prescribed by the first commandment; it is another thing to identify the idols and false gods one worships. In his analysis of the first commandment, Alistair Begg writes:

> We make a great mistake in assuming that because our houses are free of idols fashioned of metal, wood, or stone we have dealt with this and are ready to move on to the second commandment. The sobering truth to be faced up to is this: Anything or any person (including myself) that claims our primary loyalty has become "another God."[10]

WHATEVER IS LOVED, SOUGHT AFTER, SERVED, and worshipped in an ultimate sense becomes a god—even otherwise good things. In his exposition of the first commandment, the Puritan commentator Matthew Henry wrote of man's ability to idolize practically anything, noting, "Pride makes a god of self, covetousness makes a god of money, sensuality makes a god of the belly; whatever is esteemed or loved, feared or served, delighted in or depended upon on, more than God, that (whatever it is) we do in effect make a god of."[11]

The notion that anything can become an idol or a god ought to be a sobering thought for Christians. By way of example and prescription, Scripture specifically identifies a number of such false gods, and warns against them, including making an idol of one's accomplishments (cf. Dan 4:30), strength (cf. Hab 1:11), wealth (cf. Matt 6:24), food (cf. Phil 3:19), and pleasure (cf. 2 Tim 3:4). To this list could be added numerous everyday things, events, ideals, places, and people. Along these lines Peter Barnes writes: "Freedom can become a false god, and so too can a concept like world peace. The cult of health and fitness, while good within

---

[10] Alistair Begg, *Pathway to Freedom: How God's Laws Guide Our Lives* (Chicago: Moody, 2003), 57.

[11] Matthew Henry, *An Exposition of the Old and New Testaments* (Philadelphia: Haswell, 1838), 302. Puritan Thomas Watson made a similar observation, writing, "To trust in anything more than God, is to make it a god." Thomas Watson, *The Ten Commandments* (Carlisle, PA: Banner of Truth, 1965), 55.

certain boundaries, can become an idol. Philosophies which promote self-esteem, empowerment, and realization of our potential are also candidates for idols."[12] Additional prospects for idolatry include sports, success, career ambition, ministry, intelligence, academic degrees, sex, family, spouses, children, tradition, reputation, hobbies, financial security, government, political ideologies, moral agendas, and the list goes on. Surely John Calvin was correct in his observation that the human heart is "a perpetual factory of idols."[13]

It is apparent, then, that fallen humans will worship almost anything and everything except for the true God. Yet such worship is to confuse gifts and giver. Commenting on the modern worship of false gods, Michael Horton notes: "What we moderns call 'addictions' God calls 'idols,' and all of God's good gifts are meant to raise our eyes in thanksgiving to our benevolent heavenly Father, not to fix our eyes on the gifts themselves. . . . Addiction is simply a newer euphemism for idolatry."[14] Given man's tendency to worship false gods, it is not a coincidence that the Decalogue begins and ends with commands against idolatry (see Paul's teaching that coveting is equivalent to idolatry in Eph 5:5 and Col 3:5). Since moral values are derived from and contingent on whom or what is worshipped, it is imperative that believers have no other god besides the Lord. To make anything the object of one's ultimate affection apart from God is to break the first commandment.

Worship of God

ALTHOUGH THE FIRST COMMANDMENT IS STATED negatively, "Do not have other gods besides Me" (Exod 20:3), it could be stated positively as, "You shall have the LORD as your God." This is what man was made to do—that is, worship and glorify God (cf. Isa 43:7;

---

[12] Peter Barnes, "The First Commandment," in *Love Rules: The Ten Commandments for the 21st Century*, ed. Stuart Bonnington and Joan Milne (Carlisle, PA: Banner of Truth, 2004), 29.

[13] Calvin, *Institutes* 1.11.8. Horton observes, "Scripture compels us to conclude that the principal reason that people do not want to worship God is that they worship themselves instead." Michael S. Horton, *The Law of Perfect Freedom: Relating to Others Through the Ten Commandments* (Chicago: Moody, 1993), 74.

[14] Horton, *The Law of Perfect Freedom*, 44, 46. Horton has a poignant warning about personal faith becoming an idol. He writes: "We must even, as believers, beware of making our 'personal relationship with Christ' an idol. It is possible to be in love with the idea of marriage instead of one's spouse, and it is also possible to be so obsessed with one's relationship with Christ that there is not enough knowledge of and concern for Christ Himself to constitute a meaningful relationship. . . . Personal faith without a clear understanding of the object of that faith is idolatry." Ibid., 52–53.

1 Cor 10:31). While on account of the sin nature mankind resists worshipping God, believers find worship satisfying when embraced, for true morality is a reflection of the character of God in whose image man is made. John Calvin notes the first commandment requires believers "to contemplate, fear and worship his majesty; to participate in his blessings; to seek his help at all times; to recognize, and by praises to celebrate, the greatness of his works—as the only goal of all the activities of life."[15]

In commanding his people to have no other gods besides himself, the Lord was not implying that other gods can be worshipped in a secondary sense. As Barnes notes, "God was not simply saying that he is the first God to be worshipped ('no other gods before me') but the only God to be worshipped ('no other gods besides me')."[16] This is because while God will share nearly all things with man (e.g., love, power, even his Son), he will not share his glory, of which he is very jealous. The Lord declares, "I am Yahweh, that is My name; I will not give My glory to another or My praise to idols" (Isa 42:8; cf. Deut 4:24; Isa 48:11). Indeed, one day, all will recognize God and worship him as Lord (cf. Phil 2:9–11; Rev 5:13). Frame rightly observes, "As with all biblical ethics, the first commandment is a matter of lordship."[17]

Scripture is clear that no other gods exist apart from the Lord (cf. Ps 96:5; Isa 44:6, 16–20; 45:21; Acts 19:26; 1 Cor 8:4). This fact invites the question of the importance of the first commandment; for if no other gods exist, why command that counterfeit gods not be worshipped? The answer to this question is twofold. First, just as to worship a false (even nonexistent) god is to commit a sin of commission, so not to worship the true God is a sin of omission. As was discussed above, the Lord is jealous for his own glory, which is his due. Second, as Paul told the Galatian Christians, "In the past, when you didn't know God, you were enslaved to things that by nature are not gods" (Gal 4:8; cf. 1 John 5:21). In other words, the worship of even illusional, false gods can result in a type of spiritual

---

[15] Calvin, *Institutes* 2.8.16. Similarly, Edwards notes, "The command 'you shall have no other gods' is not simply a negative comment that all other religions are worthless, it is a positive statement on the exclusiveness of the one true God." Edwards, *The Ten Commandments*, 64.

[16] Barnes, "The First Commandment," 28. Edwards writes, "The phrase 'before me' clearly does not imply that we may have other gods providing he is the first." Edwards, *The Ten Commandments*, 71.

[17] Frame, *The Doctrine of the Christian Life*, 407.

imprisonment. Ryken writes: "False gods hold a kind of spiritual power over their worshippers. . . . The reason false gods have this enslaving power is ultimately because demonic forces use them to gain mastery over their worshippers."[18]

Before moving on to the second commandment, the fact that the gospel is present in the first commandment ought not to be overlooked. The first commandment calls people to put their hope and trust in God, worshipping him alone. The various false gods that vie for man's attention are really different manifestations of self. An abandonment of self and putting one's faith in God alone is part of the gospel. Horton writes: "One can even find the gospel in the [first] commandment. . . . In this commandment we find the law, forbidding us to place our faith in ourselves or in anyone or anything beside the one true God, who has reconciled us to Himself through the person and work of Jesus Christ. But it is also a gospel invitation."[19]

Common moral and theological issues where the first commandment is applicable include atheism, agnosticism, other religions, pride, selfishness, sorcery, witchcraft, secret societies, and the occult.

The Second Commandment

THE SECOND COMMANDMENT FOCUSES ON THE external worship of God. In this commandment the Lord directed his people, saying,

> Do not make an idol for yourself, whether in the shape of anything in the heavens above or on the earth below or in the waters under the earth. You must not bow down to them or worship them; for I, the LORD your God, am a jealous God, punishing the children for the fathers' sin, to the third and fourth generations of those who hate Me, but showing faithful love to a thousand generations of those who love Me and keep My commands. (Exod 20:4–6)

Even a cursory reading of these verses leads to the conclusion that there is a close connection between the first and second commandments. Taken together, these commandments stipulate that

---

[18] Ryken, *Written in Stone*, 59.
[19] Horton, *The Law of Perfect Freedom*, 47, 68.

believers are not only to worship the correct God (i.e., the first commandment); but also, they must worship the correct God correctly (i.e., the second commandment). Said differently, the first two precepts of the Decalogue teach that believers must not worship a false God, or worship the true God falsely. Indeed, in the divine economy it is clear that *how* man worships is just as important as *whom* he worships. These concepts are essentially interrelated, for one's perception of God will affect one's worship of God, as well as one's personal and moral relationship with him.[20] This commandment indicates a true external perception of God is necessary for true worship and morality. Moreover, the exhortation to right worship contained in this commandment is essential, for as Horton observes, "The human heart not only wants to worship false gods, it consistently seeks to invent new ways of worship even when worshipping the triune God of biblical revelation."[21]

Proper Worship in the Bible

A NUMBER OF BIBLICAL EXAMPLES HIGHLIGHT the importance of proper external worship and interaction with God. First, consider the account of Nadab and Abihu recorded in Lev 10:1–7. In this narrative, the Levitical priests Nadab and Abihu, who were the two eldest sons of Aaron, "presented unauthorized fire before the LORD, which He had not commanded them to do" (Lev 10:1). Because of this illicit worship, the narrative records that fire came from the LORD and burned Nadab and Abihu to death before the LORD" (Lev 10:2). From man's perspective God's lethal response to the worship of Nadab and Abihu may seem harsh. Yet this narrative clearly communicates the fact that man must approach God on God's terms. While Nadab's and Abihu's worship of God may have been heartfelt and sincere, they would never have approached God in such an impulsive and flippant manner had they possessed a proper understanding of the Lord.

A second biblical example that highlights the importance of properly drawing near to God is the account of the death of David's servant Uzzah in 2 Sam 6:1–8. This passage records that David

---

[20] In his study of the second commandment Rooker observes: "Idolatry has never been connected to ethical behavior. . . . Wrong thoughts about God lead to wrong behavior." Mark F. Rooker, *The Ten Commandments: Ethics for the Twenty-First Century* (Nashville: B&H, 2010), 54.

[21] Horton, *The Law of Perfect Freedom*, 72.

purposed to bring the ark of the covenant from Kirjath Jearim to Jerusalem. In so doing, David gathered a procession of 30,000 choice men, as well as musicians playing all variety of instruments. However, the text reports, "When they came to Nacon's thresh-ing floor, Uzzah reached out to the ark of God and took hold of it because the oxen had stumbled. Then the LORD's anger burned against Uzzah, and God struck him dead on the spot for his irrever-ence, and he died there next to the ark of God" (2 Sam 6:6–7). As with the deaths of Nadab and Abihu, God's slaying of Uzzah may seem cruel and unjust; yet this passage emphasizes the importance of proper worship and interaction with God. While Uzzah may have reached for the ark out of perceived necessity or even instinct, the fact that Uzzah allowed himself to be placed in such a position in the first place is evidence that he did not have a proper regard for the Lord. As the text says, Uzzah was slain because of his irrever-ence (cf. Num 4:5–6, 15).

Fashioning Idols

TAKEN AT FACE VALUE, AT THE center of the second commandment is the prohibition of making carved images or fashioning idols to wor-ship. In the discussion of the first commandment, it was noted that mankind is guilty of making and worshipping many different idols. Indeed, Brian Edwards rightly concludes, "Human nature is suffi-ciently perverse as to turn almost anything into an object of magical trust or worship."[22] In short, idolatry is the worship of anything or anyone other than God. In the New Testament, believers are told to flee idolatry (cf. 1 Cor 10:14), not to associate with idolaters (cf. 1 Cor 5:11), and are commended for forsaking past idols (cf. 1 Thess 1:9). Moreover, idolatry is described as being sinful in many differ-ent passages (cf. 1 Cor 6:9; Gal 5:20; Eph 5:5; Col 3:5; 1 Pet 4:3; Rev 21:8).

Idolatry, however, does not just entail the sin of devising a false god to worship; it also includes the attempt to fashion an image of the true God to worship. The second commandment indicates that any artificially devised representation of God will be deficient. Notice the scope of the prohibition, "Anything in the heavens above or on the earth below or in the waters under the earth" (Exod 20:4). Here God is saying making an idol of himself *should not* be

---

[22] Edwards, *The Ten Commandments*, 84–85.

done because it *cannot* be done. Scripture is clear that attempts to make an image of God to worship ultimately betray a fundamental misperception of the Lord, for God is beyond man's comprehension (cf. Ps 50:21; Isa 44:9–20; 46:5–9; Acts 17:24–25). John Davies observes: "God is the true and living God, and as such, his character and attributes are manifold. He is not simply the God of strength, or any other single feature. What an image conveys at one point, it obscures and distorts at another."[23] It is worth noting that on the ark of the covenant, which was built in order to hold the Decalogue, the cherubim hold their wings up in worship before an invisible throne (cf. 1 Sam 4:4; Ps 80:1).

In spite of the prohibition against idolatry in the second commandment, Scripture is full of instances of men making idols that were worshipped. Major Old Testament examples include the golden calf Aaron fashioned while Moses was still on Mount Sinai (cf. Exod 32:8), the bronze serpent Moses made (cf. Num 21:4–9; 2 Kgs 18:4), the golden calves at Bethel and Dan fashioned by Jeroboam (cf. 1 Kgs 12:28–33), as well as Gideon's ephod (cf. Judg 8:26–27) and Micah's idol (cf. Judg 18:1–31). In the New Testament the book of Acts notes the city of Athens was full of idols (cf. Acts 17:16), as was Ephesus (cf. Acts 19:23–41). Furthermore, in his letter to the church in Rome, with obvious allusion to the second commandment, Paul details how mankind has rejected God and "exchanged the glory of the immortal God for images resembling mortal man, birds, four-footed animals, and reptiles" (Rom 1:23). An ironic aspect of such idolatry is that Scripture records there is indeed one true image or likeness of God in the created order—that is, mankind himself. Genesis 1:27 notes, "God created man in His own image; He created him in the image of God." Only God can make an image of himself. Man, then, is not to fashion an image of God to worship but rather to worship the God in whose image he is made.

An issue that often arises in conjunction with the second commandment is the morality of nonidolatrous religious images. In other words, does the second commandment prohibit all physical,

---

[23] John Davies, "The Second Commandment," in *Love Rules: The Ten Commandments for the 21st Century*, ed. Stuart Bonnington and Joan Milne (Carlisle, PA: Banner of Truth, 2004), 32–33. J. I. Packer notes that when man attempts to fashion an idol of God, he always brings the Lord down to his own level. Packer writes, "Sin began as a response to the temptation, 'You will be like God' (Genesis 3:5), and the effect of our wanting to be on God's level is that we bring him down to ours." Packer, *Keeping the Ten Commandments*, 54.

religious images, such as depictions of the Lord in sculpture, illustration, and other forms of artwork? This is surely a complex issue that has sparked much discussion throughout church history. Without delving too far into this complex issue, in this introductory work several general observations are in order. First, a desire to see God in a material sense is not in itself sinful. In Scripture, even Moses requested, "Please, let me see Your glory" (Exod 33:18). Moreover, the Bible records numerous examples of theophanies, as well as the incarnation of Jesus. Second, the Bible clearly reveals the Lord is not opposed to religious artwork. For instance, God himself ordained that cherubim be depicted in the curtains of the tabernacle (cf. Exod 26:1); he gave instructions regarding adornment of the priestly garments (cf. Exod 28:33); and the Lord directed Moses to fashion the bronze serpent, which the New Testament indicates was an object lesson depicting Christ (cf. Num 21:8; John 3:14–15). It seems, then, that while God is clearly opposed to idolatry, he is not against artistry. In his study of the second commandment, Douma concludes: "What is being forbidden here are cultic images and not every image that people might carve from wood or forge from metal or sculpt from clay. . . . What emerges quite clearly from all this is that the prohibition against cultic images does not apply to the visual arts."[24]

Proper Worship

A POSITIVE WAY OF STATING THE second commandment might read, "You shall worship me properly in your external worship." Indeed, God is concerned about man's interaction and relationship with him, as well as the way in which believers' lives are manifest before him. The Bible is clear that contact between God and man must be on God's terms and in the way in which he prescribes. In the New Testament Jesus taught God is Spirit, and he desires worshippers to worship him in spirit and in truth—that is, in accord with his will as revealed in the Word of God (cf. John 4:24). The indwelling Holy Spirit teaches and guides believers in the truth of Scripture, which

---

[24] J. Douma, *The Ten Commandments: Manual for the Christian Life*, trans. Nelson D. Kloosterman (Phillipsburg, NJ: P&R, 1996), 54–55. See, also, the discussion in Frame, *Doctrine of the Christian Life*, 481–86. In his analysis Frame concludes, "The second commandment does not forbid the making of images, even of God. It forbids making images for the purpose of worshiping them." Ibid., 484.

leads to proper worship of God (cf. John 14:16–17, 26; 15:26; 16:13–15).

At first glance it may be surprising that, apart from the sacrificial system, few specific worship practices are detailed in Scripture. The lack of prescribed worship rituals is actually a reflection of God's wisdom, for man would surely turn any required worship practice into an idol. Yet some means of worship are detailed and/ or exemplified in the New Testament, including observing the ordinances of baptism and the Lord's Supper (cf. Matt 26:26–29; 28:19–20), practicing church discipline (cf. Matt 18:15–17), fasting (cf. Matt 6:16–17), giving (cf. 1 Cor 16:1–2), and ministering to those in need, including the poor, orphans, and widows (cf. Jas 1:27). Clearly the Bible teaches that proper external worship includes one's entire lifestyle and worldview, not just a set time for religious observance. This notion may seem unusual to some; yet in his analysis of the second commandment, John Davies explains:

> At any point where we fail to be the people God intended, we rob God of the glory he is due. . . . Any deviation from a full-orbed understanding of who God in Christ is, and any failure to express that in lives of consistent loving service, is a failure of true worship and a decline into an impoverished perception of the Person and work of God's Son. Any time we trim the grandeur of God's accomplishment in Christ, any time we fall short of the expression of God's will for us, any time we put up barriers or rationalize our lack of fellowship with others of God's people, we slip into the sin of idolatry.[25]

The importance of proper worship is highlighted by the divine threat that accompanies the second commandment. God warned his people, "You must not bow down to them or worship them; for I, the LORD your God, am a jealous God, punishing the children for the fathers' sin, to the third and fourth generations of those who hate Me" (Exod 20:5). Although the corporate nature of sin is affirmed elsewhere in Scripture (cf. Exod 34:6–7; Num 14:18), the threat attached to the second commandment may seem unjust in light of passages such as Deut 24:16, which reads, "Fathers are not to be put to death for their children or children for their fathers;

---

[25] Davies, "The Second Commandment," 34–35.

each person will be put to death for his own sin," and Ezek 18:20, "The person who sins is the one who will die. A son won't suffer punishment for the father's iniquity, and a father won't suffer punishment for the son's iniquity. The righteousness of the righteous person will be on him, and the wickedness of the wicked person will be on him."

Upon closer review, however, it is clear the Lord's threat of punishing future generations for violation of the second commandment is not unjust; rather, it is a display of God's grace and an encouragement to holiness. To elaborate, in this passage God is reminding his people of the fact that sin is never just personal; it always affects others, especially those to whom one is closest. This ought to be a deterrent to sin. Mark Rooker writes:

> The text does not say that God holds one's descendant, a son or grandson, personally responsible for his father's sins (Ezek 18:20). Nor does this text say that the generational extension of punishment has anything to do with the legal administration of justice. But the text does hold out the threat that one's descendants may suffer for their parent's sin.[26]

Likewise, Brian Edwards observes, "Children suffer greatly for the sins of their parents, not by some arbitrary decree of a vengeful God but by the law of cause and effect."[27]

Before turning to the third commandment, the promise appended to the second commandment must be reviewed, for it is greater than the threat of punishment it follows. In this divine pledge God refers to his "showing faithful love to a thousand generations of those who love Me and keep My commands" (Exod 20:6). Surely this promise includes immediate practical benefits, but it is also prophetic in nature. Clowney explains, "God commanded men not to make an image of him, but the implied promise in the second commandment is that God would make an image of himself. He did not want his people trying to make an image of him because his purpose was to show himself to his people in the person

---

[26] Rooker, *The Ten Commandments*, 44. Rooker continues, noting, "The threat of harm to one's descendants functions as a powerful deterrent as one naturally grieves over the affliction of his children and grandchildren more than his own hardship." Ibid., 45.

[27] Edwards, *The Ten Commandments*, 92.

of Christ. The fulfillment of the second commandment is the birth of Jesus Christ."[28] The Bible teaches Jesus is "the image of the invisible God" (Col 1:15) and in him "the entire fullness of God's nature dwells bodily" (Col 2:9). Moreover, Jesus himself taught, "The one who has seen Me has seen the Father" (John 14:9). It is through the worship of Christ, then, and not the veneration of idols, that eternal blessings come.

Common moral and theological issues where the second commandment is applicable include idolatry, church ordinances, church discipline, church worship services, fasting, false conceptions of God, the visual arts, and cultic images.

The Third Commandment

REFERRING TO HIMSELF IN THE THIRD person for the first time in the Decalogue, God declares, "Do not misuse the name of the LORD your God, because the LORD will not leave anyone unpunished anyone who misuses His name" (Exod 20:7). The focus of this commandment is on the verbal worship of God, which includes the way in which the Lord's name is used. The language of worship, especially the manner in which the Lord's name is invoked, is important, for such language reflects one's understanding of who God is. The speaking of a name is not just a sterile articulation of syllables, for words convey thoughts and names represent identities.

To many modern believers the significance of naming or speaking a name has been lost. However, in Scripture the speaking of a name can signify a relationship, be an act of authority, or even denote right of possession. Consider the following examples: the naming of creation by God (cf. Gen 1:5, 8, 10), the naming of animals by Adam, as well as the naming of Eve (cf. Gen 2:19, 23; 3:20), the naming of children by parents (cf. Gen 4:1–2), the naming of wells by their owners (cf. Gen 26:19–22), the naming of cities and lands by their conquerors (cf. 2 Sam 12:28; Ps 49:11), and the name changes that occur upon entering into a relationship with the Lord, including Abram to Abraham, Sarai to Sarah, and Jacob

---

[28] Edmund P. Clowney, *How Jesus Transforms the Ten Commandments* (Phillipsburg, NJ: P&R, 2007), 28. Clowney continues, "Jesus fulfills the second commandment in a more breathtaking way. By the power of his Spirit he unites us to himself, so that we are remade in his image. . . . Our personal union with Christ is the ultimate purpose of God's design in making us in his likeness." Ibid., 32–33.

to Israel, among others (cf. Gen 17:4–5; 32:28; 35:10). Moreover, in the Bible to cut off or to blot out a name signifies destruction or death (cf. 2 Kgs 14:27). Clearly, the speaking of a name is a significant event, for names are far more than verbal designations.

Improper Speech

WHAT IS FORBIDDEN IN THE THIRD commandment is the misuse of God's name or, as some older translations render it, taking the Lord's name in vain. Yet this commandment extends far beyond a prohibition of using God's name when cursing. Brian Edwards writes: "[The] third commandment is not merely about the misuse of a word consisting of four Hebrew consonants, but an abuse of all that the name means. To misuse his name is to tread carelessly upon God's covenant offer of salvation and to treat his holy character with contempt."[29] Similarly, Edmund Clowney teaches: "When the Bible speaks of God's name, it is not indicating that a particular set of letters carries some mystical power. The name of God is the Bible's way of speaking of God's presence in his revelation. . . . In this sense it is impossible to dissociate God's name from his person, identity, and character."[30] So, then, at the core of the third commandment is a prohibition of speaking God's name in an empty, frivolous, insincere, or superficial manner. Such talk communicates false information about God's being and effectively desensitizes both the speaker and hearer to God's holiness.[31] Given this understanding, Allan Harman suggests the third commandment can be translated, "You must not bear the character of God hypocritically."[32]

When God first revealed himself to Moses in the desert of Sinai, Moses naturally inquired about the name of the Lord. Scripture reports, "Then Moses asked God, 'If I go to the Israelites and say to them: The God of your fathers has sent me to you, and they ask me, "What is His name?" what should I tell them?' God replied

---

[29] Edwards, *The Ten Commandments*, 100. Indeed, to reject God's name is to commit the unpardonable sin (cf. Matt 12:31–32; Mark 3:28–29; Heb 10:28–29).

[30] Clowney, *How Jesus Transforms the Ten Commandments*, 40.

[31] Horton writes: "Casual use of God's name is prohibited precisely because it wears away our sensitivity to the enormous reverence we owe it. Once we are able to think lightly of God's name even in our discussions with other Christians—even when our intentions are pious—it is not so difficult to lower our perception of the market price of God's name in more pernicious respects." Horton, *The Law of Perfect Freedom*, 104.

[32] Allan Harman, "The Third Commandment," in *Love Rules: The Ten Commandments for the 21st Century*, ed. Stuart Bonnington and Joan Milne (Carlisle, PA: Banner of Truth, 2004), 40.

to Moses, 'I AM WHO I AM. This is what you are to say to the Israelites: I AM has sent me to you'" (Exod 3:13–14). God's self-disclosed name, which is equivalent to the name "Yahweh" that appears for the first time in Scripture in the following verse, is noto-riously difficult to translate. Mark Rooker suggests God's name can be translated "He causes to be" or "He brings into existence,"[33] and John Davies writes that "this name might be rendered as 'the One who is sovereignly present (with his people).'"[34] In any event, in using the first person of the verb "to be" in his self-designation, God was revealing that his name entails his self-existence and his self-sufficiency, as well as his sovereignty. Perhaps a parallel New Testament self-disclosure of God's name is Jesus' statement, "I am the Alpha and the Omega . . . the One who is, who was, and who is coming, the Almighty" (Rev 1:8).

The fact that God's name reveals his being and character is evi-dent throughout Scripture. To cite just a few examples, in the Bible the Lord's name is equated with his authority (cf. Acts 4:30), his protection (cf. Ps 20:1), his doctrine (cf. Ps 22:22), his strength (cf. Prov 18:10), his honor (cf. Ps 86:9), his glory (cf. John 12:28), his holiness (cf. Ps 111:9), his majesty (cf. Ps 8:1), his moral standards (cf. Mic 4:5), his reputation (cf. Ps 106:8), and his saving power (cf. Rom 10:13). Indeed, to misuse God's name is to place oneself in a precarious position, for as Peter preached in Jerusalem, "There is no other name under heaven given to people, and we must be saved by it" (Acts 4:12). Moreover, Paul reminded the Philippian church that one day "at the name of Jesus every knee will bow . . . and every tongue should confess that Jesus Christ is Lord" (Phil 2:10–11).

The third commandment can be broken in thought as well as in deed. As the example of the unnamed blasphemer in Lev 24:10–23 illustrates, sometimes the misuse of God's name is easy to identify. Yet, at other times, blasphemy only occurs in one's heart and is difficult to detect. Douma warns: "The name of the Lord can also be abused without even mentioning it. . . . It is not so much that someone mentions the name of the Lord, but that he thinks, speaks, and acts disparagingly with regard to Him."[35] Furthermore, it is even possible

---

[33] Rooker, *The Ten Commandments*, 60.

[34] Davies, "The Second Commandment," 20.

[35] Douma, *The Ten Commandments*, 75, 79. Similarly, Brian Edwards writes, "We may therefore break this commandment even though we never allow the words 'God' or 'Christ' to pass our lips." Edwards, *The Ten Commandments*, 100. Packer, too, warns, "Whenever

to speak the right words with the wrong heart and thus break the third commandment. Isaiah records the Lord's complaint, "People approach Me with their mouths to honor Me with lip-service—yet their hearts are far from Me" (Isa 29:13). Such ostensibly correct yet improper use of God's name is illustrated in the New Testament by the seven sons of Sceva (cf. Acts 19:13–16) and in Jesus' teaching about nominal Christians at the judgment (cf. Matt 7:21–23).

Proper Speech

STATED POSITIVELY, THE THIRD COMMANDMENT MIGHT be, "Use God's name properly" or "Revere God's name." Jesus modeled the positive use of the third commandment in the opening words of the Lord's Prayer when he prayed, "Our Father in heaven, Your name be honored as holy" (Matt 6:9). Following Jesus' example, Christians are to manifest the character of God—that is, their new character—in all they do, including their thoughts, speech, and actions. The Lord desires for his people to call upon his name and to use it properly, for such keeping of the third commandment brings honor to God (cf. Ps 50:14–15). In Scripture the Lord exhorts his people to believe in his name (cf. John 1:12), to be baptized in his name (cf. Acts 8:16), to worship his name (cf. Acts 9:14), to glorify his name (cf. Ps 29:2), to sing of his name (cf. Ps 66:2), to remember his name (cf. Exod 20:24), to bless his name (cf. Deut 10:8), to trust in his name (cf. Isa 50:10), and to fear his name (cf. Deut 28:58). Given these exhortations concerning the positive use of God's name, to use God's name in a thoughtless or trite manner is problematic at best,[36] and heresy at worst.[37]

---

sinful self-absorption makes us hate God for what he allows to happen to us or others, we break the third commandment." Packer, *Keeping the 10 Commandments*, 60.

[36] The contemporary marketing of God's name via bumper stickers and T-shirts comes close to, if not embodying, breaking the third commandment. Another area where using God's name in vain comes into view is in the use of so-called minced oaths. Minced oaths arose in English culture prior to the Victorian era as part of the cultural impact of Puritanism. Puritanism's affect on language caused people to develop a wide variety of minced oaths to avoid swearing on holy names. For example, one would say "Gosh darn" rather than "God damn," or some similar substitution of words. Minced oaths have proliferated in modern language. While some minced oaths are certainly used innocently or without thought, if such oaths stem from a heart that is turned against the Lord, then they constitute a breaking of the third commandment. Ryken writes, "[Minced oaths] are really just a more polite way to swear. They may also be a better indication of our true spiritual condition than what we say in a church." Ryken, *Written in Stone*, 95.

[37] Douma writes, "Reformed ethics [has] observed that heresy is a transgression of the third commandment." Douma, *The Ten Commandments*, 97.

One area where proper speech comes into question is the subject of Christians taking oaths in the name of the Lord. This issue arises because a number of New Testament passages appear to prohibit using God's name in oaths. For example, Jesus taught, "Again, you have heard that it was said to our ancestors, You must not break your oath, but you must keep your oaths to the Lord. But I tell you, don't take an oath at all" (Matt 5:33–34; cf. 23:16–22). Likewise, James wrote, "Now above all, my brothers, do not swear, either by heaven or by earth or with any other oath" (Jas 5:12). In light of these passages, some Christians have adopted the position that all oath-taking in God's name constitutes a violation of the third commandment.

A problem with prohibiting all oath-taking, however, is that passages in Scripture appear to allow for, encourage, or even require the practice of taking an oath. For example, in the Old Testament God's people were permitted to use the Lord's name in oaths as long as it was done with proper intent (cf. Lev 19:12; Num 5:19; 30:1–16; Deut 6:13; Ps 63:11). Moreover, examples of oath-takers in Scripture include Abraham (cf. Gen 14:22; 21:24), Joseph (cf. Gen 47:31), Paul (cf. 2 Cor 1:23), an unnamed angel (cf. Rev 10:6), and even God himself (cf. Gen 22:16; Isa 45:23; Amos 6:8; Matt 26:63–64; Heb 6:16–17). In light of the full teaching and example of those in Scripture, it seems that the aforementioned New Testament passages on oath-taking prohibit the *misuse* of God's name, not the *use* of God's name. John Frame writes that Jesus' teaching on oath-taking is aimed at "those who misuse oaths. . . . He does not intend to restrict the use of oaths by people who are aware of the solemnity and omnipresence of God's holy name."[38] Likewise, Rooker concludes, "[The third commandment] does not exclude legitimate oaths, as they were relatively common in the Old Testament (Deut 6:13; Jer 4:2) as well as the New (Rom 1:9; 9:1)."[39]

Another topic related to the proper use of God's name is praying in Jesus' name. During his incarnation Jesus instructed believers to pray in his name (cf. John 14:13; 15:16; 16:23–24), and

---

[38] Frame, *Doctrine of the Christian Life*, 499. Similarly, John Stott writes, "What Jesus emphasized in his teaching was that honest men do not need to resort to oaths; it was not that they should refuse to take an oath if required by some external authority to do so." John Stott, *The Message of the Sermon on the Mount* (Downers Grove, IL: InterVarsity Press, 1985), 102.

[39] Rooker, *The Ten Commandments*, 66.

Paul wrote of "giving thanks always for everything to God the Father in the name of our Lord Jesus Christ" (Eph 5:20). Indeed, it is common for Christians to conclude a prayer with the phrase "in Jesus' name. Amen." Yet Wayne Grudem warns that believers must keep in mind the fact that to pray in Jesus' name "is not merely . . . a kind of magical formula that would give power to our prayers."[40] Rather, in view of the third commandment, to pray in Jesus' name is to declare that one's prayer is in accord with Jesus' character and will. Therefore, to pray with selfish motives or to append mindlessly the incantation "in Jesus' name. Amen" to the end of a prayer is to break the third commandment, for it is to use God's name in vain. Brian Edwards writes, "A clear violation of the third Commandment . . . [is adding a] magical tag at end of a prayer for which we had only half a mind: 'In the name of Jesus Christ. Amen.'"[41]

Yet another area where the third commandment can be broken is in attaching God's name to false teaching. God complained through the prophet Jeremiah, "These prophets are prophesying a lie in My name. I did not send them, nor did I command them or speak to them. They are prophesying to you a false vision, worthless divination, the deceit of their own minds" (Jer 14:14; cf. Ezek 13:6). Throughout history the Lord's name has been attached to all variety of false teaching, ranging from personal scruples to public atrocities including the crusades, slavery, the holocaust, and apartheid. As he calls believers back to Scripture, Ryken summarizes this phenomenon, writing, "A more serious way to break the third commandment is by using God's name to advance our own agenda. Some Christians say, 'the LORD told me to do this.' Or worse, they say, 'the LORD told me to tell you to do this.' That is false prophecy! God has already said whatever he needs to say in his Word."[42]

In conclusion, both the threat contained in and the fulfillment of the third commandment should not be overlooked. Although not as specific as the warning contained in the second commandment, in the third commandment the Lord states that he will

---

[40] Wayne Grudem, *Systematic Theology* (Grand Rapids: Zondervan, 1994), 379. Rooker writes, "To pray in Jesus' name is to pray in accord with His purpose, His person, and His will." Rooker, *The Ten Commandments*, 72.

[41] Edwards, *The Ten Commandments*, 104.

[42] Ryken, *Written in Stone*, 95.

punish anyone "who misuses His name" (Exod 20:7). Of course, in an ultimate sense, this refers to eternal separation from God, for to reject God's name is to reject his being and offer of salvation. Yet during his incarnation Jesus declared concerning himself: "I have revealed Your name to the men You gave Me from the world. . . . I made Your name known to them and will make it known, so the love You have loved Me with may be in them and I may be in them" (John 17:6, 26). In light of Jesus' teaching, Frame rightly concludes, "So the third commandment is fulfilled in Jesus."[43]

Common moral and theological issues addressed by the third commandment include blessing, swearing, confessing, oath-taking, praying, minced oaths, cursing, coarse talk, religious humor, flippancy, hypocrisy, blasphemy, heresy, proof-texting, perjury, and claims of extrabiblical revelation.

The Fourth Commandment

THE FOURTH COMMANDMENT, WHICH FIRST APPEARS in Exod 20:8–11, is the longest of the Ten Commandments. This commandment can be summarized as, "Remember to dedicate the Sabbath day" (Exod 20:8). The focus of the fourth commandment is on the temporal worship of God, which includes the temporal rest of man. This commandment is the first commandment in the Decalogue stated positively, one of only two commandments (the other being the fifth commandment) with a positive formulation. Another significant aspect of the fourth commandment is that it is the only precept of the Decalogue that appears differently in the Exodus and Deuteronomy narratives. To elaborate, in Exod 20:8–11 the fourth commandment is rooted in God's rest at creation, while in Deut 5:12–15 the fourth commandment is connected to Israel's redemption from Egypt. This association between rest and redemption will prove important in understanding and applying this commandment.

In his exposition of the Decalogue, Douma writes, "No commandment has occasioned as much controversy surrounding its interpretation as this fourth commandment."[44] This observation is affirmed by Brian Edwards as he notes that of all the commandments,

---

[43] Frame, *Doctrine of the Christian Life*, 491.

[44] Douma, *The Ten Commandments*, 109. For a good summary of different perspectives within the discussion of the Sabbath, see Christopher John Donato, ed., *Perspectives on the Sabbath: Four Views* (Nashville: B&H, 2011).

"The fourth is the most controversial."[45] Disagreements about the fourth commandment are usually related to defining the concept of Sabbath, discerning the temporary or eternal nature of the institution, and determining the proper application of the commandment, if any at all. Indeed, some believe the notion of Sabbath-keeping is tantamount to legalism and the practice quenches Christian liberty. Yet, if the Sabbath is part of the moral law, then keeping it (or violating it) is just as important as keeping (or violating) any other part of the Decalogue. If, as Rooker notes, the fourth commandment is "the most important OT law,"[46] then it is imperative to arrive at an understanding of its meaning and application. This study begins, then, by seeking to define the Sabbath and to discern the temporary or eternal nature of the institution.

Defining the Sabbath

INTERESTINGLY, THE PRIMARY MEANING OF THE term *Sabbath* is not "seven" but "rest." The term is derived from the Hebrew verb *shabath* which means "to rest or to cease from labor." Because God rested on the seventh day of creation, the word *Sabbath* in Hebrew came to be used for the number seven. The fourth commandment specifies that this Sabbath rest was to be observed every seventh day. In the Old Testament the concept of Sabbath-keeping, or regularly resting in order to worship, was deeply entrenched in the life of God's people. For example, within the Jewish theocracy the Sabbath concept was manifest in a weekly observance of the Sabbath day. Of course, this is prescribed in the fourth commandment but is also referred to in passages such as Exod 23:12 and Lev 23:3. The idea of Sabbath-keeping was also demonstrated in the Sabbath Year, which was celebrated every seventh year (cf. Exod 23:10–11; Lev 25:1–7; Deut 15:1–11). Moreover, the Sabbath concept can be seen in the Year of Jubilee (cf. Lev 25:8–55; 27:16–25), which was observed every fiftieth year, or after seven cycles of the Sabbath Year. A commonality between each of these manifestations of the Sabbath is rest (of man, beast, and land—depending on the observance) in view of worship of the Lord.

The Sabbath day, the Sabbath Year, and the Year of Jubilee, as well as other religious festivals, show that the concept of Sabbath

---

[45] Edwards, *The Ten Commandments*, 116.
[46] Rooker, *The Ten Commandments*, 92.

was firmly entrenched in the Jewish civil and ceremonial laws.[47] Yet the question remains as to whether or to what extent the Sabbath is part of the moral law. While the various manifestations of the Sabbath in the theocratic laws of Israel may not apply in the modern context, if the Sabbath is moral in nature, then in some sense or expression, the Sabbath is eternally valid. What support, then, is there in Scripture for the temporary or eternal nature of the Sabbath? A survey of the Bible reveals several pieces of evidence in support of the Sabbath being a part of the eternal moral law of God.

The first mention in Scripture of resting on the seventh day is during the creation week at Gen 2:1–3. This passage reads: "So the heavens and the earth and everything in them were completed. By the seventh day God completed His work that He had done, and He rested on the seventh day from all His work that He had done. God blessed the seventh day and declared it holy, for on it He rested from His work of creation." The fourth commandment appeals to God's rest at creation and his sanctifying of the seventh day as a basis for Sabbath-keeping. This grounding of the fourth commandment in creation is important, for as Andrew Clarke notes, "As a part of the very order of the creation, the moral principle of the Sabbath is understood to be a 'creation ordinance.'"[48] A creation ordinance is a timeless principle established by God prior to the fall of man. John Stott claims not only is the Sabbath rooted in creation but also that the Sabbath is the pinnacle of the creation week. Stott writes, "The climax of Genesis 1 [and 2] is not the creation of man, male and female, to subdue the earth, but the institution of the Sabbath."[49] If Sabbath-keeping is a creation ordinance, or might even be considered the climax of creation, it would have to be part of the moral law which lasts forever.

---

[47] Additional passages where the Sabbath is mentioned within the Jewish civil and ceremonial laws include Exod 35:1–3; Num 15:32–36.

[48] Andrew Clarke, "The Fourth Commandment," in *Love Rules: The Ten Commandments for the 21st Century*, ed. Stuart Bonnington and Joan Milne (Carlisle, PA: Banner of Truth, 2004), 45. John Frame, too, claims, "The Sabbath is a creation ordinance." Frame, *Doctrine of the Christian Life*, 533. Additional evidence for the Sabbath being a creation ordinance is its reflection in natural law. For instance, all mankind has an inherent desire for regular worship and regular rest.

[49] John Stott, *Issues Facing Christians Today*, 4th ed. (Grand Rapids: InterVarsity, 2006), 220. Interestingly, there is no day/night demarcation on the seventh day, which is possibly indicative of the eternal application of the Sabbath.

The Sabbath is the first and one of the only impersonal objects or events that God blesses in Scripture. Moreover, nothing in Gen 2:1–3 indicates this blessing was temporary in nature or only applicable to the future nation of Israel. On the contrary, since God does not actually rest (cf. Ps 121:4; John 5:17), the grounding of the fourth commandment in the events of Gen 2:1–3 leads to the conclusion that God's rest during the creation week was likely an example for all of mankind. The Lord's Sabbath observance was the firstfruits, of sorts. In resting and blessing the seventh day, God was demonstrating a chronological pattern by which the world could be regulated. Furthermore, since man is made in the image and likeness of God (cf. Gen 1:26–27), Sabbath-keeping is one way in which man can functionally bear God's image.

The eternal nature of the moral component within Sabbath-keeping is also evident in the fact that a seven-day week was adopted by man from creation. This is repeatedly alluded to in the narrative of Scripture (cf. Gen 7:4, 10; 8:10, 12; 29:27; 31:23; 50:10). A corroborating piece of evidence for the Sabbath being part of the moral law is the reference to Cain and Abel offering sacrifices "in the course of time" (Gen 4:3). As *Young's Literal Translation* renders it, the Hebrew in this phrase can be translated "at the end of days." This, then, raises the question: At the end of what days? A logical deduction is that Cain and Abel were worshipping God by offering sacrifices at the end of the week—that is, on the Sabbath. Note, too, that Job apparently observed a regular time of worship (cf. Job 1:5; 2:13).

Perhaps the best evidence for Sabbath-keeping having a pre-Mosaic, eternal, moral dimension is present in the directions God gave Moses about collecting manna in the wilderness. These instructions and events occurred prior to the giving of the Decalogue at Sinai. The text reports Moses' telling Israel:

> This is what the Lord has said: "Tomorrow is a day of complete rest, a holy Sabbath to the Lord. Bake what you want to bake, and boil what you want to boil, and set aside everything left over to be kept until morning." So they set it aside until morning as Moses commanded, and it didn't smell or have any maggots in it. "Eat it today," Moses said, "because today is a Sabbath to the Lord. Today you won't find any in the field. For six days you may gather it, but on the seventh day, the Sabbath, there will be none." . . .

"Understand that the LORD has given you the Sabbath; therefore on the sixth day He will give you two days' worth of bread. Each of you stay where you are; no one is to leave his place on the seventh day." So the people rested on the seventh day. (Exod 16:23–26, 29–30)

Note that Moses did not give a detailed explanation of the Sabbath to the gathered people, for he assumed they were familiar with the concept. Perhaps this helps explain why in the fourth commandment God told the people to "remember . . . the Sabbath" (Exod 20:8), implying they already had knowledge of the institution.

In the New Testament the eternal, moral nature of the Sabbath can be seen in the life and teaching of Jesus. The Gospels report that Jesus faithfully kept the Sabbath, even declaring himself to be "Lord of the Sabbath" (Matt 12:8; Luke 6:5). While no charge of Sabbath-breaking was brought up at Jesus' trial, during his ministry Jesus was repeatedly confronted by the religious leaders who accused him of breaking the Sabbath. Yet each time Jesus responded by showing that the error lay with the leaders' own misunderstanding of the Sabbath, not with his or his disciples' actions (cf. Matt 12:1–13; Mark 2:23–3:5; Luke 6:1–10). Indeed, rather than teaching against the Sabbath, during one of his confrontations with the religious leaders, Jesus gave the important teaching, "The Sabbath was made for man" (Mark 2:27).[50] Later in the New Testament the writer of the book of Hebrews affirms Jesus' teaching on the relevance of the Sabbath, writing, "Therefore, a Sabbath rest remains for God's people" (Heb 4:9).[51]

Some have appealed to passages such as Rom 14:5; Gal 4:9–11; Col 2:16–17 to argue that the Sabbath is not part of the moral law, or to teach that the Sabbath has been abrogated. Yet the context of these passages reveals that these texts most likely refer to the civil and ceremonial Sabbaths, not to the moral Sabbath.[52] In these

---

[50] Of course, Jesus was not speaking contrary to the Old Testament teaching that the Sabbath is God's Sabbath (cf. Exod 31:13; Lev 19:3; Isa 56:4; Ezek 20:12). Rather, Jesus was probably alluding to man being made on the sixth day and the Sabbath being instituted on the seventh day. As such, God's Sabbath was given to man for his benefit. Note that the Sabbath is referred to in the context of the new heavens and the new earth, too (cf. Isa 66:22–23; Ezek 46:1–12; Matt 24:20).

[51] Note that the term translated "Sabbath" in Heb 4:9 is unique in the New Testament.

[52] For a contrary view, see Thomas R. Schreiner, *40 Questions About Christians and Biblical Law* (Grand Rapids: Kregel, 2010), 212, 216.

passages, as he confronts a group known as the Judaizers who were trying to impose theocratic laws upon the church, Paul teaches that the various expressions of the Sabbath in the theocratic civil and ceremonial laws do not apply to Christians, especially as a means of sanctification. Yet the moral Sabbath is not explicitly mentioned in these passages.[53] As with other Old Testament civil and criminal laws, just because the theocratic laws are no longer applicable does not mean that the moral underpinnings of the law are no longer relevant.

Keeping the Sabbath

THE MORAL DIMENSION OF SABBATH-KEEPING, THEN, relates to rest and to worship. Yet the question still remains as to how this applies—that is, how is the Sabbath principle manifest in daily living? In addressing this issue, recall that in support of the fourth commandment the Decalogue appeals both to God's rest (in the Exodus narrative, cf. Exod 20:11) and to the redemption of Israel (in the Deuteronomy narrative, cf. Deut 5:15). As he explained the connection between rest and redemption, Horton wrote: "When the Jews celebrated the Sabbath, they looked forward to the end of their suffering and labor, sacrifices and ceremonies, to the final rest. God would come at the end of the age (week) and set things right."[54] For the Jews, then, the Sabbath pictured the eternal rest and redemption that was promised at Messiah's advent. Indeed, God instructed Moses to teach the Israelites that the Sabbath "is a sign between Me and you throughout your generations, so that you will know that I am Yahweh who sets you apart" (Exod 31:13; cf Isa 56:4–6; Ezek 20:12, 20). In examining the fourth commandment, Edmund Clowney noted: "God's creation rest and the Sabbath that marks it point to another rest—the rest of redemption. . . . The Sabbath is a sign not only for Israel, but also for the other nations whom God will incorporate in his rest."[55] For Christians, then, the Sabbath is a

---

[53] Brian Edwards writes: "In Romans 14 Paul is referring to the observance of both Jewish and Christian festival days which we are at perfect liberty to invent and observe if we wish—providing we do not make them mandatory for others. . . . The same point is reiterated by Paul in Colossians 2:16." Edwards, *The Ten Commandments*, 127.

[54] Horton, *The Law of Perfect Freedom*, 116.

[55] Clowney, *How Jesus Transforms*, 55–56. Frame observes, "The Sabbath introduces eschatology into Scripture for the first time. . . . The Sabbath in Genesis 2 does have an eschatological meaning." Frame, *Doctrine of the Christian Life*, 529, 533.

sign of redemption and, as such, it depicts the eternal rest they have received from Jesus in salvation.

Keeping the Sabbath ought not to be a legalistic burden, characterized by lists of permitted and forbidden activities. Rather the Sabbath ought to be a joyous celebration and a blessing (cf. Isa 58:13–14; Amos 8:5). In a broad sense, as Jesus taught, Christians are to keep the Sabbath every day by living lives characterized by hope, trust, and resting in the Lord, not by worry and anxiety (cf. Matt 6:25–34; 11:28–30). In a specific sense the fourth commandment calls believers to observe a regular day of worship—a day Christians have called the "Lord's Day." This ought to be a day on which God's people can gather together in order to rest in God, worship him, and express corporately thanksgiving for the redemption God supplies (cf. Heb 10:25). Christians can follow the example of Christ, who on the Sabbath engaged in worship of God, service to those in need, and fellowship with other believers (cf. Matt 12:1–13; Mark 1:21–39; 2:23–28; 6:1–11; Luke 4:16–27; 6:6–10; 13:10–17).[56] In fact, not to observe the Sabbath, in either a broad or a specific sense, is to behave in a distinctly un-Christlike manner, undermining the message of hope in the gospel.[57]

In seeking to keep the Sabbath in a specific sense, many believers ask the question of the correct day of observance. The Jews clearly kept the Sabbath on the seventh day of the week, which is Saturday. In the New Testament, however, the early church moved the day of Sabbath observance to the first day of the week, which is Sunday (cf. John 20:26; Acts 20:7; 1 Cor 16:2). Apparently in reference to this day of worship, the apostle John referred to Sunday as "the Lord's Day" (Rev 1:10; cf. Ps 118:24). A survey of historic Protestant catechisms, creeds, and confessions shows that the terms *Sabbath, Christian Sabbath,* and *Lord's Day,* with various interpretations, have been commonly used in the church, often being employed interchangeably.[58]

[56] J. I. Packer writes: "If the Lord's day is the Christian Sabbath, how do we keep it holy? Answer—by behaving as Jesus did." Packer, *The Ten Commandments,* 67.

[57] Perhaps this is why even within the theocratic laws, Sabbath-breaking so upset God (cf. Exod 16:28–29), even being identified as a cause of the Jewish exile (cf. Lev 26:32, 35; 2 Chron 36:21; Neh 13:17–18; Jer 17:19–21; Ezek 20:12–13). Note that Sabbath-breaking receives severe penalties in the Jewish civil law (cf. Exod 31:13; Num 15:32–36) and is frequently addressed by the prophets (cf. Isa 56:2; Ezek 22:8; 23:38).

[58] For historical examples see *The Baptist Confession of Faith* (1689); *The Philadelphia Confession* (1742); *The New Hampshire Confession of Faith* (1833). For a contemporary example see *The Baptist Faith and Message* (2000) which uses Exod 20:8–11 as a supporting

Certainly there were some practical reasons for moving the day of Sabbath observance, such as differentiating the Christian faith from Judaism or perhaps even logistical factors. Yet the main reason for this change was that all of Jesus' named postresurrection appearances occurred on Sunday (cf. Matt 28:9–10; Mark 16:12–14; Luke 24:13–51; John 20:11–23, 26–29; Rev 1:12–20). Moreover, the promised Holy Spirit came on Sunday (cf. Acts 2:1–4; Lev 23:15–16). In light of these factors, as well as others,[59] with their realization that the Sabbath was not a day but an event, changing the day of Sabbath observance was natural for the early church.

As with other aspects of the moral law, there are certain practical benefits to keeping the Sabbath. For example, resting from work prevents men from making work their ultimate source of security and affords them the opportunity to rely on and to worship God. Moreover, resting from work allows man to enjoy that which has been produced through his labor (cf. Eccl 2:17–26) and helps mitigate the effects of the fall, which turned work into toil (cf. Gen 3:19). Yet, ultimately, as Horton observes, the Sabbath "is a call of salvation, a shadow of the gospel proclamation, that was to go out to the people of God and, through them, to the whole world."[60] Indeed, as Mark Rooker writes, "The Sabbath is a type of Christ."[61] Therefore, Sabbath-keeping ought not to be viewed as a laborious

---

proof-text for its article on the Lord's Day. Using the terms "Sabbath" and "Lord's Day" (sometimes interchangeably) has also been common in Southern Baptist resolutions. For an interpretation of the Sabbath that sees the "Lord's Day" as a distinctly Christian concept, see D. A. Carson, ed., *From Sabbath to Lord's Day* (Grand Rapids: Zondervan, 1982). For a broader historical discussion, see the Sabbath-related materials in Timothy George, *Baptist Confessions, Catechisms, and Creeds* (Nashville: B&H, 1999).

[59] Some in the early church gave theological reasons for the change in day of Sabbath observance, such as: (1) Israel looked forward to Messiah, hence their rest on the seventh day; Christians look back to Messiah, hence their rest on the first day; (2) the Father finished his work of creation and rested on the seventh day; Jesus finished his work of new creation and rested on the first day; and (3) Jesus claimed to be the "light of the world" (John 8:12; 9:5) and called his followers by the same title (cf. Matt 5:14); since light was made on the first day, it was natural to worship on Sunday.

[60] Horton, *The Law of Perfect Freedom*, 116. Similarly, Ryken writes: "The way for us to find rest is by trusting in Christ alone for our salvation, depending on his work rather than our own. . . . This is the primary fulfillment of the fourth commandment." Ryken, *Written in Stone*, 110.

[61] Rooker, *The Ten Commandments*, 97. Clarke writes: "The identification of the Sabbath with redemption is completed with Jesus' resurrection. . . . It begins, on the first day of the week, with the victorious rest provided in Christ's finished work, continues with the creation of a new people, and will culminate at the end of history in the final renewal of the heavens and the earth." Clarke, "The Fourth Commandment," 46.

duty but rather should be a natural desire of the heart that reflects the eternal rest and redemption made possible through the cross.

Common moral and theological issues addressed by the fourth commandment include anxiety, industry, labor, recreation, employers/employee rights, public worship, private worship, and retirement.

Conclusion

THIS CHAPTER HAS SOUGHT TO INVESTIGATE the scope and moral implications of the first table of the law. In reviewing the first four commandments in the Decalogue, it was shown that by properly manifesting internal, external, verbal, and temporal love for God, believers keep the greatest commandment, which is, "Love the Lord your God with all your heart, with all your soul, and with all your mind" (Matt 22:37). Indeed, loving God properly is at the core of biblical ethics.

Summary Points

- The First Commandment—No Other God
  - ○ Four variations on the God-man relationship include universalism, pluralism, inclusivism, and exclusivism.
  - ○ Even otherwise good things can become gods when they are improperly loved, served, or worshipped.
  - ○ The human tendency to worship false gods is highlighted by the content of the first commandment.
  - ○ Above all, the first commandment demands radical monotheism.
- The Second Commandment—No Graven Images
  - ○ *How* humans worship is just as important as *whom* they worship.
  - ○ A true external perception of God is necessary for true worship and morality.
  - ○ Idolatry is the worship of anything or anyone other than God.
  - ○ Humans are not to fashion an image of God to worship but are to worship the God in whose image they are made.

- ○ Contact between God and humans must be on God's terms.
- ○ The second commandment does not prohibit religious art.
- The Third Commandment—No Misuse of God's Name
  - ○ The speaking of a name is not a sterile articulation of syllables—words convey thoughts and names represent identities. God's name reveals his being and character.
  - ○ The core of the third commandment is a prohibition of speaking God's name in an improper manner because such talk communicates false information about God.
  - ○ The third commandment can be broken in thought as well as in deed.
  - ○ Christians are to manifest the character of God in all they do, including their thoughts, speech, and actions.
- The Fourth Commandment—Keep the Sabbath
  - ○ The focus of the fourth commandment is on the temporal worship of God, which includes the temporal rest of man.
  - ○ The fourth commandment is the first commandment that is stated positively.
  - ○ "Sabbath" is derived from *shabath* which means "to rest or to cease from labor."
  - ○ The Sabbath is rooted in creation; it is the pinnacle of the creation week.
  - ○ Sabbath-keeping is one way in which man can functionally bear God's image.
  - ○ For Christians the Sabbath is a sign of redemption and depicts the eternal rest they have received from Jesus in salvation.

Chapter 8

The Second Table of the Law

I n the gospel narrative, after instructing the unnamed Pharisee about the greatest commandment of the law, which is to love God with all one's heart, Jesus continued his teaching as he noted, "The second is like it: Love your neighbor as yourself" (Matt 22:39; cf. Lev 19:18). With this teaching Jesus was emphasizing and summarizing the importance of what has become known as the second table of the law—that is, commandments five through ten of the Decalogue. As this chapter will demonstrate, each of these commandments addresses an area of moral dealings between individuals where love must be manifest. In summary, the fifth commandment addresses the sanctity of *human authority*; the sixth commandment addresses the sanctity of *human life*; the seventh commandment addresses the sanctity of *relational intimacy*; the eighth commandment addresses the sanctity of *material steward-ship*; the ninth commandment addresses the sanctity of *truth*; and the tenth commandment addresses the sanctity of *motives*.

The Decalogue specifies love of God before it addresses love of neighbor, for as Edwards has observed, "There is no value talking about loving our neighbor who is next door whilst all the time we are out of line with our Creator who is in heaven."[1] Assuming love for God, then, the second table of the law begins by addressing love of neighbor in the context of rightly ordered family relations. Indeed, this is natural, for family is the first arena where others are

[1] Brian Edwards, *The Ten Commandments for Today* (Surrey, UK: DayOne, 2002), 116.

encountered. If a man has a rightly ordered relationship with the neighbors who make up his family, then he will be more likely to love the neighbors who reside beyond his family.[2] Along these lines, in his exposition of the Decalogue, Ryken writes:

> The relationship between parent and child is the first and primary relationship, the beginning of all human society. Under ordinary circumstances, the first people a child knows are his parents. God intends the family to be our first hospital, first school, first government, first church. If we do not respect authority at home, we will not respect it anywhere.[3]

So the second table of the law begins as it does, for if one truly understands what it means to submit to authority, as well as what it means to protect and to provide for those under one's authority, one will not murder, commit adultery, steal, bear false witness, or covet.[4]

The Fifth Commandment

THE FIFTH COMMANDMENT READS, "HONOR YOUR father and your mother so that you may have a long life in the land that the LORD your God is giving you" (Exod 20:12). This commandment addresses the sanctity of *human authority*. As was noted above, relationally speaking, it is natural for the fifth commandment to address family affairs, for family is the first context in which others are encountered. Structurally speaking, as it stands at the head of the second table of the law, the fifth commandment is parallel to the first commandment. Just as the first table of the law begins with a command to honor God, so the second table of the law begins with a command to honor man. Moreover, the fifth commandment helps bridge the gap

---

[2] Interestingly, Paul cites this as a moral characteristic of those who are qualified for spiritual leadership (cf. 1 Tim 3:4–5).

[3] Philip Graham Ryken, *Written in Stone: The Ten Commandments and Today's Moral Crisis* (Wheaton, IL: Crossway, 2003), 119.

[4] Martin Luther observed: "From this [fifth] commandment we teach that after the excellent works of the first three commandments there are no better works than to obey and serve all those who are set over us. This is why disobedience is a sin worse than murder, unchastity, theft, dishonesty, and all that goes with them." LW 44.80–81. Similarly, Frame observes, "So the second table, like the first, begins with the specification of a heart attitude, a deference that leads to service." John Frame, *Doctrine of the Christian Life* (Phillipsburg, NJ: P&R, 2008), 576.

between the two tables of the law. On this topic Goswell writes: "The fifth commandment . . . helps to bind the first four and the last six commandments together. It is the commandment that is most similar to the first four, because it presents parents as authority figures, and to that extent 'God-like.'"[5]

Taken at face value, then, the fifth commandment requires that honor be shown to one's parents. Conversely, the command implies parents must properly care for their children. The word translated "honor" (*kaved*) in this commandment literally means heavy or weighty. The use of the term here calls for showing respect, reverence, deference, and esteem, as well as valuing, prizing, and submitting to one's parents. By way of application, the relational order prescribed in this commandment extends to all areas of human existence. As Peter wrote in his exposition of this commandment, "Submit to every human authority because of the Lord" (1 Pet 2:13). The fifth commandment, then, applies to the relationships that exist between God and believer (cf. Exod 20:3), state and citizen (cf. Rom 13:1–7; 1 Pet 2:13–14), judge and defendant (cf. Prov 24:23; John 7:24), master and slave (cf. Eph 6:5–9; Col 3:22–4:1), pastor and layperson (cf. 2 Tim 5:17; Heb 13:17), teacher and student (Jas 3:1), husband and wife (cf. Eph 5:22–33; Col 3:18–19; 1 Pet 3:1–7), and parent and child (cf. Lev 19:3; Prov 23:22; Eph 6:1–4; Col 3:20–21), as well as in other relational contexts.[6]

Honor and Obedience

THE FIFTH COMMANDMENT DOES NOT REQUIRE blind obedience to authority within any given relationship. Rather, this precept of the moral law calls for honor, which is an attitude or disposition usually manifested by obedience. Yet it is possible to obey without honoring, as well as to honor without obeying. In the book of Ephesians, Paul clarifies this concept in his comments on the fifth commandment as he notes that children are to obey their parents "in the

---

[5] Greg Goswell, "The Fifth Commandment," in *Love Rules: The Ten Commandments for the 21st Century*, ed. Stuart Bonnington and Joan Milne (Carlisle, PA: Banner of Truth, 2004), 53. Likewise, Begg notes, "How could we ever claim to honor God, whom we have not seen, if we fail to honor our parents, whom we do see? Parental authority is divinely delegated and is an integral part of our reverence for God." Alistair Begg, *Pathway to Freedom: How God's Laws Guide Our Lives* (Chicago: Moody, 2003), 119.

[6] The authority/submission paradigm of the fifth commandment can even be applied to immaterial relationships, such as the one between mankind and the created order (cf. Gen 1:26–28; Ps 8:6–8).

Lord" (Eph 6:1 ESV). In other words, the authority to which one shows honor is only legitimate as long as it does not cause one to sin or prevent one from righteousness. Since all authority is derived from God (cf. Matt 28:18; John 19:11), immoral authority is no authority at all. Therefore, while it may seem counterintuitive, the way to honor an authority that is leading one toward sin is to disobey mournfully. Conversely, as Jesus taught in his comments on the Pharisees' practice of Corban (cf. Matt 15:3–6; Mark 7:9–13), by obeying authorities who prescribe sinful practices, one can actually dishonor others who are in authority, thereby breaking the fifth commandment.

The importance of keeping the fifth commandment is evident in the Old Testament, as the breaking of this precept under the civil law engendered some of the swiftest and harshest penalties, including death of the perpetrator (cf. Exod 21:17; Lev 20:9; Deut 21:18–21). In the New Testament the significance of this commandment can be seen in Jesus' teaching that a mark of end-times apostasy is, "Children will even rise up against their parents and have them put to death" (Matt 10:21; cf. Luke 21:16). This same idea is present in Paul's instructions to Timothy as he wrote, "But know this: difficult times will come in the last days. For people will be lovers of self, lovers of money, boastful, proud, blasphemers, [and] disobedient to parents" (2 Tim 3:1–2; cf. Mic 7:6).[7] Note that rebellion against authority is seldom limited to one relationship. Those who rebel against God often rebel against parents and others, too.

In the presentation of this norm in Scripture, the honor specified is not contingent upon the worthiness of the one in authority. Rather, it is based on the position into which the Lord has placed an individual. Concerning those in authority, Ryken observes, "Our respect is not based on their personal qualities or professional qualifications, but on the position God has given them."[8] This helps explain Jesus' teaching and example of submitting to the governing authorities (cf. Mark 12:17; John 19:11), as well as Paul's seemingly blanket command to do the same (cf. Rom 13:1). Of course, this means that at times one may have to honor an incompetent authority, as long as the authority is not leading one into sin. Such

---

[7] Of course, one should not confuse the breakdown in family structure that is caused by rebellion with Jesus' teaching that the gospel may divide a family (cf. Matt 10:34–36; Mark 3:31–35).

[8] Ryken, *Written in Stone*, 124.

arrangements are often opportunities for personal sanctification. On this issue Goswell writes: "God does not say only honor 'good' parents. If we want to be happy and healthy we must forgive our parents for sinning against us and be still willing to learn from them."[9] Note, too, that the duty to honor those in authority does not expire as long as those in authority retain their position, which may be lifelong (cf. 1 Tim 5:4).

The Promise

IN HIS COMMENTS ON THE FIFTH commandment, Paul notes this precept should be obeyed because it pleases God (cf. Col 3:20) and because it is right (cf. Eph 6:1). Additionally, Paul observes that the fifth commandment "is the first commandment with a promise" (Eph 6:2). The stated promise for keeping this commandment is "a long life in the land that the LORD your God is giving you" (Exod 20:12). Additionally, in the Deuteronomy restatement of the Decalogue, Moses adds the phrase "that you may prosper" (Deut 5:16). While a general promise is attached to keeping all of the moral law (cf. Deut 5:29), and long life is a frequently cited biblical reward for obedience to God (cf. Deut 4:40; Ps 91:16; Prov 10:27), the fifth commandment is unique among the precepts of the Decalogue in that it contains an explicitly stated reward. It seems best to view this promise not as a supernatural guarantee but rather as a divine principle describing the natural result of rightly ordered relationships.

As with each of the Ten Commandments, Jesus is the perfect example of obedience. Christ demonstrated fidelity to this command by obeying his parents (cf. Luke 2:51) and later by arranging for care of his aging mother Mary (cf. John 19:26–27). Jesus also obeyed his heavenly Father, even at the cost of his life (cf. Luke 22:42). In this sense Christ is not only man's example but also man's substitute. Concerning Jesus' keeping of the fifth commandment, Ryken writes:

> From the manger to the cross, Jesus was an obedient son who brought honor to his earthly parents and his heavenly Father. In respecting his parents' authority he is more than our example: He is the perfect child that God demands we should be. Everyone who trusts in Jesus has offered perfect

---

[9] Goswell, "The Fifth Commandment," 55.

obedience to the fifth commandment, because when Jesus obeyed his parents, he was keeping God's law on our behalf.[10]

Common moral and theological issues where the fifth commandment is discussed include: parenting, family issues, authority, discipline, obedience, submission, child abuse, parent abuse, gender roles, capital punishment, church-state relations, civil disobedience, societal rebellion, rebellion in the church, church discipline, care of aging parents, nursing homes, workplace relations, slavery, prejudice, and racism, among others.

The Sixth Commandment

THE SIXTH COMMANDMENT, WHICH ADDRESSES THE sanctity of *human life*, reads, "Do not murder" (Exod 20:13). This is among the shortest of the Ten Commandments, consisting of only two words in the original Hebrew. Unlike the fourth commandment, the Lord gives no rationale for keeping this commandment; and unlike the fifth commandment, no explicit reward is mentioned for obeying it. This lack of rationale and reward within the Decalogue notwithstanding, the sixth commandment is the only part of the moral law with which nearly everyone agrees. Laws against murder are usually incorporated into modern civil laws without debate. Of course, this is because most people are confident they themselves have not broken the sixth commandment, and no one has a desire to be the victim of someone else's transgression of this precept.

In order to get to the heart of the sixth commandment, the meaning of the term usually translated "murder" in this verse needs investigation. Note that at least eight different words in the Hebrew language communicate the act of killing. The specific term employed in the sixth commandment is the word *ratsach*. This term, which occurs for the first time in the Old Testament at Exod 20:13 and appears dozens of times thereafter, specifically refers to the unlawful, malicious taking of innocent human life. Indeed, after an extensive discussion of the term, Rooker defines *ratsach* as "any act of violence against an individual out of hatred, anger, malice, deceit, or for personal gain, in whatever circumstances and by

---

[10] Ryken, *Written in Stone*, 132. Similarly, Clowney writes, "In Christ, the commandment to honor father and mother is fulfilled." Edmund P. Clowney, *How Jesus Transforms the Ten Commandments* (Phillipsburg, NJ: P&R, 2007), 69.

whatever method, that might result in death."[11] So then, rendering the term *ratsach* "murder,"[12] as do most modern translations (i.e., ESV, HCSB, NASB, NIV, NKJV), is preferable to the translation "kill," which is found in some older versions of the Bible, including the KJV, RSV, and ASV. On this topic Frame writes: "The [sixth] commandment does not forbid all killing. It forbids killing that is illegitimate according to the law . . . . 'Thou shall not kill' is a somewhat misleading translation of the commandment. It forbids killing that is not authorized by God."[13]

As was mentioned above, no rationale for keeping the sixth commandment is given within the Decalogue. Earlier in the Pentateuch, however, when murder is first mentioned in a judicial sense, the basis for the sixth commandment is disclosed—that is, the image of God. This passage, Gen 9:5–6, reads: "I will require the life of every animal and every man for your life and your blood. I will require the life of each man's brother for a man's life. Whoever sheds man's blood, his blood will be shed by man, for God made man in His image" (Gen 9:5–6; cf. Gen 1:26–27). As was noted in chapter 1 of this book, the *imago Dei* is surely a complex theological issue. The complexity of this topic notwithstanding, Scripture clearly teaches that man is made in God's image (Psalm 8; 1 Cor 11:7; Eph 4:24; Col 3:10). In light of this fact, Edwards writes, "To destroy a human being is to smash the image of God."[14] Similarly, Kaiser notes that murder is "tantamount to killing God in effigy."[15] Murder is prohibited, therefore, for human life is sacred; it is both a gift from God (cf. 1 Sam 2:6; Ezek 18:4) and a reflection of God's

---

[11] Mark Rooker, *The Ten Commandments: Ethics for the Twenty-First Century* (Nashville: B&H, 2010), 112. A possible exception to the normal usage of the term *ratsach* is at Num 35:27 where the killing described does not appear to be unlawful. This passage describes a scenario where someone guilty of accidental killing leaves a city of refuge prematurely. Numbers 35:27 states that if "the avenger of blood finds him outside the border of his city of refuge and kills [*ratsach*] him, the avenger will not be guilty of bloodshed." Yet Rooker explains, "In Num 35:26–28 the use of *rsh* is a play on words indicating that the death of a murderer corresponds to his own devious deed: the avenger of blood will kill (*rsh*) the murderer (*rsh*), according to witnesses he will kill (*rsh*) the murderer." Ibid., 126.

[12] Douma suggests the translation, "You shall not kill unlawfully." Yet this still seems to be a more cumbersome rendering than "murder." J. Douma, *The Ten Commandments: Manual for the Christian Life*, trans. Nelson D. Kloosterman (Phillipsburg, NJ: P&R, 1996), 216.

[13] John M. Frame, *The Doctrine of the Christian Life* (Phillipsburg, NJ: P&R, 2008), 694, 701.

[14] Edwards, *The Ten Commandments for Today*, 182.

[15] Walter C. Kaiser Jr., *Toward Old Testament Ethics* (Grand Rapids: Zondervan, 1991), 91. Likewise, Rooker writes, "Because a murderer strikes at the image of God borne by a human being, murder is an attack on God's dominion." Rooker, *The Ten Commandments*, 128.

image. This is why Rooker notes that the image of God is "the theological foundation of the sixth commandment. . . . The only way to understand the sixth commandment is to view the sanctity of human life as a fundamental principle."[16]

What Is (and Is Not) Prohibited?

TAKEN AT FACE VALUE, THE SIXTH commandment prohibits all murder—that is, the unlawful, malicious, taking of innocent human life. This includes the first murder, which was Cain's killing of Abel (cf. Gen 4:10), through the murder of those in the end times just prior to Jesus' return (cf. Rev 6:11; 11:7). Yet, as Jesus taught in the Sermon on the Mount, that which is prohibited by the sixth commandment extends far beyond murder. Christ preached: "You have heard that it was said to our ancestors, Do not murder, and whoever murders will be subject to judgment. But I tell you, everyone who is angry with his brother will be subject to judgment. And whoever says to his brother, 'Fool!' will be subject to the Sanhedrin. But whoever says, 'You moron!' will be subject to hellfire" (Matt 5:21–22). Here Jesus teaches the sixth commandment prohibits malice and murder—a teaching that is found in the Old Testament, as well (cf. Lev 19:17–18). Moreover, John taught that malice and murder are functionally equivalent (cf. 1 John 3:15), and James wrote that gossip and malice violate the image of God within others (cf. Jas 3:9). The sixth commandment, then, not only addresses one's actions, but also it intends to govern one's heart. Begg reminds his readers: "We kill people all the time with our contemptuous anger, our animosity and malice, our hostility and gossip. Little hidden murders."[17]

In order to avoid confusion, it may be helpful to identify acts involving or related to the taking of life that are *not* prohibited by the sixth commandment. For example, this moral precept does not forbid the killing of animals since the sixth commandment

---

[16] Rooker, *The Ten Commandments*, 126, 131. Note Begg's teaching, "The Bible says life is sacred because it is God's gift. Human life is the most precious thing in all the world, and to end it or direct its ending is God's prerogative alone." Begg, *Pathway to Freedom: How God's Laws Guide Our Lives*, 138.

[17] Begg, *Pathway to Freedom*, 135. Similarly, Horton writes, "We disobey the sixth commandment by tolerating whatever attitude might produce either active injury or passive apathy toward our neighbor's good." Michael S. Horton, *The Law of Perfect Freedom: Relating to Others Through the Ten Commandments* (Chicago: Moody, 1993), 168.

specifically addresses the killing of human beings.[18] Furthermore, the sixth commandment does not prohibit the accidental killing of a human being. Under Jewish civil law, the inadvertent killer was innocent of murder. In fact, the law included provisions to preserve his life. To elaborate, the civil law specified that the accidental killer was to flee to a city of refuge and was to stay there until the death of the high priest (cf. Exod 21:13; Num 35:9–28; Deut 4:41–43; 19:1–7; Josh 20:1–9).[19] The purpose for residing in a city of refuge was not incarceration but rather protection of the inadvertent killer from the avenger of blood (cf. Deut 19:6).

The biblical narrative is also instructional in that it shows the sixth commandment does not prohibit certain types of purposeful killing aimed at the protection or preservation of life. Ryken asks: "Why does God permit some forms of killing? What makes them lawful? The answer is that their goal is not the destruction of life, but its preservation."[20] Examples of such acts include killing in self-defense (cf. Esth 8:11–12) as well as defending one's home at night (cf. Exod 22:2).[21] Moreover, government-initiated killing in just wars is not prohibited by the sixth commandment. Paul taught the Christians in Rome: "Government is God's servant for your good. But if you do wrong, be afraid, because it does not carry the sword for no reason. For government is God's servant, an avenger that brings wrath on the one who does wrong" (Rom 13:4; cf. 1 Pet 2:13–17). While the specific ethics of warfare are a debatable topic, both the example and the teaching of Scripture reveal that wars aimed at protecting and preserving life are morally permissible, if not morally required.

A related act that is not prohibited by the sixth commandment is the practice of state-sponsored capital punishment for murder. As the prior citation of Gen 9:5–6 revealed, not only is capital punishment allowed under this moral law, but it is actually the

---

[18] Observe that even God killed animals (cf. Gen 3:21) and commanded man to do the same (cf. Acts 10:13–15).

[19] Concerning the death of the high priest, Frame writes: "We see here how seriously Scripture takes the loss of human life. It is significant that the slayer is not finally released until the death of the high priest, indicating that, even in the case of accidental killing, only death can deal with death. The high priest stands in effect as a substitute for the slayer, fore-shadowing Christ. . . . It is only because the priest dies that the slayer can live in freedom." Frame, *Doctrine of the Christian Life*, 688.

[20] Ryken, *Written in Stone*, 137.

[21] Exodus 22:3 teaches that killing an intruder during daytime was prohibited. The text reads, "But if this [i.e., home invasion] happens after sunrise, there is guilt of bloodshed" (Exod 22:3).

violation of the sixth commandment that makes capital punishment necessary. Douma writes, "What is clear in Scripture is the basis for capital punishment, namely, respect for human life."[22] In other words, if someone breaks the sixth commandment, he has shown such disregard for human life and the image of God that he forfeits his own life. This may seem counterintuitive at first glance; yet it becomes clear upon understanding the difference between vengeance and justice, retribution and reckoning, as well as deterrence and example.

What Is Required?

As WITH ALL OF THE PRECEPTS of the moral law, the sixth commandment could be formulated positively. In the Decalogue this law reads, "Do not murder." Yet it could be stated, "Preserve innocent human life," or "Protect the life of your neighbor." So the sixth commandment not only prohibits murder, but also it requires respect for the sanctity of human life. In his exposition of the sixth commandment, Martin Luther wrote:

> This commandment is violated not only when a person actually does evil, but also when he fails to do good to his neighbor, or, though he has the opportunity, fails to prevent, protect, and save him from suffering bodily harm or injury. If you send a person away naked when you could clothe him, you have let him freeze to death. If you see anyone suffer hunger and do not feed him, you have let him starve. Likewise, if you see anyone condemned to death or in similar peril and do not save him although you know ways and means to do so, you have killed him. It will do you no good to plead that you did not contribute to his death by word or deed, for you have withheld your love from him and robbed him of the service by which his life might have been saved.[23]

As Packer notes, keeping the sixth commandment requires "consistently preserving life and furthering each other's welfare in

---

[22] Douma, *The Ten Commandments*, 234.

[23] Martin Luther, *The Large Catechism*, trans. Robert H. Fischer (Philadelphia: Augsburg, 1959), 33.

all possible ways."[24] This includes actions such as taking precautions against the loss of life, being alert to life-threatening situations, and showing kindness and love to those in need. More importantly, however, the sixth commandment calls for the cultivation of a mind-set that seeks to preserve and respect the sanctity of human life in all areas of activity.[25] The development of an outlook toward life that seeks the flourishing of the lives of others, as opposed always to acting out of self-interest, is only possible through the redemptive work of Christ. Clowney writes: "Jesus himself shows us the right view of human life. Jesus does not place a distorting value on his own physical life, for he is ready to lay it down voluntarily for the sake of our salvation. . . . Jesus transforms this [commandment] by more than his condemnation of murderers. He provides the very Life that can rescue us from our murderous selves."[26] Because of Jesus' work on the cross, believers can truly keep the sixth commandment.

Common moral and theological issues addressed by the sixth commandment include murder, suicide, revenge, unrighteous anger, jealousy, self-love, discrimination, media violence, aggression, hatred, gossip, warfare, terrorism, capital punishment, abortion, euthanasia, torture, physical fitness, care for the needy (orphans, widows, the homeless, etc.), and any type of bodily abuse.

The Seventh Commandment

THE SEVENTH COMMANDMENT IS, "DO NOT commit adultery" (Exod 20:14). This moral precept addresses the sanctity of *relational intimacy*. If *adultery* is defined as "the act of a married person willfully engaging in sexual intercourse outside of the bonds of marriage," then Ryken is correct in his observation, "The primary purpose of

---

[24] J. I. Packer, *Keeping the Ten Commandments* (Wheaton, IL: Crossway, 2007), 78. Similarly, Ryken writes: "This is the positive side to keeping the sixth commandment. At the same time that God forbids us to take life unjustly, he commands us to guard it carefully. We are called to protect life, one life at a time. . . . Keeping the sixth commandment means more than not murdering anyone. It means loving our neighbor. It means showing kindness to strangers and mercy to our enemies." Ryken, *Written in Stone*, 144–45. Edwards asserts, "God urges his people to live in such a way that they cannot be the cause of the death of another person." Edwards, *The Ten Commandments*, 186.

[25] Frame calls this the doctrine of carefulness. Cf. Frame, *Doctrine of the Christian Life*, 688.

[26] Clowney, *How Jesus Transforms the Ten Commandments*, 82, 84.

this commandment is to protect marriage."[27] Indeed, this command is logical, for marriage is a fundamental institution that, while divine in origin (cf. Gen 2:18, 24), is a basic component of all human society. Therefore, to undermine married relationships is to erode the core of civilization itself. The divine institution of marriage ought to be respected and protected. In fact, the seventh commandment puts preservation of the marriage bond on the same level as not committing murder, for the penalty for either sin within Jewish civil law was death (cf. Lev 20:10–12; 21:9). Note, too, that avoidance of adultery is the subject of many of the Proverbs (cf. Prov 2:16; 5:20; 6:24, 32; 7:5; 23:27; 27:13; 30:20).

Defining Adultery

THE DEFINITION OF *ADULTERY*, HOWEVER, CANNOT be limited to the physical act of sexual intercourse outside the bounds of marriage. Jesus was clear on this point as he taught, "You have heard that it was said, Do not commit adultery. But I tell you, everyone who looks at a woman to lust for her has already committed adultery with her in his heart" (Matt 5:27–28). What the seventh commandment prohibits, then, is not just (or even primarily) illicit sexual intercourse. Rather, this moral precept is aimed at one's inner being—that is, one's thoughts, motives, and emotions that bear upon relational intimacy. In his exposition of the seventh commandment, Christian writes that this law "has a much wider application than just the physical act of intercourse. . . . It is addressing our whole attitude to commitments and relationships, warning us against the abuse of one another's persons, emotions, trust, and so on, for the sake of gratifying our own desires and lusts, in the spiritual as well as the physical realm."[28] In short, then, to break the seventh commandment is to fail to love one's neighbor as oneself by violating an aspect of relational intimacy (cf. Rom 13:9).

---

[27] Ryken, *Written in Stone*, 153. In his exposition of this law Christian notes, "To break the seventh commandment is to commit an act of betrayal in the most intimate human relationship we can have." Bruce Christian, "The Seventh Commandment," in *Love Rules: The Ten Commandments for the 21st Century*, ed. Stuart Bonnington and Joan Milne (Carlisle, PA: Banner of Truth, 2004), 67.

[28] Christian, "The Seventh Commandment," 68. Similarly Begg writes, "But even if we have managed to gain mastery over our bodies and our speech, we dare not rest content in the assumption that we have thereby obeyed the seventh commandment. God is not merely concerned to forbid the act of adultery but also to forbid the indulgence of evil affections." Begg, *Pathway to Freedom*, 160.

The internal orientation of the seventh commandment makes this moral precept much more challenging than if it were merely an external regulation. Yet understanding the inward essence of this law is important, for James taught: "But each person is tempted when he is drawn away and enticed by his own evil desires. Then after desire has conceived, it gives birth to sin, and when sin is fully grown, it gives birth to death. Don't be deceived, my dearly loved brothers" (Jas 1:14–16). In other words, the heart must be properly ordered for spiritual life to flourish. A disordered heart will lead to a disordered life, which will ultimately lead to death. This commandment references adultery, for relational intimacy is an area where many are challenged, and adultery is a clear indicator of spiritual failure within the inner man. The seventh command-ment, then, is a call to sanctification of heart. Viewed internally, adultery is a topic to which many people can relate. Douma rightly observes, "It is no mere coincidence that the sins of sexual immo-rality regularly head the lists of sins summarized in the Bible (i.e., Rom 1:26; 1 Cor 6:10; Gal 5:19)."[29]

Christ-Church Relations

THE SEVENTH COMMANDMENT HAS PRACTICAL IMPLICATIONS both for human society and for personal sanctification. Furthermore, this moral precept is theologically significant, for as Frame reminds his readers, "The marriage covenant is also an image of the divine covenant."[30] Since the marriage covenant images the divine covenant (cf. Ezek 16:8, 60–63; Hos 3:1; Eph 5:22–33), any violation of the husband-wife relationship will metaphorically impact the integrity of the Christ-church relationship. On this topic Ryken writes: "Another reason God forbids adultery is because there is a close connection between our sexuality and our spirituality. The union between a hus-band and wife is intended to exemplify the exclusive relationship between God and his people."[31] Therefore, to distort marriage by violating the relationships contained therein is necessarily to distort

---

[29] Douma, *The Ten Commandments*, 282.
[30] Frame, *Doctrine of the Christian Life*, 750.
[31] Ryken, *Written in Stone*, 156. Similarly, Rooker notes, "Adultery is the social equivalent of the religious crime of having other gods (Exod 20:3) since marriage is a mirror of God's covenant with His people." Rooker, *The Ten Commandments*, 143. Cf. David W. Jones, "The Asperity of Sexual Sin: Exploring the Sexual-Spiritual Nexus," *Faith and Mission* 22, no. 1 (Fall 2004): 3–22.

the revelation of God available through the institution. Clowney explains further:

> God did not fish around for some image to use to show his people what his love is like, and then stumble on marriage as the best one to convince them to return to him in covenant devotion. He did not recognize the power of married love and determine to use sexuality as the strongest figure. No. God planned it the other way around. The Lord placed in us at creation deep sexual emotions so that we might understand the jealousy of his love for us and the joy of jealousy for him.[32]

Scripture is clear concerning God's standards for marriage, as Paul wrote that "sexual immorality and any impurity or greed should not even be heard of among you, as is proper for saints" (Eph 5:3). Not only is sexual immorality improper, but avoidance of it is God's will for all people. Paul instructed the church in Thessalonica, "For this is God's will, your sanctification: that you abstain from sexual immorality, so that each of you knows how to control his own body in sanctification and honor, not with lustful desires, like the Gentiles who don't know God" (1 Thess 4:3–5). Additionally, the writer of Hebrews warns, "Marriage must be respected by all, and the marriage bed kept undefiled, because God will judge immoral people and adulterers" (Heb 13:4). This is the standard to which God calls mankind with the prohibition of adultery in the seventh commandment.

In light of the divine standards for marriage, then, as well as the societal, personal, and theological implications of the seventh commandment, adultery must be guarded against. Edwards makes the sobering observation: "[Adultery] is an act that once committed can never be uncommitted, paid for, or even adequately apologized for. Even love will not cover it. It is the most serious breach of trust that anyone can commit. It is beyond human cure."[33] Yet Jesus made possible the forgiveness of this sin, even telling the woman who was caught in adultery, upon her presumed repentance: "Neither do I condemn you. . . . Go, and from now on do not

---

[32] Clowney, *How Jesus Transforms*, 95. Likewise, Christian writes, "God's institution of marriage is clearly intended to help us understand our spiritual relationship with him." Christian, "The Seventh Commandment," 71.

[33] Edwards, *The Ten Commandments*, 215.

sin anymore" (John 8:11). Moreover, the Corinthian congregation included some who were guilty of the sin of adultery (cf. 1 Cor 6:9); yet Paul reminded them, "But you were washed, you were sanctified, you were justified in the name of the Lord Jesus Christ and by the Spirit of our God" (1 Cor 6:11).

Common moral and theological issues commonly discussed under the seventh commandment include adultery, polygamy, pedophilia, bestiality, harlotry, premarital sex, lust, pornography, sexual violence, sexual harassment, rape, incest, homosexuality, prostitution, modesty, divorce, masturbation, birth control, dating/courtship, sexual abuse, sexually transmitted diseases, cohabitation, celibacy, singleness, in vitro fertilization, surrogate pregnancy, and genetic engineering.

The Eighth Commandment

THE EIGHTH COMMANDMENT, WHICH ADDRESSES THE sanctity of *material stewardship*, simply reads, "Do not steal" (Exod 20:15). Given the succinctness of this law, it may be tempting to conclude this moral precept is easy to observe, yet Packer reminds his readers, "Temptations to steal property—that is, to deprive another person of what he or she has a right to—arise because fallen man always, instinctively, wants more than he has at present and more than others have."[34] Additionally, this commandment contains no direct object; man is not told what not to steal. The implication being that man will be inclined to steal many different things. This insinuation is confirmed by a perusal of the Hebrew civil law where, among other items, the Lord specifically instructed his people not to steal livestock (cf. Exod 22:1–4), pasture land (cf. Exod 22:5), possessions (cf. Exod 22:6–8), persons (cf. Deut 24:7), or goods that were lost and found (cf. Exod 23:4).

Under the Old Testament civil law, the penalty for violating the eighth commandment ranged from various forms of restitution to death of the perpetrator (cf. Exod 21:16; 22:1–15); yet in the New Testament the cost of breaking this moral law is even higher, as Paul taught that neither "thieves, greedy people . . . or swindlers will inherit God's kingdom" (1 Cor 6:10). The magnitude of these penalties invites the question, "What, precisely, is prohibited by

---

[34] Packer, *Keeping the Ten Commandments*, 90.

the eighth commandment?" Within the Jewish tradition this law was understood to forbid kidnapping (i.e., the stealing of another human being) because the Hebrew word translated "steal" in this verse can also be translated "kidnap" (cf. Exod 21:16; Deut 24:7; 1 Tim 1:10).[35] Yet, as even the rabbis understood, stealing extends far beyond kidnapping. Rooker offers the following definition, "The act of stealing is the secret taking of another's property without the owner's knowledge or permission."[36] So, while kidnapping human beings may be the worst kind of stealing, the eighth commandment prohibits the misappropriation of anything over which man is a steward.

Ownership Versus Stewardship

RYKEN WRITES, "THE EIGHTH COMMANDMENT ISN'T just about stealing; it's also about stewardship."[37] This is because the Bible describes God as the true owner of all things. David declares, "The earth and everything in it, the world and its inhabitants, belong to the LORD" (Ps 24:1), and God himself proclaims, "Every animal of the forest is Mine, the cattle on a thousand hills. I know every bird of the mountains, and the creatures of the field are Mine . . . for the world and everything in it is Mine" (Ps 50:10–12). The fact that God is the true owner of all things leads to two conclusions. First, man is merely a steward or a caretaker of what belongs to God. This role is not to be taken lightly, for Jesus taught that God will hold mankind accountable for his stewardship (cf. Matt 25:14–30; Luke 19:12–27). Indeed, God cares about material things and will one day redeem the created order (cf. Rom 8:18–22). Second, since God is the true owner of all things, to steal anything from anyone is ultimately to steal from God. In his exposition of the eighth commandment, Begg teaches, "It is God who grants to us the ability to get wealth and accumulate worldly goods. Consequently when we invade another's property and steal from them, we sin against God."[38]

---

[35] Cf. Rooker, *The Ten Commandments*, 146–48.

[36] Ibid., 148. Similarly, Edwards writes, "Stealing is to take without permission that which rightly belongs to another person." Edwards, *The Ten Commandments*, 218. Likewise, Ryken writes: "The Hebrew word for stealing (*ganaf*) literally means to carry something away, as if by stealth. To give a more technical definition, to steal is to appropriate someone else's property unlawfully." Ryken, *Written in Stone*, 170.

[37] Ryken, *Written in Stone*, 174.

[38] Begg, *Pathway to Freedom*, 175.

The fact that God ultimately possesses all things heightens the importance of keeping the eighth commandment, yet it ought not to diminish the concepts of temporal human ownership and private property. Frame writes, "The eighth commandment assumes that God has given human beings ownership of property,"[39] and Horton notes, "The prohibition of theft presupposes the right of private property."[40] Indeed, apart from the idea of man's temporal ownership, the concept of stealing makes no sense. So, while God is the ultimate owner of all things and man is his steward, man is to treat that over which he is a steward as if it were his own. Moreover, in regard to the eighth commandment, man is to respect others' temporal possession of things, realizing God is the true owner of the world.

In light of the discussion above, the eighth commandment might be stated positively as, "Be a good steward." Stewardship implies the development and application of an honest work ethic. In writing to the church in Ephesus, Paul instructed, "The thief must no longer steal. Instead, he must do honest work with his own hands, so that he has something to share with anyone in need" (Eph 4:28). In his comments on this moral law, Frame writes: "The eighth commandment also presupposes a work ethic. . . . Work is the antithesis of theft."[41] Keeping the eighth commandment, then, entails not only avoidance of theft but also proper stewardship of one's possessions and the application of a good work ethic (cf. 2 Thess 3:10; Titus 1:12). Rather than stealing from others, believers are to provide for those in need out of that which they steward, which may increase with honest work. In sum, then, keeping the eighth commandment has at least three aspects: not stealing from others, stewarding one's own possessions, and providing for those in need.

---

[39] Frame, *Doctrine of the Christian Life*, 797. Likewise, Rooker writes, "At the philosophical and foundational base of the eighth commandment is the right to own property." Rooker, *The Ten Commandments*, 151.

[40] Horton, *Law of Perfect Freedom*, 198. Oakes asserts that the eighth commandment "affirms a person's right to own private property." Barry Oakes, "The Eighth Commandment," in *Love Rules: The Ten Commandments for the 21st Century*, ed. Stuart Bonnington and Joan Milne (Carlisle, PA: Banner of Truth, 2004), 75.

[41] Frame, *Doctrine of the Christian Life*, 798. Later Frame accurately observes, "A man's righteousness is defined by his treatment of the poor." Ibid., 813. In a similar manner to Frame, Oakes writes, "The commandment affirms the virtue of earning a living by honest work, and the responsibility to use all that we have wisely, not just for our own benefit, but also for the well-being of those in need." Oakes, "The Eighth Commandment," 75.

Jesus, Our Ultimate Treasure

TO BREAK ANY ASPECT OF THE eighth commandment is to act unlike Christ and displays distrust in God. Ryken writes: "Stealing is a sin against God. . . . Every theft is a failure to trust in his provision. Whenever we take something that doesn't belong to us, we deny that God has given us or is able to give us everything we truly need."[42] Believers need to accept Jesus' teaching regarding God's care for his children and provision of necessary goods (cf. Matt 6:19–34; 10:29–31; Luke 12:22–34). On this topic Rooker claims: "The antidote for stealing is found in Phil 4:19: 'And my God shall supply all your needs according to His riches in glory in Christ Jesus.'"[43] Understanding the Lord's providential care for the world will lead to an embrace of the eighth commandment.

As with all of the commandments, many times believers fail to keep aspects of the eighth commandment and thus become thieves. It is important to remember, however, that Jesus died on the cross between two thieves, and his death was for mankind (cf. Matt 27:38). Ryken teaches: "When Christ died on the cross, he died for thieves, so that every thief who trusts in him will be saved. The first thief to be saved was the one hanging next to him on the cross."[44] Through Jesus' atonement lawbreakers can become law-keepers in both an imputed and an imparted sense, as did Zacchaeus (cf. Luke 19:8–9). This is possible because through the cross Christ became man's treasure. Clowney writes:

> Jesus transforms the eighth commandment, "You shall not steal," by helping us to set our hearts on true treasure. . . . Jesus himself brought the treasure of heaven to us by coming to establish a lasting kingdom, in which we have an inheritance. That inheritance is his very presence, for he is himself the treasure that we must value above all others. . . . Our inheritance is more than the blessings of glory, more than the new heavens and earth. It is the Lord, who gives himself to us, that we may be one with him. Yes, Jesus Christ does all this in transforming the

---

[42] Ryken, *Written in Stone*, 174. Similarly, Oakes observes, "At the heart of this commandment is the requirement to trust in our covenant Lord for all our needs, recognizing that the God who feeds the birds of the air and clothes the lilies of the field will also see that our needs (not our wish-lists) are met." Oakes, "The Eighth Commandment," 78.

[43] Rooker, *The Ten Commandments*, 151.

[44] Ryken, *Written in Stone*, 183.

commandment of property rights, "You shall not steal."
He gives himself as our treasure.[45]

Common moral and theological issues addressed by the eighth
commandment include idleness, laziness, stealing, burglary, rob-
bery, larceny, hijacking, shoplifting, pick-pocketing, embezzlement,
extortion, racketeering, private property, deceptive merchandising,
time management, greed, price-fixing, selfishness, borrowing, slan-
dering, taxes, advertising, merchandising, fraud, gambling, debt,
usury, copyright violation, identity theft, stewardship, tithing,
bribery, plagiarism, cheating, insurance fraud, generosity, wealth,
poverty, and benevolence.

The Ninth Commandment

THE NINTH COMMANDMENT IS, "DO NOT give false testimony against
your neighbor" (Exod 20:16). This moral precept, which addresses
the sanctity of *truth*, is needed by God's people, for false testimony,
dishonesty, and the like are a constant temptation and challenge for
mankind. To illustrate the extent of this problem, in Scripture false
witnesses spoke—with lethal results—against Naboth (cf. 1 Kgs
21:13), Jesus (cf. Matt 26:60–61), and Stephen (cf. Acts 6:13–14).
False witnesses are a frequent topic in the Proverbs, indicating a need
to guard against this sin (cf. Prov 6:19; 12:17; 19:5, 9). Additionally,
Paul cited the breach of this commandment in his letters to Corinth
(cf. 2 Cor 12:20), Galatia (cf. Gal 5:19–20), Ephesus (cf. Eph 4:31;
5:4), Colosse (cf. Col 3:8), and Thessalonica (cf. 2 Thess 2:9), as well
as in his instructions to Timothy (cf. 1 Tim 6:4–5) and Titus (cf.
Titus 1:12). Of course, violation of this commandment is a familiar
sin, and numerous examples could be cited from both history and
contemporary life.

In order to understand the importance of the ninth commandment, it must be noted that truth is held up and praised in the
Bible. For example, Scripture teaches Jesus is full of truth (cf. John
1:14), being truth himself (cf. John 14:6). Moreover, Christ identified the promised Holy Spirit as the Spirit of truth (cf. John 14:17)
and notes that an aspect of the Holy Spirit's ministry is to guide
believers in truth (cf. John 16:13). Paul wrote that truth must be
spoken in love (cf. Eph 4:15), and Jesus taught that those who

---

[45] Clowney, *How Jesus Transforms the Ten Commandments*, 108, 114.

speak truth will dwell with God (cf. John 8:32). Conversely, the Bible teaches that Satan is the father of lies (cf. John 8:44) and that God, who cannot lie (cf. Titus 1:2), hates lies and delights in truth (cf. Prov 6:17, 19; 12:22). Scripture also teaches that the tongue is vile (cf. Rom 3:13; Jas 1:26; 3:1–12) and that believers should not lie to one another (cf. Lev 19:11; Col 3:9). In the book of Revelation, John noted that liars are among those whose "share will be in the lake that burns with fire and sulfur, which is the second death" (Rev 21:8).

As it is given in Scripture, the ninth commandment focuses on truth-telling in a legally binding format, such as in a court of law before a judge, where another's well-being is at stake. Douma writes, "The ninth commandment involves first of all judicial or courtroom matters,"[46] and Frame observes, "The context is that of legal testimony."[47] Indeed, this is logical since all of the commandments, as stated, speak to the most extreme violation of the moral norm they address (e.g., murder violates life, adultery violates intimacy). False testimony in a court of law violates truth to such a degree that one's life may be at stake. Furthermore, as Rooker notes: "The effectiveness of the Old Testament legal system is interwoven with the presuppositions of fidelity and trust. . . . A lying or false witness represents a severe threat to the entire legal system."[48] This is because the theocratic legal system rested almost entirely on the testimony of eyewitnesses. Unlike modern legal systems ancient courts did not have lengthy trials, forensic evidence, sealed private records, or prolonged appeals processes. Rather, the theocratic legal process was short and public as court was held daily before an assembly of elders at the city gates. Sentences were generally carried out immediately. Understandably, not bearing false witness in such a legal context was extremely important.

What Is a Lie?

SCRIPTURE RECORDS MANY EXAMPLES OF INDIVIDUALS lying, where the event is clearly presented as sinful and destructive. Instances include Satan's lie to Eve about the effect of eating the forbidden

---

[46] Douma, *The Ten Commandments*, 313.

[47] Frame, *Doctrine of the Christian Life*, 830. Similarly, Rooker writes, "The primary focus of the ninth commandment would appear to be its use in the legal context." Rooker, *The Ten Commandments*, 160.

[48] Rooker, *The Ten Commandments*, 155.

fruit (cf. Gen 3:4–5), Cain's lie concerning the death of Abel (cf. Gen 4:9), Saul's lie about his lack of patience and disobedience (cf. 1 Sam 15:13), Gehazi's lie to Elisha regarding his whereabouts and greed (cf. 2 Kgs 5:22), and Peter's lie about his knowledge of Jesus (cf. Matt 26:72), as well as Ananias and Sapphira's lie concerning the sales price of their land (cf. Acts 5:1–10).

Yet there are other occasions in Scripture where nontruth-telling occurs, and it is not explicitly condemned. Examples include Abraham and Sarah's lie before Pharaoh and Abimelech (cf. Gen 12:10–20; 20:2–18), the Hebrew midwives' lie about the birth of male babies (cf. Exod 1:15–20), Rahab's lie concerning the location of the spies (cf. Josh 2:1–14; 6:25; Heb 11:31; Jas 2:25), Michal's lie about David's escape (cf. 1 Sam 19:14), Jonathan's lie concerning David's whereabouts (cf. 1 Sam 20:27–29), David's lie about his mission (cf. 1 Sam 21:2), Samuel's lie concerning his intentions (cf. 1 Sam 16:1–5), and a spirit's lie through false prophets concerning Ahab's victory in warfare (cf. 1 Kgs 22:21–23; 2 Chr 18:20–22), as well as lying in military contexts, including lies told by Joshua, Gideon, David, Elisha, and many others (cf. Josh 8:3–8; 1 Sam 19:12–17; 27:10; 2 Sam 5:22–25; 17:19–20; 2 Kgs 6:14–20).[49]

These seemingly conflicting examples of the ethics of truth-telling invite the question, "What, then, is a lie?" In looking more closely at the ninth commandment, it should be noted that this moral law does not say, "Always tell the truth," or "Never say anything untrue." Rather, using the example of courtroom perjury, the ninth commandment prohibits malicious nontruth-telling—that is, purposefully jeopardizing truth with the intent of personal benefit or injury to others.[50] As Packer notes, men tell malicious lies for many reasons, including pride, avoiding exposure, furthering self-interests, fear, revenge, conceit, and fraud.[51] The ninth commandment prohibits all nontruth-telling that is motivated by such

---

[49] Note Rooker's observation about these types of biblical examples, "While not all these practices are necessarily condoned in the Old Testament, they appear to differ from the offense of false testimony that the ninth commandment prohibits." Rooker, *The Ten Commandments*, 158.

[50] Hodge's exposition of the ninth commandment is helpful. He writes: "It is not every *enunciato falsi* which is a falsehood. This enunciation may be made through ignorance or mistake, and therefore be perfectly innocent. It may even be deliberate and intentional. This we see in the case of fables and parables, and in works of fiction. . . . Intention to deceive, therefore, is an element in the idea of falsehood." Charles Hodge, *Systematic Theology*, vol. 3 (Grand Rapids: Eerdmans, 1873), 440.

[51] Packer, *Keeping the Ten Commandments*, 96.

reasons. On this topic Frame writes that the ninth commandment "does not mandate truth in an abstract way, but in the concrete relationships between believers and their neighbors. . . . The sin of false witness is that of distorting the facts in such a way as to harm one's neighbor."[52] Similarly, Rooker observes, "Exodus 20:16 is not directed to the problem of truth versus lying. It has much rather to do with the person's relationship with his neighbor. It addresses the question: what happens through a lying witness? The ninth commandment has to do with caring for the neighbor."[53]

Malevolent nontruth-telling is clearly sinful. Yet, just as killing can occur in different contexts (e.g., murder vs. capital punishment), and sexual intercourse can occur in different contexts (e.g., rape vs. marital intercourse), so can nontruth-telling occur in different contexts (e.g., slander vs. fiction). The ninth commandment addresses malicious nontruth-telling, not the telling of all nontruths. Recall from the discussion about the three parts of morality in chapter 1 of this book that knowledge of conduct alone is insufficient to assign moral praise or blame. Conduct, character, and goals—that is, the entire moral event—must be weighed in the process of ethical evaluation. In regard to the ninth commandment, this has led ethicists to identify three different types of nontruths: jocular lies (e.g., jokes, fictions), lies of necessity (e.g., lies in warfare, sports), and malicious lies (e.g., perjury, slander).[54] The difference between these events is not the communication of nontruth; rather, it is the composition of the entire moral event. This ought not be confused with casuistry.[55] As with the biblical examples cited earlier, then, that which turns a nontruth into a lie is the intent to glorify oneself or to harm one's neighbor.[56] So, what is a lie? The words of Frame, cited in chapter 4 of this book are a

---

[52] Frame, *Doctrine of the Christian Life*, 834, 830.

[53] Rooker, *The Ten Commandments*, 155. Likewise, Douma asserts, "The ninth commandment aims at preserving the reputation, the good name, of the Israelite." Douma, *The Ten Commandments*, 316.

[54] For this terminology see Douma, *The Ten Commandments*, 324. Horton prefers humorous lies, helpful lies, and hurtful lies. Horton, *The Law of Perfect Freedom*, 229.

[55] *The Westminster Dictionary of Christian Ethics* defines *casuistry*, which is usually associated with the Middle Ages, Roman Catholicism, and canon law, as "any form of argument, usually about moral or legal issues, that employs subtle distinctions and twisted logic in order to justify some act that would be generally considered disreputable." *The Westminster Dictionary of Christian Ethics* (1986), s.v. "casuistry." Used in this pejorative sense, the component of casuistry that makes it immoral is malicious intent.

[56] Theologically speaking, the opposite of God being truth is to make oneself the source of truth. A sign of this shift in allegiance is the glorification of self rather than God.

good summary: "I would say that a lie is a word or act that intentionally deceives a neighbor in order to hurt him. . . . The sin of false witness is that of distorting the facts in such a way as to harm one's neighbor."[57]

Douma warns, "Agreeing that lying is sometimes permissible is dangerous,"[58] and, perhaps overstating his position, Edwards notes, "We must tread a careful line, it is a rare thing for a lie to be justified."[59] Indeed, these admonitions must be taken carefully, for as Begg reminds his readers, "We sin most easily in our words."[60] While the difference between the rape of a stranger and intercourse with one's spouse is unmistakable, and the difference between stealing and borrowing is generally understood, the line between speaking gossip and sharing a prayer request can become blurry, even to the speaker. Believers must keep in mind James's teaching that "no man can tame the tongue. It is a restless evil, full of deadly poison" (Jas 3:8). Indeed, it is the experience of most believers that the ninth commandment is broken more regularly than other parts of the moral law. Yet Horton offers the encouraging words, "For those of us who have violated the [ninth] commandment . . . there is refuge in the righteousness of the one who is the Truth. In Christ, our deceits, errors, hypocrisy, lies, gossip, and slander are not charged to us."[61]

Common moral and theological issues addressed by the ninth commandment include sports, games, jokes, honest mistakes, fictions, magic tricks, lying, perjury, bribery, gossip, rash judgments, twisting words, candor, slander, idle talk, exaggeration, backbiting, favoritism, flattery, libel, rumors, misquoting, misinterpretation, misleading, half-truths, and hypocrisy.

The Tenth Commandment

THE TENTH COMMANDMENT READS: "DO NOT covet your neighbor's house. Do not covet your neighbor's wife, his male or female slave, his ox or donkey, or anything that belongs to your neighbor" (Exod

---

[57] Frame, *Doctrine of the Christian Life*, 830, 835. Similarly, Hodge writes that in order to break the ninth commandment "there must be an intention to deceive when we are expected and bound to speak the truth." Hodge, *Systematic Theology*, 443.

[58] Douma, *The Ten Commandments*, 329. Douma continues, "A lie of necessity may be used only in dire circumstances. . . . Situations where the lie of necessity may be used are rare, if we deal honestly with the ninth commandment." Ibid., 330.

[59] Edwards, *The Ten Commandments*, 241.

[60] Begg, *Pathway to Freedom*, 192.

[61] Horton, *Law of Perfect Freedom*, 236.

20:17).[62] This moral law addresses the sanctity of *motives*. This commandment is unique in that it is the only precept in the second table of the law that is solely internal. In this way the tenth commandment is an appropriate conclusion to the Decalogue. This is so because it sheds light on how the other nine commandments are to be kept, for all sinful acts begin with sinful desires.[63] As James wrote: "But each person is tempted when he is drawn away and enticed by his own evil desires. Then after desire has conceived, it gives birth to sin, and when sin is fully grown, it gives birth to death" (Jas 1:14–15; cf. 1 Tim 6:9). Interestingly, Rooker notes that no other culture in biblical times had a law against coveting.[64]

What Is Coveting?

GIVEN ITS INTERNAL NATURE, PERHAPS IT is easy to view coveting as a less serious sin than other transgressions of the moral law. Yet Jesus lists coveting alongside other egregious sins such as adultery and murder, and Paul taught that covetousness is a cause of God's wrath and that breaking this commandment can keep one from the kingdom of God (cf. 1 Cor 6:9–10; Eph 5:5; Col 3:5). What, then, is coveting? In short, coveting is an ungoverned, illegitimate, selfish desire to possess that which belongs to another. Said differently, to covet is to long for something that would require a violation of part of the moral law in order to obtain it. The tenth commandment specifically cites the three things that are most often coveted: money (i.e., neighbor's house), sex (i.e., neighbor's wife), and means to power (i.e., neighbor's servant, ox, or donkey). So, then, that which

[62] Unlike most of the laws in the Decalogue, the tenth commandment has slight differences in its statement in Exod 20:17 and Deut 5:21. In Exod 20:17 and Deut 5:21 Moses inverts the order of "neighbor's house" and "neighbor's wife." Additionally, on account of the fact that Israel was about to enter the Promised Land, in Deut 5:21 Moses adds "his field" to the tenth commandment.

[63] Concerning this commandment, Rooker observes: "It is the commandment most at the root of covenant disobedience in that it logically precedes the rest. It is to be a restraint upon evil desires before they prevail. . . . This last commandment could be viewed as the interpreting clause of the whole Decalogue. . . . This law forms a suitable conclusion to commandments six through nine, but it may be viewed as encapsulating all ten of them." Rooker, *The Ten Commandments*, 172–73. Similarly, Bird notes: "In many ways the commandment can be seen as a summary of the preceding ones because it goes behind the act to the thoughts and motives of the heart. Hence, it is the only commandment which can never be enacted into human law codes. No law can stop people's greed, and no one can witness it, save the individual." Tony Bird, "The Tenth Commandment," in *Love Rules: The Ten Commandments for the 21st Century*, ed. Stuart Bonnington and Joan Milne (Carlisle, PA: Banner of Truth, 2004), 90.

[64] Rooker, *The Ten Commandments*, 164.

is coveted can be material or immaterial. The point is that the object of desire becomes ultimate in one's life. Bird observes, "Covetousness is a form of idolatry because it elevates something else into the place that only God deserves."[65]

In Scripture, examples of coveting abound. Major examples include Eve's coveting of the forbidden fruit (cf. Gen 3:6), Achan's coveting of material goods (cf. Josh 7:20–21), David's coveting of Bathsheba (cf. 2 Sam 11:1–4), Ahab's coveting of Naboth's vineyard (cf. 1 Kgs 21:1–24), Gehazi's coveting of material wealth (cf. 2 Kgs 5:20), Judas's coveting of money (cf. John 12:6), Ananias and Sapphira's coveting of reputation (cf. Acts 5:1–11), and Demas's coveting of the things of this world (cf. 2 Tim 4:10). The sin of coveting also seems to have been prevalent in the life of Paul, for the apostle notes that knowledge of this commandment was used by the Lord in the process of his conversion (cf. Rom 7:7–12).[66]

Coveting, then, is usually presented in Scripture negatively, as an act of rebellion against God; yet a number of passages in the Bible describe or prescribe what could be called meritorious coveting. For example, after discussing the Holy Spirit's gifting of the church for effective ministry, Paul encouraged the Corinthian church to "covet earnestly the best [spiritual] gifts" (1 Cor 12:31 KJV; cf. 1 Cor 14:39). Additionally, Scripture commends or commands believers in the coveting of a spouse (cf. Prov 18:22), in the coveting of ministerial leadership (cf. 1 Tim 3:1), and even in the coveting of Scripture itself (cf. 1 Pet 2:2). So, as with each part of the moral law, the conduct of coveting cannot truly be evaluated apart from knowledge and consideration of the character and goals of the one who is coveting.

Overcoming Coveting

IN HIS EXPOSITION OF THE TENTH commandment Packer writes: "Put positively, 'you shall not covet . . . anything that is your neighbor's' is a call to contentment with one's lot. The contentment that the tenth commandment prescribes is the supreme safeguard against temptations to break commandments five to nine."[67] Indeed, not

---

[65] Bird, "The Tenth Commandment," 92.

[66] In view of Rom 7:7–12, Rooker observes, "This commandment thoroughly convinced Paul that he was a sinner." Rooker, *The Ten Commandments*, 171.

[67] Packer, *Keeping the Ten Commandments*, 102. Similarly, Begg writes, "If we are to say no to covetousness, we must learn to say yes to contentment." Begg, *Pathway to Freedom*, 215.

only is contentment "great gain" (1 Tim 6:6), as Paul observed, but also it is the way to overcome coveting. Ryken calls contentment "the remedy for covetous desire,"[68] and Rooker teaches that contentment is "the cure for covetousness."[69] This is so, for it is impossible to be both content and covetous at the same time.

For believers and unbelievers alike, contentment is not natural, nor can it be generated circumstantially. Indeed, contentment—the antidote to coveting—must be cultivated and continually fostered in the life of a believer. As Paul wrote, "I have learned to be content in whatever circumstances I am" (Phil 4:11). However, given the fallen condition of the human heart, how can contentment be learned? The answer to this question is found in the book of Hebrews as the writer addresses the issue of not coveting wealth. Hebrews 13:5 states: "Your life should be free from the love of money. Be satisfied with what you have, for He Himself has said, I will never leave you or forsake you." In other words, the way to achieve contentment, and thus avoid coveting, is to be satisfied with God's sovereign and providential provision for each of his children. Such contentment will remedy covetousness. On this topic Ryken writes:

> The truth is that if God wanted us to have more right now, we would have it. If we needed different gifts to enable us to glorify him, he would provide them. If we were ready for the job or the ministry we want, he would put us into it. If we were supposed to be in a different situation in life, we would be in it. Instead of saying, "If only this" and "If only that," God calls us to glorify him to the fullest right now, whatever situation we are in.[70]

The tenth commandment is a logical conclusion to the Decalogue, for there is a sense in which it encapsulates all nine prior commandments. For example, the tenth commandment

---

Bird, too, observes: "Discontentment is the primary symptom of coveting. . . . The underlying value of this commandment is contentment." Bird, "The Tenth Commandment," 89.

[68] Ryken, *Written in Stone*, 212.

[69] Rooker, *The Ten Commandments*, 174.

[70] Ryken, *Written in Stone*, 212. In view of Heb 13:5, note Horton's observation on this topic, "At the bottom of it, coveting is a theological problem. . . . The writer of Hebrews bases his call to contentment, not on some airy, sentimental, blind command, but on the promise God has made to never leave us nor forsake us." Horton, *The Law of Perfect Freedom*, 247–48.

shows that coveting autonomy will lead to the breaking of the fifth commandment, coveting a neighbor's spouse will lead to the breaking of the seventh commandment, coveting the material goods of another will lead to the breaking of the eighth commandment, and so on. Indeed, perhaps the tenth commandment highlights mankind's spiritual condition and need in a more effective way than any other part of the moral law. Considered positively, though, this commandment ought to be an encouragement to believers. Clowney writes, "When we consider how Jesus has transformed this commandment we realize that Jesus is asking of us not less desire, but infinitely more! Jesus commands us to seek the kingdom of God and his righteousness with all our heart."[71]

Common moral problems that arise in discussions of the tenth commandment include coveting, gambling, idolatry, discontentment, greed, and envy.

Conclusion

THIS CHAPTER HAS SOUGHT TO INVESTIGATE the moral implications of Jesus' statement that the second most important commandment in the law is, "Love your neighbor as yourself" (Matt 22:39). In exploring this divine directive, the six commandments that comprise the second table of the law were analyzed. This chapter demonstrated that these precepts in the moral law address major areas in which neighbor love must be manifested in Christian living. These areas include maintaining the sanctity of human authority, the sanctity of human life, the sanctity of relational intimacy, the sanctity of material stewardship, the sanctity of truth, and the sanctity of motives. The second table of the law provides a comprehensive rubric through which one can manifest neighbor love and engage in biblical ethics.

Summary Points

- The second table of the law is summarized by Jesus' statement of the second greatest commandment, "Love your neighbor as yourself" (Matt 22:39).
- The Fifth Commandment—Addresses the sanctity of *human authority.*

---

[71] Clowney, *How Jesus Transforms the Ten Commandments*, 145.

- o Requires that honor is shown to one's parents and other authorities regardless of their apparent worthiness.
- o Honor is an attitude *typically* manifested by obedience, except where obedience would cause sin or prevent righteousness.
- o Unique among the precepts of the Decalogue in that it contains an explicitly stated reward.
- The Sixth Commandment—Addresses the sanctity of *human life*.
  - o Forbids the unlawful, malicious taking of innocent human life.
  - o Murder is prohibited because life is sacred and man is made in God's image.
  - o This command does not prohibit wars aimed at protecting and preserving human life or state-sponsored capital punishment.
  - o Stated positively, the sixth commandment is "Preserve innocent human life."
- The Seventh Commandment—Addresses the sanctity of *relational intimacy*.
  - o This command addresses physical and mental adultery.
  - o The seventh commandment is a call to sanctification of heart as it focuses on purity in one's thoughts, motives, and emotions that bear upon relational intimacy.
  - o Since the marriage covenant images the divine covenant, any violation of the husband-wife relationship will metaphorically impact the integrity of the Christ-church relationship.
- The Eighth Commandment—Addresses the sanctity of *material stewardship*.
  - o Prohibits the misappropriation of anything over which man is a steward.
  - o While God is the ultimate owner of all things and man is his steward, man is to treat that over which he is a steward as if it were his own.
  - o Keeping the eighth commandment involves at least three aspects: not stealing from others, stewarding one's own possessions, and providing for those in need.
  - o Breaking the eighth commandment demonstrates lack of faith in God's provision.

- The Ninth Commandment—Addresses the sanctity of *truth*.
    - Prohibits malicious nontruth-telling that will purpose-fully jeopardize truth with the intent of personal benefit or injury to others.
    - Truth is extolled by Scripture with Jesus describing him-self as the truth.
    - Conduct, character, and goals must be weighed in the process of evaluating nontruth-telling to determine if it violates the ninth commandment.
- The Tenth Commandment—Addresses the sanctity of *motives*.
    - The only commandment in the second table that is solely internal, it acts as a summary of the whole second table of the law.
    - To covet is to long for something that would require a violation of part of the moral law in order to obtain it.
    - Contentment—the antidote to covetousness—must be cultivated and continually fostered in the life of the believer.

Chapter 9

Conclusion

The first chapter of this book gave the following definition of biblical ethics: Biblical ethics is the study and application of the morals prescribed in God's Word that pertain to the kind of conduct, character, and goals required of one who professes to be in a redemptive relationship with the Lord Jesus Christ. In the unpacking of the component parts of this definition, it was noted that biblical ethics is deontological in orientation, for it looks to the objective norms in Scripture for moral guidance. This means the Word of God is the source of moral authority within a system of biblical ethics. Furthermore, the place of importance the three parts of morality—conduct, character, and goals—occupy within this approach to moral reasoning was also discussed. Indeed, proper moral conduct must conform to biblical norms, be motivated by love for God and neighbor, and have the glorification of God as its goal.

Chapters 2–5 in this text analyzed various aspects of the moral law, which is the central element and the source of moral authority, in a system of biblical ethics. Chapter 2 looked at the relationship between the law and God as the nature of the law was discussed. Chapter 3 examined the relevancy of the law as it focused on how the law relates to the gospel. The subject of chapter 4 was the relationship between various parts of the moral law as the coherency of the law was studied. Finally, in chapter 5 the structure of the law was reviewed as it focused on how the law relates to man. In addition to showing the foundational nature of the moral law for biblical ethics, these four chapters sought to demonstrate the comprehensiveness of the law for moral reasoning.

The sixth through eighth chapters of this book were more practical in orientation as they looked at the giving and content of the moral law itself. Chapter 6 focused specifically on the giving of the moral law as it is communicated by the Ten Commandments. Within this chapter the delivery, essence, enumeration, and interpretation of the law were covered, as well as a review of the prologue to the Ten Commandments. Focusing on the relationship between God and man, chapter 7 gave a brief exposition of the first table of the law, which addresses the internal, external, verbal, and temporal worship of God. Finally, chapter 8 of this book covered the second table of the law as various aspects of neighbor love were reviewed, including showing respect for the sanctity of authority, human life, relational intimacy, material stewardship, truth, and motives.

Practicing Biblical Ethics

IN CONCLUDING THIS STUDY, SEVERAL ADMONITIONS about the practice of biblical ethics are in order. First, while a simple ethical methodology was detailed in chapter 5 of this book, believers ought not to expect simplicity or ease in the practice of biblical ethics. Although God's moral standards are not hidden or complex, discerning the applicable biblical norms in any given scenario can prove difficult. Among other reasons this difficulty arises because of humanity's sinful estate, man's finite intellect, and the compounding nature of sin in the fallen world. The correct moral choice will not always set everything right—that is, produce a state of sinless perfection or complete restoration in the present. Sometimes the consequences of sin are lifelong, and even correct moral choices are made in the fallen world. As such, biblical ethics is rewarding, yet it is a challenging, lifelong discipline.

Second, as has been explored over the previous chapters, moral norms are not simply rules to follow but are a revelation of God's own moral character and being. This truth ought to be an encouragement for believers as well as a motivator to pursue the practice of biblical ethics. Yet believers ought to keep in mind Jesus' words:

"Remember the word I spoke to you: 'A slave is not greater than his master.' If they persecuted Me, they will also persecute you. If they kept My word, they will also keep yours" (John 15:20). The implications of Jesus' words for biblical ethics are far-reaching. Since biblical ethics reveal Christ, believers ought not to expect God's moral norms to be immediately embraced by the fallen world. Indeed, refutation of biblical ethics is the natural reaction of many. Surely such rejection can be discouraging; however, the Bible teaches persecution that arises because of faithful witness to Christ is actually a blessing that will ultimately bring glory to God (cf. Matt 5:11–16; 1 Pet 3:14). Rejection of biblical ethics by the lost world is not a reason to neglect the discipline; rather, it ought to be a motivation to pursue biblical ethics.

Finally, in studying biblical ethics, one must keep in mind that this approach to morality is not just one way of doing ethics among a pool of competing options. Indeed, since biblical ethics is the application of eternal, divine, moral laws to everyday living, biblical ethics is not just an academic discipline; it is the substance of the Christian worldview. Inwardly, biblical ethics entails the embodiment of God's moral character by God's image bearers in the world God made. Externally, biblical ethics provides a way for believers to engage the lost world, regardless of whether moral norms are accepted or rejected. This is done both naturally, as believers' lives reflect the hope of their salvation, and verbally, by way of expressing moral truth. This can be direct or indirect, written or spoken. Indeed, believers must keep in mind the fact that, in comparison to the world's ethics, biblical ethics are not just different or correct (although they are); rather, God's moral standards are the only pathway that can provide hope for the lost world.

Glossary

Antinomianism – The term literally means "against the law." There are no moral absolutes in an antinomian ethical system.

Atonement – Jesus' substitutionary death on the cross in order to provide salvation for all who will believe.

Axiomatic – Self-evident.

Ceremonial Laws – Laws that were given for the functioning of the sacrificial system, including tabernacle/temple operations, religious festivals, and dietary regulations.

Christian Essentialism – The view of the nature of law that understands the moral law to be a reflection of God's own moral character.

Christian Reconstructionism – An approach to the Bible and politics that seeks to govern via applying theocratic civil laws in the contemporary setting.

Civil Laws – Laws given for the governance of the Hebrew theocracy.

Conflicting Absolutism – The view that moral laws can and do conflict. In such cases this position teaches that one is to commit the lesser evil and repent of the sin.

Consequentialism – A system of ethics that assigns moral praise or blame based on the end results of moral events.

Continuity Approach – The approach to the law-gospel question that teaches that the Old Testament law, with the exception of the ceremonial law, and civil laws that have become technologically outdated, is binding upon Christians.

Convictional Use of the Law – When serving in this capacity, the moral law convicts men of sin by becoming a mirror that reflects man's sinful condition in light of God's holiness and moral standards.

Covet – To long for something that would require a violation of part of the moral law in order to obtain it.

Creation Ordinance – A timeless principle, institution, or practice established by God prior to the fall of man.

Decalogue – A term meaning "10 words." This word is often used to refer to the Ten Commandments.

Deontological Ethics – A system of ethics that assigns moral praise or blame based on the conformity of acts to fixed moral norms.

Discontinuity Approach – The approach to the law-gospel question which generally holds that the New Testament alone is normative for the Christian life.

Dispensational Theology – The theological system that divides history, as presented in Scripture, into several distinct phases. Within each phase the economy of God's dealings with man are managed differently.

Dominion theology – A theological system that seeks to establish the kingdom of God on earth usually via a theonomic form of government.

Epistemology – The study of the nature of knowledge.

Esoteric – Tangential, mysterious, difficult to understand.

Ethical Methodology – The practice of applying and using a system of ethics.

Ethical Nonvoluntarism – The idea that the rightness or wrongness of the law is determined solely by its own internal nature.

Ethical Rationalism – A deontological approach to ethics that attempts to discern moral norms solely through the created order.

Ethical Voluntarism – The idea that the rightness or wrongness of the law is determined by its being willed by God.

Euthyphro Dilemma – A conversation between Socrates and Euthyphro, reported by Plato, about the nature of law and its relationship to God.

Exclusivism – The theological system that teaches only one God exists and man must be knowingly reconciled to God through the cross of Christ.

Existential – Derived from experience or existence.

First Table of the Law – The first four of the Ten Commandments.

General Revelation – God's revelation of himself to all peoples, at all times, in all places. Classic modes of general revelation include creation, the conscience, and history.

Graded Absolutism – The view that many universal moral norms can and do conflict; yet ethical norms are hierarchical, and thus one can obey a higher norm while breaking a lower norm without sinning.

Inclusivism – The theological system that teaches there is only one way to be right with God; yet the application of the atonement of Christ may include people who are not practicing Christians.

Legalism – A tendency to define ethics as rule-keeping.

Lie – Malicious nontruth-telling; purposefully jeopardizing the truth with the intent of personal benefit or injury to others.

Moral Laws – Laws that are based on, reflect, and demand conformity to God's moral character. The moral law is summarized in the Ten Commandments.

Moral Norms – Objective ethical standards.

Moral Philosophy – A term sometimes used to describe secular approaches to moral reasoning.

Moral Theology – An older name for the field of study known as Christian ethics.

Murder – The unlawful, malicious taking of innocent human life.

Natural Law Theory – A deontological approach to ethics that attempts to discern moral norms solely though the created order.

Nonconflicting Absolutism – The view that moral laws cannot conflict since they reflect the nonconflicting character of God. Apparent conflict betrays a misunderstanding of moral norms or a misperception of a moral event.

Normative Use of the Law – When the moral law functions in this capacity, it acts as a lamp to instruct believers in righteousness. This use of the law is identified by most Protestant thinkers as the main use of the moral law.

Ontology – The study of the nature of essence, being, existence, or reality.

Pluralism – The theological system that teaches there are many ways to be right with God.

Postmillennial Eschatology – The belief that Christ's triumphant return and the final resurrection will occur after a period of biblical peace on earth.

Providence – God's intervention and working in the world.

Redemption – To purchase or deliver from sin and death.

Sabbath – The event or act of resting or ceasing from labor.

Sanctification – To be set apart, to become holy, to become Christlike in character.

Second Table of the Law – The last six of the Ten Commandments.

Semi-Continuity Approach – The approach to the law-gospel debate, which holds that only the moral law is applicable to New Testament believers.

Situationalism – An ethical system that affirms only one moral norm exists, which must be kept in all situations. The moral norm is defined by the moral agent and varies in application by situation and person.

Social Use of the Law – When functioning in this manner, the moral law serves as a barricade or a bridle that restrains men from sin.

Special Revelation – God's revelation of himself in the Bible and other supernatural, scriptural means of divine communication.

Summum Bonum – Latin term meaning "highest good."

Synecdoche – A figure of speech meaning "a part for the whole."

Theocracy – A God-centered form of government.

Theonomy – A system of government characterized by being governed by divine law.

Universalism – All humans stand in the same relationship with God.

Utilitarianism – A system of ethics that assigns moral praise or blame based on the end results of moral events.

Name Index

Subject Index

Scripture Index